D0881458

MARÍA OF GUADALUPE

PAUL BADDE

MARÍA
OF GUADALUPE

Shaper of History, Shaper of Hearts

Translated by
Carol Cowgill

IGNATIUS PRESS   SAN FRANCISCO

Original German edition:
Maria von Guadalupe:
Wie das Erscheinen der Jungfrau Weitgeschichte Schrieb
© 2004 by Ullstein Buchverlage GmbH, Berlin

Translated from the Spanish edition:
La Morenita:
Cómo la aparición de la Virgen configuró la historia universal
Translated by Pedro V. Escobar Illanes, S.J.
© 2005 by Buena Prensa, Mexico City

Cover art: Image of Our Lady of Guadalupe (detail)

Cover design by John Herreid

© 2008 by Ignatius Press, San Francisco
All rights reserved
ISBN 978-1-58617-241-1
Library of Congress Control Number 2008926717
Printed in the United States of America ∞

To Ellen and Raam

At that hour there was a great earthquake, and a tenth of the city fell; seven thousand people were killed in the earthquake, and the rest were terrified and gave glory to the God of heaven.

The second woe has passed; behold, the third woe is soon to come. . . .

And a great portent appeared in heaven, a woman clothed with the sun, with the moon under her feet, and on her head a crown of twelve stars; she was with child and she cried out in her pangs of birth, in anguish for delivery.

(Rev 11:13–14; 12:1–2)

Images are one road to reality. . . . But there has to be a place where a person can find them untouched, not he alone, a place where anyone who feels unsure can find them . . . There, experience holds still, there he sees into its face. . . . The image needs his experience in order to awake. This is why images slumber for generations, because no one can see them with the experience that awakens them. . . .

Images define what a person experiences. . . . They are incorporated into him as a kind of base and ground. Indeed, the images that constitute a person make his life unique. . . . The person who finds the images his experience requires will feel strong.

Elias Canetti, *The Torch in My Ear*

CONTENTS

CHAPTER ONE

A DELECTABLE FRUIT OF THE CACTUS FOR THE EAGLE

With wood from the Santa María, Christopher Columbus built the first house in America. Hernán Cortés conquered Mexico. The growling of dogs on the beach and the dawn of the modern era lie heavy over the cities of New World and Old.

On the morning of August 3, 1492, sails billowing in the first wind, Columbus sailed from Andalusia in the *Santa María*, together with the *Niña* and the *Pinta*, in order, as he confides in the ship's log, to search for a westerly sea route to Jerusalem. If the names of his ships had been listed in another way, they would have made the phrase "Holy Mary (*Santa María*) paints (*pinta*) the girl (*niña*)". In itself, this would have been striking. However, this was only the beginning of the incredible story of the dark Lady, who, five hundred years after the discovery of America, still waits to be discovered by Europe, Asia, Africa and other parts of the world.

Historians say that, on Christmas night, 1492, the *Santa María* ran aground on a sandbar off of Haiti. Columbus decided to dismantle the grounded flagship and "build a fort out of what was salvaged". However, some years ago on the docks of the port of Barcelona, I saw an exact reproduction of the caravel *Santa María*. I doubt that with the planks and masts of this nutshell anyone could have managed to construct a fort. Two or three huts, perhaps, or a house—or even a small barricaded chapel. There was not

enough material for more. The one thing that seems sure is
that from the remains of the *Santa María* the first European
house was raised in the New World. A year later it was
pulled down and reduced to ashes.

Twenty-seven years later Hernán Cortés, a native of the
city of Medellín, in Spain, disembarked from the *Santa María
de la Concepción* onto the shore of the American continent.
It was Good Friday of 1519, in the area of what would
later become the port of Veracruz. A small expeditionary
flotilla accompanied the *Santa María de la Concepción*. Two
days later, Cortés asked two Franciscans, Diaz and Olmedo,
to celebrate Easter with a high Mass on the beach. "The
Spaniards planted a cross in the sandy ground", writes Francisco López de Gómara in his history of the conquest of
Mexico. "They prayed the rosary and the Angelus as a bell
was rung." To anyone familiar with Catholic liturgy, this
seems somewhat confused. But there is no doubt that, after
the liturgical service, Cortés, in a brief speech, took possession of an immense territory in the name of the Spanish
Crown. Needless to say, the king of Castile was totally ignorant of who Cortés was and what he was doing there. The
"Captain General" had taken on himself the responsibility
of a royal commission.

Thus he resembled the immortal Don Quixote de la Man-
cha, who in Cervantes' book, written years later, would assume
the fight against the forces of evil and defend the honor of
the pure and lovable Dulcinea, who unfortunately existed
only in the poor knight's addled brain and overheated imagination. But, unlike Don Quixote, "the Knight of the
Woeful Countenance" with his nag Rocinante and his rusty
lance, Cortés set upon his mission with a sharp sword and
well-fed horses. Hernán Cortés' countenance was by no means
woeful; he was an elegant man who dressed in silk and velvet. The natives could not comprehend what he might

represent, and they observed in wonder the solemn ceremony of the occupation of Mexico. They were baffled as they observed these pale, well-armed men bow their heads and kneel before a wooden cross.

Along the coast, next to the conqueror's flagship, were anchored three other caravels and six small brigatines that had transported 530 men in the prime of their lives. They were natives of Spain, Genoa, Naples, Portugal and France. Among them were fifty sailors, the two Franciscans already mentioned, thirty crossbow-men and twelve harquebus-men. Among their armaments the expeditionary force had many swords and lances, sixteen horses, numerous Irish wolfhounds and mastiffs, ten long-range cannons, four falconets and various small Lombard cannons, as the new firearms were named in those days. Some of the men had mutilated ears—the punishment for those who had been caught robbing and convicted in Castile. Be that as it may, the gold chain around the neck of the self-proclaimed Captain General Cortés bore a medal with the Virgin Mary on the front and Saint John the Baptist on the back. On the mainmast of the flagship waved a golden pennant with a blue cross and the Latin inscription: "Amici, sequamur crucem, et si nos fidem habemus, vere in hoc signo vincemus": Friends, let us follow the cross. If we believe in it, truly in this sign we will conquer.

In spite of everything, a few weeks later, some of the conquistadors no longer held such a belief and had lost faith in the leader's good luck; they mutinied and took over a brigantine in order to sail back to Cuba. Cortés hanged two of the ringleaders, mutilated the foot of a third and had the rest publicly flogged. Then he gave orders that, with the whole expeditionary force looking on, nine ships should be grounded in the bay of Villa Rica, in order that even the most cowardly among them would have only one way open, through all their fears: the road to Tenochtitlán, the Aztec capital. In those days it was as large and as populated as ancient Naples or Constantinople and was even more beautiful than Venice. Cortés left only one ship in navigable condition, the *Santa María de la Concepción*.

As all of this was going on, in far-away Europe Leonardo da Vinci was dying and the seven German electors were electing Charles I of Castile as Charles V of that Holy Roman Empire over which, it would later be said, the sun never set. With the addition of Mexico and the Philippines, this empire would cover the globe.

Within a mere two years of disembarking, Cortés had conquered the mighty Aztec empire. According to one variant, the word "Mexico" meant the "Land of the Moon". An actual conquest of the moon would not have come as a greater surprise. Nothing could have prepared the Europeans for the discovery of a New World or for the natives, whose human sacrifices terrified and revolted the Spanish adventurers from the first moment they witnessed the Aztecs take a flint knife to carve out the heart of a living victim and place it, still beating, on a black basalt altar as an offering to their god Quetzalcóatl. They called this the "delectable fruit of the cactus for the Eagle". Some of these altars of sacrifice to the Eagle still exist. After the conquest of Mexico, for example, the architects of the royal chapel nearby in Cholula imported them as holy-water fonts for the entryway.

Generally, before the sacrifice of members of the aristocracy, a drink of hallucinogenic mushrooms and a ration of obsidian wine would be given them—something, however, not disdained by many of the onlookers as well, whose deafening roars of laughter echoed unforgettably through the Spaniards' heads day and night. Less aristocratic or reluctant victims received nothing and were dragged up the pyramid by the hair. Because the priests drew blood from their own ear lobes as additional sacrifices, they were sinister-looking indeed. This was not all. They dressed in black; their hair was tangled; their faces ash-gray; their fingernails extravagantly long. Nothing could reconcile the Spaniards to Aztec sacrificial practices: not gold, not plaintive chants, not the gorgeous feathered vestments, not even the legend-ary magnificence of the Aztec cities. The blood-encrusted temple pyramids seemed to the Spaniards the very portals of hell.

In turn, to the Aztecs, the Spaniards' horses, which they called deer, seemed "as tall as the rooftops". The Spaniards entertained themselves by terrorizing the people with the horses' neighing, which they used tactically and strategi-cally. This was a clash of cultures for which there was no precedent: Stone Age versus Iron Age; obsidian and flint versus Toledo steel; hauling by sled or teams versus the wheel; arrows versus gunpowder and cannonballs; and finally, the recklessly bold spirit of these Renaissance Christians versus the proverbial pagan anguish of the Amerindians, who were subject to an uncountable multitude of gods.

During the conquest of Mexico, from among the 1600 Spaniards, mostly latecomers to Cortés and his expedition, about one thousand died. But the Amerindian tribes who joined the conquistadors—the Tlaxcaltecans, for example, whom the Spaniards stirred up and set against the tyrannical Aztec people—mourned many more victims. The historian Hugh Thomas concludes about their combatants and vic-tims as a whole that the Aztecs "had fought like gods" in the struggle but, in such an unequal contest, had perished by the hundreds of thousands. There had been prophecies that, in the year 1519, Quetzalcóatl, their feathered serpent-god, would return. The Aztecs had been waiting for him for gen-erations. For this reason, some suppose that the Aztecs suc-cumbed, not so much because of Spanish astuteness and their superior war machine, but rather because of an overwhelming surprise—and a profound disappointment.

Before and after the conquest of Mexico, not a single native Amerindian living on the islands of the Caribbean survived the Spanish invasion. For this reason, after their land was conquered, the situation seemed equally hopeless to the inhabitants of Mexico—Mexican, Mistecan, Cholulan, Toltecan, Chichimecan, Tlaxcaltecan, Xochimilcan, Totonacan and others. From here on we will refer to them simply as Aztecs, the name by which the Europeans identified the Amerindians who held sway over vast territories in Mexico at the time of the conquest. First, obviously, no dialogue between the cultures was likely to have been successful, even before the final victory of the military expedition, after Cortés kept the powerful ruler of Mexico, Montezuma II, under arrest in his own palace. Before he died under a rain of stones hurled by Aztec hands, a rain of stones that would erupt like a volcano against the Spaniards from their capital—before all this, the adventurer from Spanish Extremadura would sit for hours at night with the Aztec emperor, who before his accession to the throne had himself been high priest. He spoke to him not only about his sovereign, Charles, the sharpest "sword of Christendom" (to whom Cortés hoped to offer Montezuma's empire as a gift), but also about the ever-virgin Mother of God; about God: the Father, Son and Holy Spirit; about the Immaculate Conception; about the Incarnation; and about many other "interesting things". The sermons of this passionate conquistador and ladies' man were scarcely less bold than his conquest. This is something that sometimes surprises his biographers, and they refer to it frequently.

Nevertheless, for the Aztecs these sermons must have sounded more than strange. For on other days, in the plaza of the Great Pyramid, Cortés permitted the chained Aztec monarch to preside at the solemn burning of rebel Amerindian rulers. Montezuma himself did not stop having human sacrifices offered even while imprisoned. From the apex of the Great Pyramid drums sounded, as did conch horn, flutes and fifes made from bone. The earth had to keep revolving, and for this blood was needed. Also the many celebrations had to continue, and these could not be imagined in ancient Mexico without the human sacrifices that were "like flowers for the gods". The Aztecs had surrendered to bloodlust. The Florentine Codex relates that when his daughter reached the age of six or seven, an Aztec father would say to her: "An obsidian wind is blowing on us; it brushes us lightly and moves on; the earth is not a place of well-being; here there is no joy; here there is no happiness." Four hundred years later, Joseph Höffner wrote: "A dark and bloody harshness weighed down the religion, a harshness that had deprived them of any cheerful lightness of heart." The Aztecs could not imagine life without war.

In the Old World, on the other hand, especially in Spain, not only were many real or presumptive heretics being burned at the stake, but also, in Germany, this was the time when the Reformation rose and took its course, which for the first time broke the Church apart into Catholics and Protestants, so that very soon eight million Christians had cut themselves off from Rome. No bonfire, no *auto-da-fé*, with its flames, could stop this revolution. In any event, the Emperor Charles V had enough to worry about without preoccupying himself with the adventures of one of his many foolhardy subjects in some faraway New World. The dawn of the modern era, with its attendant terrors, was on the horizon.

Simultaneously something occurred in Mexico that sounds more fantastic than the most sensational account of the conquest of the Aztec empire by Cortés and his men. It was the first apparition of the Queen of Heaven in the New World. No one with any regard for his intelligence would want to put faith in this phenomenon. Perhaps only now can the scope of this event be truly seen, because, better than ever before, we can now perceive how greatly this event has changed the course of history and the balance of the world.

CHAPTER TWO

ENCOUNTER AT DAWN

Two artifacts treat of the mysterious encounter on the outskirts of Mexico City in December 1531: one is the image of a girl on a rough piece of cloth; the other is a text written in Nahuatl, the language of the Nahua Indians.

It was ten years after the fall of Tenochtitlán, the Aztec capital at the edge of a sapphire lake that surrounded the island city. At daybreak on December 9, 1531, an Amerindian named Cuauhtlatoatzin, a Chichimecan, was met high on a hill by an unknown young woman who introduced herself as "the perfect ever-virgin Mary, the Mother of the only God through whom everything lives". The man was one of the few Christian Amerindians, having been baptized seven years before and given the double name Juan Diego in honor of the apostles John and James (Jacob or Diego). The girl then spoke to the fifty-seven-year-old widower in Nahuatl: "Juanito" and "smallest of my sons". After this, he returned her greeting with no less tenderness: "My child, smallest of my daughters—mi Niña." This encounter took place on the feast of the Immaculate Conception of Mary. The Spaniards to whom Juan Diego recounted his vision concluded that, if this were not a lie, she had to be the immaculate Virgin (la Purísima), preserved from sin not only after her birth but from the very moment of her conception. The *Santa María de la Concepción*. Naturally, their first supposition was that the Amerindian was simply lying. What else could it be, especially when the encounter took

19

place at the exact spot where the Aztecs had formerly venerated Tonantzin, the mother-goddess of grain?

At this very time, in Peru, in the southernmost part of the double continent, the conquistador Pizarro, trying to imitate Cortés' heroic exploits, had begun his conquest of the Incan empire. However, it was not Cortés' feats, but this unlikely encounter between an Amerindian and a heavenly apparition that made Mexico the wellspring of the greatest mass conversion in history. Right after this event, eight million Amerindians suddenly became Catholics, people who only ten years before could imagine nothing better in the world than "to cook" Spaniards, or Catholics, "in chocolate sauce and eat them". In 1541, the Franciscan Toribio de Benavente, "Motolinía", who is credited with the baptism of Juan Diego and his wife, María Lucía, wrote that around nine million Aztecs had been baptized. He alone had administered the sacrament of baptism to 300,000 Amerindians. One of his brother Franciscans, Pedro de Gante, a nephew of Charles V, reported that on many days he guided between four and ten thousand Amerindians into the Church of the apostles. This was, perhaps, the most significant event in a thousand years. Nonetheless, it has remained largely unremarked over most of the world, even though the whole Mexican culture and the history of all other Latin American nations bear witness to it, as, in a very special way, do two amazing artifacts.

The first and more important is a perfectly preserved piece of cloth, 1.72 meters [67.72 inches] long by 1.07 meters [42.13 inches] wide, woven from usually very perishable agave fibers, with a seam across the middle. Since 1531, it has been displayed and venerated on Tepeyac Hill on the outskirts of today's Mexico City, first in various small shrines and then for centuries in the "Renowned National Basilica of Holy María of Guadalupe", a baroque basilica that was replaced in 1976 by an enormous concrete edifice, situated

next to the ancient basilica, which was in danger of collapsing. It seems that in the first decades after 1531 small
pieces were snipped from the cloth to serve as relics. The
roughly woven fabric was originally used as a tilma, a kind
of all-purpose outer garment, usually worn by the Aztecs
as a simple cloak fastened on the right shoulder like a Roman
toga. For the common people among the Aztecs, clothing
did not have to be more than knee-length.

The front of the tilma, which is displayed like an altarpiece,
is not unadorned, however, as tilmas usually were. Rather,
it is furnished with a unique image of a young woman with
hands joined. Her mestizo features led to her being called
the "holy Creole", as she was referred to as early as the
seventeenth century. She foreshadows the formation of a
new Spanish-Indian-Mexican people that had not yet come
to be in 1531. This is a lucid observation and a plausible
thought. However, anyone looking carefully at the young
woman will discover that she really does not look mestiza
or Indian or Spanish; in fact, if anything, no race can be
definitely assigned. If one takes seriously the story told of
her, however, she would have to be Jewish. She is a young
person, with an expression even more enigmatic than that
of Leonardo da Vinci's *Mona Lisa*. She is dressed in a flow-
ered gown over which she wears a green-blue cloak of ori-
ental style, decorated with forty-six stars. She is surrounded
by the golden rays of the sun. She is standing on a black
crescent moon, within a pink, almond-shaped oval that opens
into a thick layer of clouds. Because her features are in shades
of bronze and olive, Mexicans call her the *Morenita* (the
little dark-skinned girl). The birth of Mexico as a modern
nation is due to this image. Nothing in the history of peoples is comparable to this phenomenon, either in antiquity
or in the modern era. Nor is there anything comparable to
the image of the Virgin of Guadalupe.

The other artifact that introduced María of Guadalupe is a text about the origin and formation of this image, which must have been written down for the first time by one Antonio Valeriano around the middle of the sixteenth century in the imperial Indian College of the Holy Cross of Saint James of Tlatelolco, in Mexico City. It is said of this Amerindian that he was the nephew of the last Aztec emperor, Montezuma II, and was a co-worker of Father Bernardino de Sahagún, one of Cortés' companions, who later became the greatest chronicler of Aztec culture. The college where Sahagún worked until his death in 1590 was enormously important as the place where the Spanish and Aztec cultures engaged each other. The original account by Antonio Valeriano, the so-called "evangelist of the apparition", has been lost. It is said to have been written on fragile agave paper, although it is not known what the text was like. The story has been transmitted only in the Nahuatl version published later, in 1649, by the Baccalaureate Luis Lasso de la Vega, under his own name, with the title *Huei Tlamahuiçoltica Omonexiti in Ilhuicac Tlatóca Çihuapilli Santa María Totlaçonantzin Guadalupe in Nican Huei Altepe-Nahuac México Itocayòcan Tepeyacac*. It was printed in the neighborhood of the church on Tepeyac Hill, where Lasso de la Vega served as chaplain. The text is a narrative written in the Nahuatl language in which the dialogue weaves together both Spanish and Aztec stylistic elements. More important, this cross-cultural masterpiece is the birth certificate of modern Mexico. With this document, the Aztecs were suddenly inserted into the course of world history, but no longer solely as warriors, victims, slaves or cannibals, whose terror of the gods impelled them to ever more bloody sacrificial orgies. (As an aside, there also exist other narratives on the so-called "Guadalupe event", but none of the same caliber.) The most ancient copy of this text is in the New York

Public Library in the department of rare books and manuscripts. In 1648, a year before its printing, the Thirty Years' War had ended in the West, as the various peoples of the Old World, fragmented into different denominations, fought each other to exhaustion.

These two totally different artifacts are the most important documentary sources of the incredible story of the *Morenita*. It is also incredible how the second document unfolds the story of the earliest witness for the first time. Without many words, the author affirms, in effect, the following: Between December 9 and 12, 1531, Mary, Mother of God, appeared four times to an Amerindian named Juan Diego on a hill that gave access to the path leading to the destroyed capital. During the last encounter she left her image on his tilma. This rough fabric has preserved the Virgin's apparition (as in a photograph). Even today, anyone can see it for himself; it hangs in the basilica on Tepeyac Hill, now called Guadalupe.

Taken out of context, the historical narrative would perhaps be nothing but a charming fairy tale—except that it refers explicitly to that astonishing piece of cloth which can still be seen on the outskirts of Mexico City. In combination with the textile, the text is a sensation.

In the version that has come down to us, Lasso de la Vega's document consists of five and a half double-sided leaves, numbered consecutively. The typesetters of the printery of a Juan Ruiz divided the 218 verses into five enormous paragraphs of different lengths with justified lines. The third page has a line at the bottom margin. The second and fourth pages show a few unimportant areas of damage to the text. The text as a whole begins with a large, beautifully embellished initial "Y". In other respects, the text is as clear and neat as scarcely any workshop in Europe could have produced in that day, since printing was still a

relatively new art at that time. The title page is decorated
with a simple black and white woodcut, which, with a few
lines, unequivocally draws the image of our Lady described
in the narrative of the apparition. She appears wearing a
starry mantle, framed by rays of the sun and surrounded by
clouds. Unlike the original image, however, this one shows
the Virgin Mary crowned.

Nahuatl was the lingua franca of imperial Mexico, a language understood and spoken today by only a few old people and the population living in Tula, in the state of Hidalgo.
They describe it as "stately, elegant, rich and flexible". Until
the Spaniards arrived, it was, above all, a spoken language
that could be written only in pictographs or ideograms.
Here, the narrative of the "miraculous apparition of the
Mother of God" in America was finally written down in
the sober Latin letters that the conquistadors had brought
along to the New World in their baggage. One thing dis-
tinguishes this narrative from any other well-documented
apparition of Mary—from the records of La Salette and Lourdes to the official account of the events at Fatima. In these
latter, with serious warnings, the Virgin Mary almost always
expresses a great concern about the dangers and threats to
which the world is exposed. In the narrative of the apparition of the Virgin of Guadalupe, there is no word about
this, even though she appears as the apocalyptic woman of
the book of Revelation, "clothed with the sun, with the
moon beneath her feet". Subsequent manifestations are almost
always to children, perhaps because of their purity. But in
this first truly great narration of a Marian apparition, she
appears as a beloved mother to a man, a widower, to one
who characterizes himself with enigmatic modesty as nothing but "a nobody, a piece of string, the tail-end".

Because of the opening two words in Nahuatl, the narrative is called the *Nican Mopohua*, which means "here is

related". So now we need to continue by reproducing the entire ancient Mexican narrative, with all its attendant embellishments and self-deprecations, which have continued to be a peculiarity of Amerindian rhetoric to this day. The narrative is not one of the most sensational works, but it is one of the most uplifting testimonies of world literature.

CHAPTER THREE

CONQUISTADORA OF HEARTS

The complete 1649 text by Luis Lasso de la Vega of a narrative written by Antonio Valeriano a century before about the fantastic events surrounding the encounter of the Virgin Mary with a widower in December 1531.

Here is set forth in an orderly way the marvelous manner in which the ever-virgin Holy Mary, Mother of God, our Queen, lately appeared on Tepeyac Hill, now called Guadalupe. First she revealed herself to a poor Indian named Juan Diego; and later her precious image appeared before the new bishop Friar Juan de Zumárraga. And all the miracles she performed [will also be related].

Ten years after the conquest of the City of Mexico, shields and arrows were put aside, war ceased, and there was peace at sea and on land among the peoples, as faith began to spring up, knowledge of the true God through whom everything lives. At that time in the year 1531, a few days into December, there was a poor Indian known as Juan Diego, a native of Cuautitlán. Tlatelolco was the center of all things spiritual, and it was to there on this Saturday, long before daybreak, that he was walking to divine worship and praise.

As he reached the little Tepeyac Hill, dawn broke, and he heard singing up on the hill like the song of a variety of wonderful birds; sometimes the singers' voices were still, and then it seemed as if the mountain itself answered them. Their song was sweet and delightful, surpassing that of the *coyoltótotl* and *tzinizcan* and other beautiful song birds.

Juan Diego stopped to attend to this and said to himself: "Am I worthy or deserving of what I am hearing? Or am I dreaming? Perhaps I will soon awake from this sweet dream. Where am I? Perhaps in the earthly paradise of which our ancestors have spoken? Is this the country of flowers, the country of corn and fleshpots? Am I perhaps already in heaven?" He was looking eastward up the hill from where the wonderful heavenly song was coming, when it suddenly ceased and all grew still. Then he heard someone calling him from up the hill: "Juan, dear. Dearest Juan Diego." He then ventured to go where the voice was calling him.

He was not a bit alarmed: on the contrary, he very happily climbed the hill to see from where the voice was calling him. At the top he saw a Lady standing there, telling him to come closer. Once in her presence he was astonished at her splendor, which surpassed anything he had ever seen. She was perfect; her dress was radiant as the sun; the stones and rocks on which she stood were shot through with brilliance, like a bracelet of precious stones, and lit the earth like a rainbow. The mesquite, prickly pear and other chaparral that grow there seemed like emerald; their foliage, fine turquoise; and their branches and thorns gleamed like gold.

He bowed to her and listened to her soft and courteous voice. Love and peace came from her. Her affection was compelling in drawing him to her. She said to him: "Listen, Juan, dear, smallest of my sons, where are you going?" He replied: "My Lady, my Queen, and my little girl, I am going to your house in Mexico-Tlatelolco, to praise and serve God as taught us by our priests, the representatives of our Lord."

She then spoke to him and revealed her holy will: "Know and understand, smallest of my sons! I am the ever-virgin, holy Mary, Mother of the true God; the life-giving Creator of all people; the Lord of what is near and what is far, of heaven and earth. I deeply desire that a chapel be built to me here where I can show, praise and testify to him forever. Here I will give people all my love, compassion, help, comfort and salvation. For I am truly your compassionate Mother: your Mother and the Mother to all who dwell in this land and to all other nations and peoples who love me and call and entreat me. I am the Mother of all who seek me and place their trust in me. Here I will hear their cries and listen to their complaints. Here I will console them in their suffering and relieve their pain. Here I will heal them in their anguish, their affliction and distress. To bring about all that my tenderness wants to achieve, go to the palace of the bishop of Mexico and tell him how I am sending you to make known to him my great desire that he build me a chapel here. On this flat place he should build me a chapel. Tell him in detail what you have seen, wondered at and heard. Know assuredly that I will reward you richly and will repay you. I will know how to thank you. Yes, I will make you happy and give you great joy. For the reward you will earn for this service is great. I will repay you for your labor and fatigue. Now, you have heard my command, my son, my smallest. Go and give your best effort to this task."

At this point, he bowed before her and said: "My Lady, my child, I am going to carry out the splendid command voiced by your perfect breath. I will say good-bye for now, I, your humble servant." Then he went down to carry out her orders, coming out at the path that was the direct route to Mexico. Upon entering the city, he went directly to the palace of the bishop, a prelate just recently arrived, named Friar Juan de Zumárraga, a religious of Saint Francis.

Arriving, he tried to see the bishop; he begged his servants to announce him. A long time later they came to call him, as the bishop had ordered him brought in. As soon as he entered, he bowed and knelt before him; then he gave him the message of the heavenly Lady. He also told him all he had wondered at, seen and heard. After hearing his speech and the message, the bishop seemed not to take him seriously and responded: "Come back some other time, my son, and I will listen to you at greater leisure. I will consider from the very beginning all the reasons you have brought me and think about your wishes and desires."

He went away from there. Sad because he had not been able to carry out his task, he returned that very day to the top of the hill and was fortunate to find the heavenly Lady, who was waiting for him at the very spot where he had first seen her. Catching sight of her, he prostrated himself before her and said: "My Señora, Lady, Queen, smallest of my daughters, my littlest one, I went where you sent me immediately to carry out your orders voiced by your sweet breath. Although it was difficult, I gained entry to where the prelate was sitting; I saw him and gave him your message, as you instructed. He received me kindly and listened attentively, but by the way he responded it seemed that I had not been able to convince him. He said to me: 'Come back some other time, my son, and I will listen to you at greater leisure. I will consider from the very beginning all the reasons you have brought me and think about your wishes and desires.' By the way he responded, I understood perfectly well that he thinks that it is perhaps some invention of mine that you want them to build you a chapel and that the command did not come from your lips. Therefore I earnestly beg you, my Lady and my littlest child, to send one of the noblemen, someone who is known, respected and esteemed, to take your message, so that your mission will be accomplished and the words that come from your sweet lips will be believed. Because I am only a man of the fields, a poor creature. A piece of string, the tail-end, a peon, a slave, a rope, dirt, a leaf, the bottom of the pile. I must be led myself. I must be carried on the back. My littlest Virgin, smallest of my children, you have sent me to a place where I do not belong. My child! My Lady and Queen! I beg you to release me from your demand. For I am grieving your face and your heart. I will only cause disappointment and anger if I go, my Lady and mistress."

The venerable, most holy Virgin answered him: "Listen, my littlest one, my son! Understand that I have many servants and messengers whom I could send to deliver my message and do my will. But it is absolutely necessary that you yourself go and make the request. Through your mediation should my heart's wish and will be accomplished. I earnestly beg you, my son, my smallest, and strictly command you from my heart to go again tomorrow to see the bishop. Speak in my name, and make him understand completely my will that he begin construction of the chapel I am requesting. And tell him again that I, the ever-virgin, holy Mary, Mother of God, am sending you."

Juan Diego answered. "My Lady, Queen, my little one, let me not cause you pain or sadden your heart. Very willingly will I go to carry out this task, deliver the words of your breath. In no way will I neglect doing it or think the way too arduous; I will go to do your will, even though he may perhaps not want to hear me, or hears me but still does not believe. Tomorrow afternoon, when the sun goes down, I will come back to tell you the bishop's answer. And now I say good-bye to you, my little one, good Lady and Queen. My child! In the meantime, rest a little." Then he made his way home so that he, too, might rest.

The next day, Sunday, long before dawn, he left his house and went straight to Tlatelolco, to be instructed in the things of God, put his name on the list of the baptized, and see the bishop afterward. He arrived just before ten. He was ready. He went to Mass and had himself inscribed in the list of the baptized. The crowd had already dispersed when Juan Diego went to the bishop's palace. As soon as he arrived he made every effort to see the bishop and with great difficulty, succeeded. He knelt at his feet and sadly wept as he repeated the command of the heavenly Lady—that he would believe the message and will of the Immaculate One, that he should build a small chapel at the location she had chosen. To get at the facts, the bishop asked him many things: where he had seen her and what she looked like. And Juan Diego gave a perfect accounting to the bishop. Even more, he described her precisely and all he had seen and wondered at, and how everything about her showed her to be the ever-virgin, most holy Mother of the Savior, our Lord Jesus Christ. Still, the bishop did not believe him.

He told him that he could not do what he was requesting simply on his word and because of his insistence. It was very necessary to have a sign, so that he could believe that the heavenly Lady herself was sending him. As he listened, Juan Diego said to the bishop: "My lord, what sign do you want? I will go to the heavenly Lady who sent me and ask her for it." The bishop noted that he was consistent in his story, without uncertainties or hesitations, then sent him away.

But right away he ordered some trustworthy people of his household to follow him and find out where he went and whom he saw and to whom he talked. They complied. Juan Diego came straight back along the path. Those who followed him lost him at the ravine near the Tepeyac bridge; and although they looked for him everywhere, they never saw him. So they returned, not only because they were tired of searching, but also because they were frustrated, which made them angry. They went to report all this to the bishop, telling him not to put his faith in Juan Diego, as he was simply deceiving him; he was making up the story he had come to tell or perhaps had only been dreaming and what he had asked for was a fantasy. Finally they agreed that if he came again, he should be taken and punished severely, so that he would never again lie or deceive in order to create a sensation.

Meanwhile Juan Diego was with the most holy Virgin, giving her the bishop's answer. Upon hearing it, the Lady and Queen said: "Very well, my son, my dearest child, come back here tomorrow so that you can take to the bishop the sign of truth he has asked for. Then he will believe you and will stop doubting and being suspicious of you. And you, my little son, know that I will repay your concern and the work and fatigue that you have expended for me. So go now. I will await you here tomorrow."

The next day, Monday, the day on which Juan Diego was supposed to take some sign back as proof, he did not return. For when he arrived home, he found that his uncle, Juan Bernardino, had fallen sick and already lay near death. First Juan Diego called a physician, but, in spite of the doctor's efforts, nothing more could be done, since he was so deathly ill. During the night his uncle begged him to go out, before daybreak, to Tlatelolco to call a priest who would hear his confession and prepare him for dying, because he was very certain that death was upon him and that he would never again rise or be healed.

Tuesday, long before daybreak, Juan Diego left his house for Tlatelolco, to call the priest. When he approached the path that follows the contours of Tepeyac Hill, along his usual route on the west side, he said to himself: "If I go straight, the Lady might see me and detain me, so that I take the bishop the sign of which she spoke. First, we have to deal with our affliction and call the priest. My poor uncle is anxiously waiting for him." He turned toward the hill

and climbed it on the eastern side, so that he could get to
Mexico more quickly without the heavenly Lady delaying
him. He thought that from where he turned off, she, who
sees well everywhere, would not be able to see him. At this
very moment, he saw her coming down from the top of
the hill, looking toward the spot where he had seen her
before. She came to meet him at the side of the hill and
said to him: "What is happening, my son, my smallest? Where
are your steps headed? Where are you going?"

Was he a little embarrassed or ashamed or startled? Or
even scared or taken by fright? Juan Diego bowed before
her and greeted her: "My little one, my dear little daughter, my child and my Queen! I hope you are happy. How
are you today? Did you rest well, and has the day begun
well? Are you in good health, my Lady and child? I have
to cause you some pain, and that makes me sad. Know,
my little girl, that one of your poor servants, my uncle, is
very ill; he has a terrible sickness and is on the point of
death. Now I am rushing to your house in Mexico to call
one of the priests, beloved by our Lord, to go hear his
confession and prepare him, for from the day of our birth,
we approach the hour of a good death. When I have ful-
filled my duty, I will be right back again to go again to
take your message, my Lady and beloved child. Please forgive me. Have patience with me now. I am not deceiving
you, my child, my smallest daughter. Tomorrow I will hurry
back here to you."

After listening to Juan Diego's speech, the most kindly
Virgin answered: "Hear and understand, my smallest and
dearest son, that what is alarming and afflicting you is nothing. Do not let your countenance or your heart be disturbed. Do not fear this illness or any other illness or
suffering. Am I, your Mother, not here? Are you not under
my shadow and protection? Am I not the source of your

joy? Are you not in the folds of my mantle, in the crossing of my arms? What more do you need? Let nothing else disturb or distress you. Do not worry about your uncle's illness. He will not die from it today—be assured that he has been cured." (At that precise moment, his uncle was healed, as it was later learned.) When Juan Diego heard these words of the heavenly Lady, he was greatly reassured and was at peace. He begged her to send him as soon as possible to see the bishop and take him the sign and proof, so that he would believe.

The heavenly Lady then told him to climb to the top of the hill where he had seen her before, saying: "Climb, my son, my smallest, to the top of the hill, where you saw me and received my errand. There you will find various flowers. Cut them, gather them and put them together. Then come right down and bring them before me." Juan Diego immediately climbed the hill and when he got to the top he was greatly astonished that so many varieties of exquisite Castilian roses had bloomed, with their petals wide open, so long before their season, for at this time of the year everything was covered with frost. They were very fragrant, drenched in dew that looked like precious pearls.

Right away he began to cut them and gather them up into the folds of his tilma. The top of the hill was certainly not the place where flowers bloomed. There were just stones, thistles and thorns, mesquite and cactus. Now and then herbs grew, but not in December, when the frost destroyed all life. He went down immediately, bringing the colorful flowers he had gone to cut to the heavenly Lady. When she saw them, she rearranged them with her precious hands and put them back in his tilma, saying: 'My son, my smallest, this variety of flowers is the proof and sign you are to take to the bishop. Tell him in my name to see my desire in them and do my will and wish. You are my ambassador, most worthy of my trust. I strictly command you to open your tilma and reveal what you carry only in front of the bishop. Give him a full account. Tell him that I commanded you to climb to the top of the hill to cut the flowers; tell him all you have seen and wondered at, so that you can persuade the prelate to do what he can to make and erect the chapel I have asked for."

After the heavenly Lady had advised him, he set out on the path that leads directly to Mexico. He was at peace and sure of a good outcome, holding with great care what he carried in his tilma, taking care to drop nothing and rejoicing in the fragrance of the variety of beautiful flowers. When he arrived at the bishop's palace, the porter and other servants went out to meet him. He entreated them to tell the bishop that he wanted to see him, but not one of them would do so, pretending that they could not hear him— either because it was very early or because they perceived him as a nuisance or because their companions had told them about losing sight of him when they had tried to follow him the day before.

He waited a long time. When they saw that he had been standing there a long time, barefooted, head bowed, not doing anything, in case he were called, and noticed that he seemed to be carrying something in his tilma, they approached to see what he carried and satisfy their curiosity. So, in the end, Juan Diego let them glimpse the flowers because it was clear to him that he could no longer conceal his miraculous gift and in order to keep them from harassing him further or evicting or flogging him.

And when they saw that they were genuine Castilian roses, which did not bloom at that time of year, they were greatly astonished, since, besides, they were fresh-picked, completely open, very fragrant and very beautiful. They tried to grab and take some three times but had no luck, because, as they grabbed, the flowers no longer seemed real, but painted, embroidered or appliquéd on the tilma.

They hurried to the bishop to tell him what they had seen and that the humble Indian, who had come so many times, wished to see him. He had already waited a long time. The bishop realized that this had to be the proof needed to certify and act on the humble Indian's request. He immediately ordered that he be admitted.

Upon entering, Juan Diego bowed humbly before the bishop as he had done before and retold the story of all that he had seen and wondered at and repeated the message: "My lord, I did what you commanded me. I went to tell my mistress, the heavenly Lady, holy Mary, the beloved Mother of God, that you asked her for a sign so that you might believe me that you are to build a chapel where she asks you to. I also told her that I had promised to bring you the sign and proof of her will that you asked me to bring. And she has well received the word of your breath. She was well pleased by your request for a sign and proof, so that her beloved will may be done. Very early today she commanded me to come see you again. I asked for the sign that would make you believe me, that sign which she had promised to give me. She sent me to the top of the hill, where I had seen her before, to cut some Castilian roses. I knew well that the top of that hill was not a place where flowers could grow, since it is a place of rocks, thistles, thorns, cactus and mesquite, but I did not doubt. As I approached the top of the hill I saw that I was in paradise, where there were exquisite Castilian roses, brilliant with dew, which I proceeded to cut. When I had cut them, I brought them down; she took them in her hands, rearranged them, and placed them in my tilma, so that I might bring them and give them to you in person. She told me that I must deliver them to you, as a sign of the truth of my word and my message to have her will be done. Here they are. Please receive them."

Then he unfurled his white tilma in which he had folded the flowers. As the different Castilian roses scattered over the floor, there was suddenly imprinted, visibly, the wonderful image of the ever-virgin, holy Mary, Mother of God, as it is now preserved and on display in her chapel on Tepeyac, now called Guadalupe.

As soon as the bishop and others present saw it, they fell to their knees. They were overwhelmed with amazement and awe. They became sad, and their hearts and minds were in ecstasy. The bishop, crying tears of repentance, prayed and asked pardon for not having begun to carry out her will and command. Standing, he untied from Juan Diego's neck the tilma on which the heavenly Lady was made manifest. Then he took it and placed it in his chapel. The bishop asked him to stay, so Juan Diego remained one more day in the bishop's house. The next day the bishop said: "Now let us go see where the heavenly Lady wants her chapel built." And he immediately invited everyone who might be concerned with its construction to go along.

As soon as Juan Diego showed him where the heavenly Lady had commanded that her chapel be raised, he asked permission to leave. He now wanted to go home to see his uncle, Juan Bernardino, the one who was so sick that he had left him to go to Tlatelolco and call a priest to hear his confession and prepare him for death, the one whom the heavenly Lady had declared already cured. However, they would not let him go alone, but accompanied him to his home.

Arriving, they saw that his uncle was happy and free from pain. He was astonished that his nephew arrived in such state, with so many people, and asked him why they did this and why they were showing him such respect. His

nephew answered that when he left to call the priest to
hear his confession and prepare him for death, the heavenly
Lady had appeared to him on Tepeyac Hill, telling him not
to be upset, that his uncle was cured, which greatly com-
forted him; she sent him to Mexico to see the bishop so
that he would build her a house on Tepeyac Hill. The uncle
revealed that he was sure that he was cured at that moment
and that he saw her at the same moment in the same image
as she appeared to his nephew. He had learned from her
that she had sent his nephew to see the bishop in Mexico.
The Lady also told him that when he should go to see the
bishop, he should make known what he had seen and the
miraculous way he had been cured and that the blessed image
should always be called and she should be worshipped there
as the ever-virgin holy María of Guadalupe.

They then took Juan Bernardino before the bishop to
report and bear witness before him. When he and his nephew
arrived together, the bishop offered them hospitality in his
house for a few days, until a shrine to the Queen of Tepeyac
could be built where she had appeared to Juan Diego. The
bishop moved the holy image of the beloved heavenly Lady
to the cathedral, taking it from the chapel in his palace, so
that all the people could see and wonder at her blessed image.
The whole city was deeply moved: they came to see and
wonder at her revered image, whose divine origin they recognized, and pray to her. Many were astonished at the miraculous way she had appeared, for no person in this world
had painted her beloved image.

Luis Lasso de la Vega, *Nican Mopohua*, Mexico City, 1649

CHAPTER FOUR

THE MYSTERY IN THE VIRGIN'S EYES

A modern convergence between the image, the Nican Mopohua *and historical probability. Vivid colors and photos of the Lady's iris, in which can be seen twelve men and a black servant named María.*

This is the story in full. It is clearly so amazing and wonderful that it comes as no surprise that many serious people immediately classify it as a mere fantasy. Could it be anything but a charming lie? Such suspicions surfaced immediately. In the sixteenth century itself, some reputable monks and other devout people held that a truly unique painting had surfaced and that some other person invented a story to go with it. Others held that someone invented the story and that another person, unknown, had painted the picture to fit it. Such arguments remain unchanged to our own day, as have the reasons behind them. Such a fraud could have emerged only from the very lowest motives and from the greedy desire for donations; it had to have arisen to deceive poor, innocent country people, to keep them in ignorance. This is self-evident. The presumption of evil is always convincing.

But during the twentieth century, two previously unknown photographs came to light that investigators of previous centuries had not been able to consider—more evidence validating María of Guadalupe. In them can be seen something like a modern convergence, which in a singular way—and with historical probability—joins and binds together the image of the Virgin and the *Nican Mopohua*, and vice versa. For these are photographs of the "photographs" within the Virgin's eyes, in which the final scene of the narrative of the apparition in the *Nican Mopohua* has been recorded. This is, naturally, even more incredible than the story itself. Strictly speaking, the images are not photographs, but reflections, mirror images, in the pupils of María of Guadalupe's eyes. At the very instant of the miracle of the roses, her eyes recorded and preserved the scene of the unveiling of her image before Bishop Zumárraga on December 12, 1531. Recent enlargements of photographs of her pupils made this discovery possible. However, I learned that a photographer had revealed the interior of her eyes in 1929. Later, an oculist, examining the eyes of the image yet again, "dropped the magnifying glass upon seeing it and gave a cry", as Christine related it to me (about whom more later): "'These are real, living pupils!' he exclaimed, as he discovered the reflections of some people in the iris."

The first photographs of the *Morenita* come from the late nineteenth century, although the first high-quality photos of the image of the Virgin were produced only on May 18, 1923, by Manuel Ramos. A 1929 report by Alfonso Marcué González, the official photographer of the Basilica of Guadalupe, first mentioned that the examination of the photo negative of the Lady's right eye revealed something like the figure of a bearded man. Nevertheless, because of the political situation, the then bishop of Mexico asked him not to make this discovery public. A fierce and furious persecution of Mexican Catholics raged in the years 1926 to 1929. Even the image of the Virgin had to be hidden far from the basilica, in order to protect it. When it was returned, on the occasion of the imminent celebration of the fourth centenary of the apparitions, Abbot Cortés Mora commissioned new photographs.

On July 5, 1938, Berthold von Stetten took the first color photos of Our Lady of Guadalupe. Finally, on May 29, 1951, José Carlos Chávez made the same discovery as Alfonso Marcué González had in 1929—but this time in both eyes—after which the archbishop of Mexico, Luís María Martínez, commissioned him to do scientific studies of the image. Just before the anniversary of the apparitions, on December 12, 1955, it was first announced officially that the reflected image of a man, probably Juan Diego, had been discovered in the Virgin's eyes. In May 1956, Dr. Javier Toroello Bueno and Dr. Rafael Torija, oculists, discovered similar images reflected in the corneas of both eyes. They identified shapes of reflected light as these would appear in human eyes, according to Helmholtz's discoveries in the 1880s. Ever since the discoveries of Doctors Torroello Bueno and Torija, the eyes of the *Morenita* have become a favorite study of ophthalmologists who were then permitted to examine the painting with microscope and ophthalmoscopes, without its protective glass. In 1958 they discovered in Mary's eyes the "Purkinje-Sanson effect", in which objects seen by the eye are reflected on three different places in the human eye, twice vertically, upward (that is, with the head at the top), and once vertically, downward (with the head downward, or upside down). This is a phenomenon observable in the human eye or in photographs, but never in paintings. In 1963 Kodak specialists examined the image once again and generally agreed that it had the "characteristics of a photograph".

In May 1979, making infrared studies, Philipp Serna Callahan and Professor Jody Brant Smith from Florida discovered that the pink color of the dress becomes transparent in this light, even though pink pigments ordinarily remain totally opaque. They declared that this was a "mystery".

All this finally came into the hands of José Aste Tönsmann, who, in his study of the image of the Virgin, had

access to the most recent digital technology. Señor Tönsmann is an engineer from Lima, Peru. Before arriving in
Mexico as a distinguished data-processing and computer spe-
cialist, he had studied and taught in various cities in South
and North America. He recalls that "Then I knew nothing
about the Virgin. When I came to Mexico I was looking
for a symbol typical of Mexican culture, which I could dig-
itize and store. I thought about the famous Aztec calendar
stone, or something similar. Then by chance I read a magazine article about the studies Carlos Salinas Chávez had
made of the right eye of the Virgin of Guadalupe. This
awakened my curiosity." Thus began José Aste Tönsmann's
studies of the Virgin's eyes, which still continue. Although
the archbishop of Mexico opened all necessary doors, Tönsmann got the most help from modern technology, which
has undergone a revolution in recent decades. Instrumen-
tation with which the team at NASA evaluates satellite images
permitted this Cornell University scientist to magnify micro-
scopic segments of the iris and pupil of the photo's eyes by
2,500, with a resolution of 25,000 pixels per square milli-
meter. He was asking himself: "How is it possible that the
colors retain their power to reflect light and shine when
there is no paint detectable in the image?" Callahan and
Smith had also proven that the colors of the Virgin's image
change depending on the angle from which the spectator
approaches. In biology this phenomenon is called "irides-
cence"; we know animals who use this as camouflage, yet
how does this phenomenal artifact come to be iridescent?
Nothing of this kind had been reproduced by men before.

Finally, more intriguing than these questions were his
own discoveries in the eyes. After passing the photographs
through a variety of filters and analyzing the results, he
demonstrated that there were not just one or two figures
reflected in the eyes, but a whole group of people. Among

these, he believed he could identify a seated Amerindian, Bishop Zumárraga and his translator, Juan González, then Juan Diego with tilma unfurled, a woman, a bearded Spaniard, a group of Indians, including a child—in a word, a true-to-life depiction of the final scene in the *Nican Mopohua*: "Then he unfurled his white tilma in which he had folded the flowers.... As soon as the bishop and others present saw it, they fell to their knees. They were overwhelmed with amazement and awe ... , and their hearts and minds were in ecstasy." He deduced that the image was the result of the Virgin's eyes preserving the discovery scene at the moment of greatest astonishment. Each person was frozen in time, caught in different places and gestures. There is a half-naked Aztec, with long black hair in a ponytail, seated with legs crossed; he wears a clearly visible earring and a ring on his finger. At his side is an old bald man with a white beard, straight nose and heavy eyebrows, a tear running down his right cheek—with a strong resemblance to a portrait of Bishop Zumárraga. Next to him is a young man; then, in profile, a man in a tall hood, bearded and mustached, with a Roman nose and protuberant cheekbones, deep-set eyes and lips half closed, who holds out some kind of scarf to the bald man. Also represented is a young black girl. A little apart, in the background, there is a small group, perhaps a family: the father wearing a hat, a young woman carrying an infant at her shoulder, the grandparents and three children. Thirteen persons in all are captured and preserved in the eyes.

I had read José Aste Tönsmann's book on the eyes of the Virgin; I had examined the many beautiful images and drawings that supported his conclusions. But I still had some questions. Could not the identification of such tiny figures be some elaborate fraud? Could these not be simply vague objects interpreted subjectively, like the blurred figures of a Rorschach test, in which a person is invited to see something in the inkblots, enabling him to know himself better, depending on what he sees? Señor Tönsmann just smiles and declares indulgently: "Do you know something? If there were only one 'photo', I would have to admit you were right. But here, in two different eyes, we have two snapshots that are not identical, each of which corresponds precisely in its refraction and proportion, exactly as your two eyes would divide up and refract a single, identical scene. In the eyes of María of Guadalupe we have two snapshots from different angles, shifting the angle of refraction, exactly as happens when a single image is reflected differently in each of a person's eyes. This is the evidence that these images provide. A single image could be attributed to chance or subjective interpretation. But two images bring all the laws of reason and probability into play. The correspondences and the distortions resulting from the curve of the cornea are too complex to be mere chance. And they would remain completely inexplicable if the figures depicted a scene totally different from what I believe I am seeing."

Nonetheless, could not this scene have been painted on the Virgin's irises? "No. Such precise technology did not exist, neither fine metal points, nor brushes nor pen. A single hair would have been too thick for many of the details. This is even more true because, at that time, the connections among the laws of optics, here offered as proof, were unknown. No human being could have painted anything like it—or could produce anything similar even today. For the fine touches are revealed only by magnification."

"But you speak also of identifying a person of color among those present. You assume it is a servant of the bishop. But in 1531 there was as yet not a single Negro in the Caribbean. The importation of black slaves in the Caribbean took place much later, only after the extermination of whole populations on the islands."

"You are right. However, in the General Archives of the Indies, in Seville, Bishop Zumárraga's will has been discovered, in which he mentions a black female slave, whom he wished to free before he died as a token of his gratitude for her great service. We even know her name—María."

CHAPTER FIVE

NOT PAINTED BY HUMAN HAND

Photograph of Turin. Pure Edessa cloth. Thomas, the skeptical apostle and, in Jerusalem, a stone burial chamber covered with roses. The first trace of María of Guadalupe in a journey to the end of the millennium, across three continents and world history.

I had never in my whole life either heard or seen anything about the "beloved image" that has impacted the world for over four hundred years. Not one word, one picture of a tanned or dark-skinned Mary. I first became acquainted with the image in the spring of 1988, not through José Aste Tönsmann's book or that of any New or Old World historian, but by chance in Turin, where, as a reporter, I had to do a piece on the authenticity of the Shroud, which many consider to be a life-size photograph of Jesus of Nazareth. All the arguments for and against its authenticity were familiar to me before I arrived, but I had never actually seen it. On landing at the airport, I immediately took a taxi to the cathedral and hurried up the stairs to the main entrance. I entered the shadowy church and stood spellbound before the enormous piece of cloth displayed above the altar in the semi-darkness. At that very moment a group of young nuns, in an alcove off to the right, broke into song: "Benedetto il Signore Dio d'Israele" (Blessed be the Lord God of Israel). A priest in a brocade chasuble shining with gold incensed the altar with a censer that raised waves of thick smoke to the steady rhythm of its softly clanking chains as it moved back and forth. Early morning Mass had begun. But all my attention was on the poorly lighted shroud behind the choir, the shroud first mentioned by the first-century evangelists Matthew, Mark, Luke and John.

In chapter 15 of his Gospel, Mark says that after Jesus' crucifixion, Joseph of Arimathea, a distinguished member of the Sanhedrin, who looked forward to the Kingdom of God, "bought a linen cloth, and taking [the body] down, wrapped him in the linen shroud, and laid him in a tomb which had been hewn out of the rock". When two nights had passed, "the [disciple] whom Jesus loved" came running to the tomb, says John's Gospel, bent down to look in and saw "the linen cloths lying there". Simon Peter, who was right behind him, saw the burial cloths in the tomb, but not Jesus, whose corpse had been laid there. In the first centuries of the Christian era, in the ancient city of Edessa in what is today eastern Anatolia, Turkey, there was preserved an image of Christ not painted by human hand. The Shroud of Turin, or Shroud of Jesus, underwent all kinds of tests that indicate it is identical with this piece of "pure linen" from Edessa. It has been a long time since it was "pure", since in Jerusalem it was stained with blood and water. Since then the stains have remained dry. Later fires have burned and charred the linen here and there. But this piece of cloth shows the viewer still more. Among the stains caused by fire, blood and water, there stands out a faint but clear negative reproduction of a man with eyes closed, laid on half the cloth, with the other half covering him, so his front and back are visible.

The image seems to have been breathed onto the linen cloth. From a distance, at first glance, the delicate contours of the frontal and dorsal images of the man look like the fully outstretched arms of a human being. Seen up close, the image is covered with wounds; there is no part of the body intact. The man has been flogged like a slave. The

dorsal view is on the right-hand side of the piece of fabric.
The left-hand side is the frontal view of the face; the hair,
matted and clumped; the thorax; legs and arms; with thin
hands that some compassionate person has crossed over the
genitals. The right cheek is swollen and smeared with blood;
the nose is swollen as if broken at the base. The beard, also
matted and clumped, has been partially pulled out. The shoulder has been severely damaged. A wound appears in the
carpal bone of the right hand. From this wound blood has
trickled up the forearm. Blood is flowing from the hair onto
the brow and the nape of the neck, as if nails or thorns have
been driven into the head. Over one of the burned spots on
the fabric, on the left in the general area of the chest, there
is a blood stain so large that a hand could be inserted into
the wound that had once been covered by the fabric. In the
middle of the right side of the Shroud, the hair, fixed in a
sort of ponytail, is so soaked that blood has trickled down
the nape of the neck to the shoulder. The shoulders and
extremities are covered with the crisscross lines left by whip-
ping. From the large wound in the chest, blood and water
have flowed down to the lower back and have pooled there.
On the left foot there is a three-inch space without wounds.
Otherwise, no part of the body is unbloodied. It is as if he
had sweated blood from his shoulders, buttocks, arms, legs,
above and below, in front and in back. A stream of blood
has flowed from the sole of his foot onto the Shroud. This
strong man was like a piece of raw meat when he was placed
naked onto the Shroud. It is totally inexplicable how he can
appear so unscathed here, his face so full of peace.

I had heard that this is the oldest authentic picture of a
human being, one that had been neither painted nor drawn.
It is said that it is the earliest "photo" in history, to which
men and women flock from all over the world. Perfectly
lighted, the yellowed background gleams gold. "Behold the

Lamb of God", says the priest from the altar directly in front of the Shroud as he elevates the Host.

The man with the short gray hair is Giuseppe Ghiberti. With the full authority of the cardinal of Turin, he is responsible for the world-famous *Santa Sindone*, as the Italians refer to the Shroud. He is probably the greatest living expert on this piece of cloth. His reception room is on the other side of the Po River, in an extensive complex of an art academy; and it is totally austere: a table, two chairs and a crucifix hanging on the wall. The only luxury is a half-open window. He is pressed for time when I first meet him here on a bright spring day. All his time is taken in organizing the exhibition of the Shroud for the innumerable visitors. Most of the questions he has answered hundreds of times, and I already know his answers by heart. I do not expect my interview with him to be at all sensational, so I finally ask him: "But, Don Giuseppe, is there a definitive explanation of how the image was imprinted on the cloth?" "No," he says with a tired smile, "but this piece of fabric is not alone in that respect. Think about the origin of the image of the Virgin of Guadalupe. Who painted it?"

"What does the Virgin of Guadalupe have to do with this?" I had heard the title somewhere, but nothing else. He replied: "Right now in Mexico there is another image whose origin no one can explain. It, however, is an image of the Mother of God." I straightened up in my chair. "Can there really be a second image like the Shroud?"

"No, that's not the right way to put it. The image in Mexico is a real picture, not a poor shadow with a few blood and water stains, like the Shroud of Turin. Neither is it locked up in a vault, to be exhibited every twenty years or so. There it hangs out in the open in a basilica, where anyone who wants to can look at it at any time. It represents a young woman in great detail, and it is in color.

But in this case, too, how it came to be is totally inexplicable."

"Please tell me more. I want to know more about this."

Don Giuseppe looked at his watch. "There isn't much to tell. A few centuries ago the Mother of God appeared to an old Amerindian and sent him to the bishop to ask that a shrine be built on the site of the apparitions. Naturally, the bishop did not believe him and wanted to see a sign first. The Amerindian reported this to the Virgin. So she told him that, as a sign that he was telling the truth, he should gather some flowers growing on a small hill and take them to the bishop. So he did. He cut the roses, wrapped them in his tilma and went to the bishop, saying as he unfolded the tilma: 'Here is the sign.' The roses fell out, and the image appeared on the fabric. That's the whole story. The miracle of the roses is known throughout Latin America."

I looked at Don Giuseppe, not believing my ears. This professor of theology is a sober, educated, sensible man, speaking perfect German. "This is a fairy tale, a legend," I countered, "the opposite of the Shroud of Turin, which is a completely real piece of cloth."

"So is the image of the Virgin of Guadalupe. Reason is on your side; the story does sound like a fairy tale. Nonetheless, no one can account for how the image was imprinted on this piece of cloth that really exists on the outskirts of Mexico City. It is always on display, not just on special occasions. That is why ever-growing masses of people gather there, more than in Turin. It is the greatest Marian pilgrimage site in the world."

The Po River was in flood. While we were speaking, a strong wind had driven all the clouds away. Returning from Don Giuseppe's to the Via Po, bordered with porticos, I paused by a street light on the bridge of "the Great Mother of God" and braced myself on the cast-iron handrail to look at the swollen, gray waters that were shooting by and watch a branch that kept popping up and down in the water before hurling itself into the waterfall to the river below. A street-car passed behind me, leaving the bridge trembling.

A long-forgotten childhood memory surged up in me like a suddenly released stream of water. Was I four or five years old? What happened was that, once I started school, my mother stopped telling me stories as she had done before. Or, perhaps, I just did not pay attention to them anymore. Now this memory rose up like a movie. At night my mother is sitting on my bed and telling me about the death of Mary in the far-off city of Jerusalem: "All the apostles are reunited once more, and together they carry the Mother from Mount Zion to the tomb in the garden of Gethsemane. Only Thomas is missing, because, yet again, he is late. When he arrives three days later, he, too, wants to say good-bye to Mary. So the twelve apostles go back down to the Kedron valley where they have buried Mary in a tomb excavated from a rock, so as to see her one last time before they part. As soon as they roll away the stone blocking the entrance to the tomb, they are wrapped in a marvelous perfume. Then they notice: the place where Mary had lain is full of roses. But she is not there."

The floodwaters shoot past, under my feet, as if they want to carry the bridge along with them. Before I reached the other shore of the Po at the Vittorio Veneto Plaza, I had forgotten the roses of Mexico as I had the roses of Jerusalem.

CHAPTER SIX

QUEEN OF PEACE

Searching for the Queen of Peace in times of war. A pilgrimage through Balkan river valleys, meadows and hills to find answers during a personal crisis, and the unexpected discovery of my mother's old calendar.

The second time I heard about the dark-skinned María of Guadalupe was a year later in the environs of Herzegovina. War had erupted furiously in the Balkans. Hour after hour, NATO bomber squadrons took off from Italy toward the opposite shore of the Adriatic to support the Muslims in Kosovo and defend them from the Serbian military. War had also erupted in me, though on a different battlefront. Strife had cast an evil spell on my life: in my family, with my friends and with enemies. My sky was dark and seemed to be cursed. My dreams became nightmares; my hopes, frauds. All I had always considered good, important, and right now seemed to fall to pieces, like a far-distant procession, a caravan scattered in different directions and dissolving on the horizon. Conflict I had never before known took over my life, intermingled with attacks of strong death wishes. This person who suddenly found himself on the bus, leaning his head on the window and staring into the depths of the blue sea, had emerged one afternoon in December on a train from Basel to Munich, where I was living at the time.

In Basel, one of my older brothers had suffered a stroke. He was the one with whom I had had my best fights, but all that was definitely in the past. All he could do now was laugh with me. Try as he might, he could not pronounce a single word. The train was a little behind schedule, as some gauge had frozen. Snow covered the fields. From the east, cirrus clouds were tinted a silvery pink. The train ran the length of the Rhine valley. In the dining car I had drunk a cup of tea and listened in on the almost inaudible conversation of two men at the next table: "I'm going again next week", one said to the other. "I have to experience it one more time. Peace radiates from her to the whole valley." I ordered another cup of tea, lit a cigarette and glanced out the window. At that moment the full moon rose over the snow-covered fields. Nevertheless, the more quietly they spoke, the harder I found it to concentrate. I closed the book I was actually anxious to read. The older man looked like an engineer; the younger, a farmer. It seemed as if the train stopped at every little cow town. The younger man got off in the Algäu region.

Now I spoke to my only fellow traveler: "What valley were you talking about?" He turned the question back on me: "Have you never heard about Medjugorje? In 1981, the Mother of God appeared there to some children. More than that, since then she has appeared to them every day at 6:45." "Aha", I said, and opened my book again.

"You don't believe me", he persisted; "you don't need to. No one is obliged to believe it; no one is forcing you to believe. The bishop of Medjugorje is totally opposed, although other bishops do go, mostly incognito. It's not necessary to believe. In itself, there is nothing to believe. But you have to go there. It will change your life." I gave him a polite smile. Then he stood up to put on his coat and place some documents in his briefcase. "Well, what are the apparitions about? What does the Mother of God say? What does she look like?" I asked him in farewell. The man was about to button his coat. "Basically, she always says the same thing. The children say that the first time they saw her, she was dressed in a shining gray dress and a white veil. She has blue eyes and is crowned with twelve stars. 'Mir! Mir! Mir!' she cried to them in Serbo-Croatian, the first time. It means Peace, peace, peace. This happened on June 25, 1981, while the communist regime was still in full power. They built a fence around the mountain and restricted access; they nailed the door of the church shut. Police and tanks had to put brakes on the apparitions. But ten years later, war broke out in the Balkans and spread throughout all the states of Yugoslavia, one after the other, laying them waste. By some quirk of fate, this little area was untouched by all these alarms. There, no shot was fired. Peace, peace, peace has remained the keynote of all her messages to date. She is the Queen of Peace." He held out his hand. "You need to go visit her. It will change your life." He got off the train. He turned up the collar of his coat in the dimly lit station. He waved at me once more as the train set off again.

I was fifty years old. By the end of the twentieth century I had lived three lives: as a professor, as a journalist and as the father of three sons and two daughters. I had absolutely no leanings toward superstition. Marian apparitions were as alien to me as the fairy tales of my childhood. I had never made a pilgrimage (although vacationing in comfortable cars, with good wine and fine restaurants in place of prayers and litanies, I had followed in the footsteps of other pilgrims). At the Franciscan friary around the corner from my house I noted that the "monthly messages" of the Madonna of Medjugorje were formulaic: "Pray, pray, pray" and "Thank you for answering my call." Father Claus, a very trustworthy priest, looked at me out of the corner of his eye, and he responded with an indulgent smile when I asked for the latest messages from Medjugorje. The Mother of God's monthly messages to the visionaries were especially provocative. Three months later, during an attack of inner restlessness, I booked two tickets for a pilgrimage to the former Yugoslavia. "Queen of Peace"—the title resonated with promise. Who could have resisted it?

So right after Easter, my son Jakob and I caught a flight to Split. Jakob was free because he had just then lost another job. He was trying to decide whether or not he could change his luck by purchasing some risky stocks. During the flight he was lost in the handbook entitled *The Road to Financial Independence: Your First Million in Seven Years*. We had just settled ourselves into the bus that picked up pilgrims at the airport when a woman, who stood by the driver the whole length of the coastal highway, loudly intoned the first rosary. This made me shudder, and I felt worse when I took a good look at each of my traveling companions.

Eight years earlier my mother had died with a rosary in her hands. The endless murmur of one Hail Mary after another had been familiar to me from infancy. I have scarcely ever been exposed to a more monotonous formula. The first songs I heard were probably hymns to the Virgin, which my mother sang while she cleaned, ironed, washed dishes or did laundry. Just as we today organize our lives around the seasons, vacations, breakfast rituals or the nightly news, so she organized her life around the liturgical year and the feast days of the saints. One of her favorite proverbs was "A life without feast days is like hiking with no rest stops." The rest stops that most delighted her on her liturgical hike were, above all, the Marian feasts. The Annunciation to Mary (March 25), the Assumption of Mary (August 15), Our Lady of the Rosary (October 7). From her childhood in Eifel, before the two world wars, she knew that "The swallows leave on the birthday of Mary" (September 8). Another proverb from her farmer's almanac: "On the feast

of the Holy Name of Mary summer says 'Amen'"—a feast
then celebrated on September 12. Thus, my father met her,
not on December 8, but on the day of Mary's Immaculate
Conception. The word for "conception" in German is
Empfängnis, which my younger brother and I misheard as
Gefängnis, which means "prison", and I wondered about
the strange idea, which Mother never explained to us. These
feasts were the key to deciphering a world that was totally
unintelligible to us. My mother's only omission was Our
Lady of Guadalupe, probably because she had never heard
of her. However, even for her, sitting in her little room in
her old age, television and the world news had "switched
off" her rosary—until she became nearly blind. But in her
coffin she again had the rosary wrapped around her hands.

We had never thought to teach our children to pray the
rosary. Much less could we have branded on their souls or
their genes our murmured prayers when they lay in bed or
when we drove in the car or needed something—or when
they left home. Clearly, we no longer prayed the rosary.
Pope John Paul II still prayed it, calling it "an ideal way of
seeing her Son through his Mother Mary's eyes". But when
all is said and done, does a Pope not come from a different
world, almost as far from ours as was that of my mother?
Was this practice not out of the Middle Ages? In my generation the string of beads that is the rosary had been broken in almost all Catholic homes, and this began long before
the revolutionary upheavals of 1968. In the Catholic board-
ing school I attended, the rosary was not prayed. The prayer
had simply dried up like a river in the desert. No one murmured a protest—and I least of all.

Now, eight years after my mother's death, I suddenly found
myself in a small town in Herzegovina, in a region in which
the monotonous alternating prayers of the rosary can be
heard in every street and byway, in every language in the

world—as I had never experienced it as a child: in Croatian, Dutch, Korean, Italian, even Arabic and Hungarian. I was encountering a phenomenon unknown so far. It was like a Catholic Tibet with its prayer flags. But I could not offer such a subject to my glossy magazine for which I worked or to my editor-in-chief, who was one of the most open human beings I knew. The streams of pilgrims going to Medjugorje are a mass phenomenon. Yet they had remained under the radar of the media world in which I had earned my living for twenty years. What was happening here was completely unknown to me.

CHAPTER SEVEN

CLOTHED IN THE COSMOS

Fleeing from thunder, lightning and torrential rain, the first encounter with one of the visionaries: at an inn in Herzegovina, Christine talks about the conquest of Mexico and the experience of the Mother of God.

The large valley around Medjugorje was carpeted with flowers. And I quickly discovered that in these fields, praying was like breathing. Thousands came together at four in the morning; mothers carrying infants, old people leaning on their canes, some on crutches, were all on the move. In the morning twilight the birds' concert urged the travelers on. As the sun rose, clouds of butterflies began their dance around the flowers in all the fields of this broad valley. They followed the rivulets, streams, rivers of pray-ers who, for years now, have poured up over two hills before reuniting to flood the valley. Many were barefooted. However, nothing spectacular was going on, except that, truly, it was marvelously peaceful.

Jakob was unenthusiastic. Before leaving Medjugorje, we were climbing the cross-topped mountain alone, one last time, by way of a rough stairway carved into the rock and leading to the top in abrupt zigzags, when a torrential rain burst upon us. We were unable to find shelter anywhere. Our stairway was rapidly transformed into a wild mountain river. When we got back to our inn, our jackets, shirts, pants, shoes were streaming like sponges. There we met Christine.

When she saw us seated before bowls of hot soup, with scarcely dried hair, in clean shirts and sweaters, as proud of having endured the weather as if we had done something heroic, she laughed. In a bright voice she asked if she could sit with us a while. She was short, fine-boned, with large eyes, black hair, and was always laughing; she was accompanied by her parents—mountain folk from the Vorarlberg region—and by her brother who had come on pilgrimage to the hamlet of Medjugorje. The night before, her father had told her to be sure to tell us about the Virgin of Guadalupe. It was still raining buckets outside, with great lightning bolts cutting through the sky; claps of thunder came and went, rumbling over the valley; the wind whistled through all the cracks in the windows and was held back only by the cheap curtains. Then Christine began to chirp about the Virgin of Guadalupe, like a blackbird in early evening.

She had brought down from one of the second-floor doors of the inn a well-worn poster, which she hung on the dining-room wall. It was an image of our Lady in a grayish-pink oval; flowers were drawn on her robe; stars covered her blue-green mantle; sharp rays fanned out behind her; beneath her feet was a black half-crescent pointing upward; under this a small feathered man held up the hem of her robes. This was the first time I had ever seen a copy of the most mysterious image after the Shroud of Turin. Everything about it seemed alien.

"The Mother of God personally painted this image", Christine began with a quick gesture, making it impossible to slow her down. "This is our Mother of Guadalupe. She herself painted it on the mantle of an Amerindian after the conquest of Mexico, when he asked for a sign. The Aztecs called this mantle a tilma. It was a piece of white cloth that had many uses. Knotted at the neck, it served as a cloak; folded over and put on the head, it protected the person from the sun; gathered by the four corners, it could be

used as a bag or a purse; at night, it served as a blanket or
a hammock for small children. It was woven from the fibers
of the agave cactus, the cheapest fabric to be found in Mexico, which was used by the poorest and neediest. This fabric lasts twenty years, at the longest, before it rots away—in
contrast to the quetzal and duck feathers from which the
clothing of the nobility was made. It is scarcely more dura-
ble than potato sacking. Nonetheless, beneath the image,
this very cheap cloth has remained intact for five hundred
years. Naturally, the fabric has been tested more often than
can be counted. The tests showed that the material contains no pigment, no base coat, no oils, nothing. No writing instrument has drawn the image, no brush strokes are
visible on this piece of cloth. The image is simply there."

I was hanging on her words. Christine opened up the
image for us as if it were a picture book. After about five
minutes I thought: Either this is the greatest of all frauds—
even with the tough competition—or this is the story of a
lifetime, one for which I have been searching for decades!
"Of course, all this is incredible", Christine laughed. "No
one could believe such a story. As incredible as it may
seem, though, the story has one catch: The image exists!
It hangs on a wall in Mexico City. I have seen it myself.
And not just I. More than twenty million people come to
see it every year. Twenty million! The 'Villa', the Basilica
of Our Lady of Guadalupe, is the greatest place of pilgrimage in the world—greater than Rome, greater than
Mecca or Jerusalem."

Jakob had returned to his room to his handbook on stocks
and finances. Ivanka, the daughter of the house, removed
our plates; when three more guests came in to escape the
weather, her father brought yet another demijohn of house
wine from the storeroom. A new thunderclap rattled the
windowpanes. But Christine, imperturbable, continued her

story of the brilliant conquistador, Hernán Cortés, the cross on his coat of arms flying from the mast of his flagship, and of how this cross, after a good twelve years, reappeared on the brooch with which the Virgin of Guadalupe fastened the collar of her gown. "Eight years before the apparitions, the first Franciscans arrived in Mexico. Cortés, a pious Christian—who had killed his wife, Catalina, in an emotional outburst one year before—had great hopes for the missionary skills of the mendicant order. He sincerely desired a spiritual conquest to complete the worldly and material conquest of Mexico. Two years later, another two Franciscans arrived barefoot from the port of Veracruz. Cortés greeted them on his knees. But the despair of the Amerindians continued to be overwhelming. The sign of the cross only reminded them of the greatest humiliation in their history.

"Exactly ten years before, they had been brutally subjugated by Cortés. The conquest had cost them hundreds of thousands of lives. After the conquest, in order to wring out the last speck of gold from the land, the Spaniards had tortured the nobles, enslaved the men, branding them like animals. Many towns had been devastated. New types of epidemics had wiped out whole cities, killing eight million all together: smallpox, measles, plague, whooping cough, mumps and other contagious diseases the Spaniards had brought with them. Fever raged among the Amerindians, tormenting them with bone pain, stomach pain, tuberculosis. Rotting corpses, lying in the streets, reeked appallingly. There was no way to bring in the corn harvest, which rotted in the fields. Since there was no one to sow, many fields went to seed. For this reason, starvation often followed epidemic like a wildfire. That disaster claimed more victims than all the Spanish massacres combined. Tenochtitlán had become almost uninhabited; that magnificent city was a heap of ruins. The women were so sunk in despair

that they did not want to bear any more children. It was
the end. It was the turning point. For it was precisely at
this moment that the Virgin appeared with this image, whose
flowers now, suddenly, spoke to the Amerindians like an
open book."

Outside, the storm gave no signs of passing, but I was
past hearing the thunderclaps. I looked at Christine, fascinated. Where could she have learned all this?

"It's because of this image that I lived in Mexico", she
instantly replied, and continued: "But, as I've already said,
the successes of the missionaries after 1521, when Cortés
brought them to Mexico, were almost completely nullified.
Now, to the Amerindians, the cross on the Madonna's brooch
was a clear reference to the conquerors' God. The Aztecs
had always been sensitive to signs in the sky and apparitions
in the heavens. Their language and writing consisted of such
signs. For them, the rays protecting her shoulders were a
meteor, a comet cutting across the heavens. That the Virgin
blocked the sun was a clear sign that there would no longer
be human sacrifices to the sun, to whom they had in the
past sacrificed whole tribes. In the royal turquoise they identified a queen, even though she bore no crown. By the flowers, they understood that all creation was her clothing, and
in her be-starred mantle they understood that her outer garment was the whole cosmos. Nonetheless, it was obvious to
them that she could not be a goddess, since she herself was
clearly adoring someone: gods do not join their hands like
this woman, and goddesses do not bow their heads with such
humility. The image rapidly began to speak to them without a single word being uttered. They could even dance out
the rhythm of the rays surrounding the Mother of God. She
would heal their sorrows! Try to imagine this: unexpectedly,
at the time when Michelangelo was painting in Rome, Mary
herself was painting a masterpiece, with a section of gold,

on potato sacking! It was an unbelievable miracle. The Aztecs understood this right away." Christine clapped, laughed and talked on without taking a breath.

She was as breathless about Aztec polytheism as about the gods, whose names no one could possibly remember. There were about two hundred principal gods and sixteen hundred secondary gods, whom the Amerindians met at every turn. She told me about Huitzilopochtli, the sun god, whose brilliance the Madonna obscured in her apparition, as she did that of his rival, Quetzalcóatl, the moon god on whom she is resting her feet in the image. But Christine spoke with the same enthusiasm of the ancient Mexicans' exquisite sensitivity—often praised—and their love of nature: they had venerated and praised the Creator of the world in every flower and, in their longing for the living God, had offered during some weeks up to twenty thousand human victims in sacrifice.

It was for this very reason, finally, that they had waged their wars, which were by mutual agreement called the "flower wars". Not to subjugate an enemy or gain land or take a city, but to take prisoners; that is, in order to satisfy and make their god happy with the largest possible number of victims, so that he would find the energy to rise the next day. "If the Aztecs did not wage war, they felt that they had become useless", the emperor Montezuma I is said to have commented. Their poets agreed: "A battle is like a flower." Christine solemnly affirmed: "For them, the greatest glory was to die for god." All this sounded beyond fabulous. In any case, it was a belief that the Aztecs did not want to be taken from them. "After the conquest, the Spaniards tried to force them, by fire and sword, to enter the Church. But the Aztec nobility mocked the Castilians for their greed for gold, for their pale goddess, for their frightening horses and their bestial stench. The God these Spaniards worshipped—a bloodied man nailed to a crossbeam, a victim and without a priest—seemed to the Aztecs to be pure mockery. The fact that the Franciscans had learned their language did not help any, nor did the fact that some of them had their incisors filed down in order to speak to the Aztecs without mispronouncing the unfamiliar sibilants. It was all useless. 'Isn't it enough that we've lost?' they retorted to the priests trying to convert them. 'Isn't this enough for you? Do with us as you please, but don't try to change us or our beliefs.' With very few exceptions, their hearts remained immovable. Juan Diego was one of these exceptions. The widower went every day from the mainland to an island where the Franciscans were instructing him. His wife had died of smallpox."

Christine took in some air, held out her arms and related the story of the apparition in all its details, as if she had been present. Her eyes shone. She told the story as would a child who had experienced something that very morning and wanted to share it with his parents—with the same enthusiasm and excesses. A short while before computer simulation in a United States university had shown that the constellation represented on Mary's mantle corresponded exactly with the constellations filling the sky over Mexico City on December 12, 1531. These stars preserve forever the date of the apparition on this potato sack that has no expiration date. She grabbed a small pointer and went over to the poster depicting the Virgin. "Look, here is the star the astrologers followed to Bethlehem. There is Centaurus representing the sacrifices that would be abolished by this apparition. There is the Southern Cross; there, Scorpius; there, Draco. And if you wanted to complete the star map, the Northern Crown would be located on her forehead." Outside of Ursa Major, Orion and Cassiopeia, which I had learned to recognize as a boy scout, I knew no other constellations. Listening to her began to make me dizzy.

"Well, what about Medjugorje?" I asked Christine, as outside the night had long since turned raven black, and the wind and rain had finally calmed down. "Also, what about Lourdes and Fatima, and so on, where uncounted numbers of people are convinced that the Virgin appeared?" "Yes", she replied. "Two years ago a Mexican pilgrim asked the same question. She asked one of the visionaries to present her question to the Mother of God. A few days later, the visionary came with the answer. 'I am appearing here', replied the Queen of Peace, 'but I live in Mexico. Here, I appear to a few; in Mexico I am there at any time to all, to each and everyone.'"

The next morning I picked up a pink-streaked rock from the hill on which the Madonna first appeared in Herzegovina on June 25, 1981. On the return journey, in the face of the incredible story Christine had put before me, the conflict that had impelled me to Yugoslavia was as good as forgotten. Her voice was still echoing in my ears—of the flowers, of the image painted without paint, of the Amerindians who could dance the text of a gown as if it were sheet music, of the rays of the sun that marked the rhythm of the dance—as I tried, in total confusion, to relate all this to my wife, Ellen, as we sat at table back home.

"What does 'without paint' mean?" she interrupted. "The image is colored, isn't it?"

I tried somewhat helplessly to convince her. "Yes," I said, "but there is no paint on it—do you understand? No brush put the colors on the cloth. The image is just there, colored, but not with paint."

"That's not unusual", broke in Christine, our youngest daughter, the last of our children still living at home, who was sitting with us at the table. "Flowers aren't painted either. The painting of the Virgin is colored just like flowers."

CHAPTER EIGHT

YEAS AND NAYS

First inquiries into the story of María of Guadalupe, "Empress of both the Americas", research in textbooks, manuals, compendia, newspaper archives, expert circles, the Internet, and with the "Comforter of the Afflicted" in Kevelaer.

Flowers, flowers, everything in bloom. The month of the flowers came not only in Mexico. In Munich, May arrived as never before with breezes and perfumes. And I could scarcely stop recounting the incredible story to my wife, my friends, my relatives. Bocena, the young woman from Poland who helped with the housework, had probably heard more about the Virgin Mary from infancy than all the rest of us put together. While I was yet again sitting at the kitchen table talking to my wife about the Virgin of Guadalupe, who had appeared in Mexico, out of the blue Bocena just laughed, tapped a Marlboro from her pack and put it in her mouth, saying sarcastically: "What can really be known about all this? What and from whom? No one has returned from the beyond. All dead. Who knows what's there? No one really knows anything." Bocena's German was limited, but she was using the classical argument of all the enlightened since the time of Voltaire. She believed in every horoscope that appeared in the newspaper; she also believed in every promise of lower prices during the end-of-summer sales. But she did not believe in anything else. How could I answer her? Besides, she had reason on her side: no one has come back from the beyond to tell us what is there. But the story of the *Morenita* would not release its hold on me. On the contrary.

Therefore, as soon as I returned from Herzegovina, I—with some difficulty—got hold of the only book on María of Guadalupe available in Germany and devoured it. Then I arranged to have the editorial offices of the periodical for which I work send me from Frankfurt whatever they had on file. In an earlier account, a colleague in Washington had reported that, soon after the beatification of Juan Diego, the very elderly Abbot Guillermo Schulemburg, who for thirty years had been curator of the miraculous image of the Virgin in the Basilica of Our Lady of Guadalupe, began to cast doubts—from a strictly theological perspective—not only on the apparitions but also on the very existence of Juan Diego. It was a scandal that had rocked all of Mexico. The "Schulemburg case" also caused a stir in the United States. The *Washington Post* had called the Schulemburg case an event comparable to the Chief Justice of the Supreme Court declaring that the authors of the Declaration of Independence had never written it and that the Declaration had simply been invented to explain the reason for democracy in the United States. The *Independent* quoted a Mexican as saying: "This is like denying the existence of Abraham Lincoln."

At the same time, however, to the consolation of Christendom, the first well-attested miracle was admitted, a necessary step toward the later canonization of Juan Diego. This is how the events unrolled. During the process of the beatification of Juan Diego, in May 1990, a young man named Juan José Silva, living in a northern section of Mexico City, tried to commit suicide. A short time before, he had made an effort to effect a reconciliation with his father, but he had been roundly rejected. He was at his mother's house, heavily drugged and in tremendous distress, and had climbed onto the ledge of a balcony, ready to jump. The poor woman could do no more than grab the leg of his trousers and cry, "Help me, Juan Diego. Give me a sign. Save my son." But the youth jumped. He weighed about 140 pounds and fell thirty feet, on a 70° trajectory. He hit the ground with nothing to diminish the impact. His head was unrecognizable. In the Durango Hospital the doctors could not explain how he could even have survived the fall. It was May 6, 1990. Three days later, in the Basilica of Guadalupe, Pope John Paul II inscribed Juan Diego among the community of the blessed. Shortly after the beatification, Juan José Silva awoke in the hospital and asked for something to eat. A week later he left the hospital completely healed. Tests showed no effects of the fall. The case could not be explained by autosuggestion. To the doctors, the cure was scientifically inexplicable. It seems that God has a sense of humor.

But, of course, so do God's critics, in varying degrees. Thus, for almost five hundred years, there has been a rumor that the image of the Virgin is a painting crafted by the Spaniards to dupe the Amerindians. Ingenious Franciscans had hatched this plan and spread the corresponding legends among the people. That is why they had deliberately placed the apparition on Tepeyac Hill, site of the ancient temple of Tonantzin, Aztec goddess of fertility: to provide the Amerindians a very easy mnemonic bridge to facilitate their conversion from their old form of worship to faith in the "Creator of heaven and earth". Smart missionaries had done nothing but "baptize" the site of the goddess of vegetation, who was always surrounded by flowers, by narrating the poor, widowed Juan Diego's visions of Mary.

The Internet has a great number of websites relating to the Virgin of Guadalupe, and naturally there are sites that "prove" with scientific precision that it is all a fake. According to them, the image was nothing but the banner Cortés flew on the flagship he landed in Mexico. This was the flag used by the Spaniards on their first campaigns against the Aztecs by land. According to other sources, the Spaniards had commissioned the painting of our Lady from an Amerindian from Tlaxcala named Marco Zipaktli (or Siptlal or Cipac) in order to bewitch the Amerindians by painting in their own style. On September 8, 1556, Francisco Bustamante, the Franciscan provincial, preached an irate sermon in fierce opposition to the excessive veneration of the Virgin of Guadalupe, just as he also fulminated against Zumárraga's successor as bishop of Mexico City, Alonso de Montúfar. The cult on Tepeyac Hill "did not have a great beginning and had no sound basis", he railed at the time. He advocated a punishment of one to two hundred lashes for anyone who would spread the idea that the image could work miracles. This superstition wipes out the Franciscan missionary effort, he said, and confuses the Amerindians anew, leading them to fall back into the paganism from which, with enormous effort, his brothers in religion had freed them. Instead they should cling to their new faith and, preferably, keep away from images, whether painted or sculpted. The veneration of the Virgin had to be monitored very critically. After all, she is not God! It would be much better if the gifts and alms were given immediately to the poor and the hospitals. Bustamante's sermon is well documented as is the acute difference of opinion between the Franciscans and the Dominicans. Friar Francisco Bustamante was a Franciscan; Alonso de Montúfar was a Dominican. This sermon, however, already brings up a basic motive for all later disputes about the image of the Virgin of Guadalupe: Pious wonder may be understandable in country folk or Amerindians, but it is strictly forbidden in a critical thinker! As I have said, the modern age had already begun.

Thus, as other sources indicate, in 1787 a certain José Ignacio Bartolache reexamined the image and discovered that it was not painted on agave cloth and was heavily retouched and strewn with patches. Moreover, it was falling to pieces in some places, devoured by mildew and moisture. In short, more than one person painted it, and it was in terrible shape. Again, in 1883, a certain Joaquín García Icazbalceta examined the image and discovered it was a clumsy, botched piece of work. In 1895 it was so hopelessly rotted away that it had been replaced by a copy by a Father Antonio Plancarte. Later, in 1928, this "new" image was examined by the "great painter" Dr. Atl, who handed down the final verdict: "The image in Guadalupe is a plagiarism of a picture hanging in a church in Fuenterrabla, Spain, which is, in turn, an amateurish imitation of various decadent Byzantine pictures of the Madonna." In short, "The Virgin of Guadalupe is a purely decorative and occasional work, produced by someone gifted with a very mediocre imagination." Besides, infrared photographs show beyond doubt that it has been repeatedly retouched. These retouchings affected the "angel", "the elongated fold of the mantle in the angel's hand", the "rays of the sun", "the golden network" over the Virgin's robe, the belt, the cuffs and the hands of the Virgin. Everything, of course, had been fabricated solely to attract more donations. With reference to the *Nican Mopohua* and Archbishop Zumárraga, however, it turns out that he was from the Basque city of Durango and was one of the most evil and fanatical conquistadors and murderers. Moreover, he was not even in Mexico when, according to the whole fraud, the image appeared. He had been recalled to Spain between 1531 and 1534. And Juan Diego—like all Amerindians—had not in any way been admitted to the Church until 1540.

I can find no place called Fuenterrabla in any atlas or road map of Europe. A review of Bishop Zumárraga's journeys quickly establishes that he embarked from Veracruz for Spain in May of 1532, that is, five months after the events at Tepeyac in December 1531. All the documents show that he advocated passionately, though in vain, for the rights of the Amerindians. He founded the famous Tlatelolco College and, with it, the first university in Mexico, along with many schools for indigenous girls, various hospitals, and the first printery in the New World. He died in June 1548. But the debate about the image continues unabated.

I still had never seen Mexico. However, through other reports I had in the meantime discovered that Pius XI had declared Our Lady of Guadalupe Queen of Mexico and Patroness and Protectress of Latin America and the Philippines. Then, in 1945, Pius XII named her Defender and Empress of both Americas. She is painted by a brush not of this world, the Pope had declared. The writer Octavio Paz thinks that "the inspired story of the Virgin" is "impressed on the heart of Mexico.... No one understands our land and history if he does not understand what is and has been the veneration of Guadalupe. The Virgin is the solace of the poor, the shield of the weak and oppressed. In a word, she is the Mother of orphans." This is the reason that all Mexican revolutionaries carried her image onto the battlefield.

The priest Miguel Hidalgo, who took the first steps to separate Mexico from Spain, carried her on his flag, and the legendary Emiliano Zapata sewed the Virgin as an emblem on his sombrero. As is obvious, she is swinging in every taxi and is enshrined in every bar in Mexico, "outlined in pink and yellow neon lights and surrounded by bottles of whisky, rum and cognac". This is in no way a form of blasphemy, but a sense that "the Virgin is the Mother of all, including the late-night crowd." She is the Mother who satisfies all desire, who does not allow anyone to sink into sadness or bitterness, and who cares for each person in a unique way.

In Mexico reproductions of the image of the Virgin Mary can be found on every street corner, bus, train station, store, church, chapel, home; it appears on postcards, bullfighters' costumes, promotional and publicity ads. María of Guadalupe is better known than any pop star. She is the soul of Mexico. In a book of photographs I found a painting by Alejandro von Waberer O'Gormans, a contemporary of Frida Kahlo, who painted the Virgin Mary in the act of enveloping herself with the night sky as with an immense dark-blue mantle.

I had read everything I could find. The thousands of citations and bits of information could easily be put back together into the whole image, like a glimmering mosaic. On Internet search engines I found innumerable websites. How was it possible that I had never heard of her before? How did it happen that in Europe the Virgin of Guadalupe seems to be practically unknown?

Meanwhile, during a short trip back home, I also visited Kevelaer for the first time. For many Marian pilgrims, Kevelaer is the heart of the left bank of the lower Rhine river. The walls of the church were covered with votive bulletin boards, which, with ever-changing pictures of those helped by her, proclaimed one central thing: "Mary has helped!" In the face of sickness, death, need, accidents, exams, missing children, lost wealth, broken axles, war, catastrophe, all affliction and misfortune—Mary has helped over and over again.

It was overwhelming. The town on the border of the Netherlands and Germany had a parish church built on the model of the Sainte-Chapelle in Paris; it was next to a baroque chapel whose magnificence equalled those of Rome. As a matter of fact, there is only one miraculous image in this shrine: a tiny piece of paper from the time of the Thirty Years' War, a small copperplate engraving depicting Mary as *Consolatrix Afflictorum*, Comforter of the Afflicted. This is all. Yet because of it, even today, 600,000 pilgrims a year travel to Kevelaer. Because of this small, yellowed engraving, my parents had set out on foot along a difficult and exhausting road. Given all this, how is it possible that none of them had ever heard anything about the image in Mexico, a hundred times bigger and more impressive? I could not figure it out.

CHAPTER NINE

THE NAME OF THE ROSE

A hymn about the Mother of God clothed with the sun, a song written in Munich in 1638, and an evening's conversation about William of Ockham, the medieval dispute about universals, the matrix of the modern era and the forgotten entryway into freedom.

Yet again I inquired among my scattered friends and acquaintances in Munich, with the same results. No one was familiar with the story, not even the pastor. I kept asking myself: How could it be possible that not one of them—myself included—had heard about her? "Why hasn't the history of the Virgin of Guadalupe landed long since in newspaper headlines, if what you say is true?" a colleague, who published a prominent monthly magazine in the United States, asked me with incredulous astonishment when I told him the story. This was some time after I had begun to write down my notes on the amazing story, of course. One May evening, as I was shutting down my computer, I heard bells ringing over the rooftops. Saint Anna Kloster was just three blocks down from our house. I looked at the clock. The bells would be calling people to May devotions, which, as a child, I had attended with my mother. I put on my fleece jacket and leaped down the stairs.

Father Claus, the guardian, was introducing May as "Mary's month". He began by calling attention to the marvelous flowers with which Norbert, his brother in religion, had decorated the church. But, to be truthful, he said, he could not say much about either the month of May or Mary.

Nevertheless, he continued, if he were even more truthful, he would have to tell us how once, in his beloved Africa, he came to be involved in a real war. Shells were falling all about him. With great difficulty he saved himself by getting into a cellar, grenades exploding on the ground around him, closer and closer. Then all he could think to do was pray to the Mother of God, as his mother had taught him to do as a boy. "When nothing else remains, *she* is there": that is what he could say about Mary. "When I, with all my theology, intelligence and wisdom, was at an end, only Mary came to my mind, about whom I ordinarily never think."

But that May night he seemed more moved by the new organ in the choir loft at the rear of the church, whose music he never tired of hearing. He had mobilized half the city of Munich to finance the new instrument, which was resonating proudly for the handful of elderly ladies and gentlemen who had come to the church that evening, a home for the aged being next door. Nevertheless, the organist intoned the final hymn with a passion that made the little rococo church seem filled to overflowing:

> Proclaim: Who is she who is born before the day,
> Who rises like daybreak over Paradise?
> She comes from afar
> Adorned with moon and stars,
> Raised up amid the splendor of the sun—
> The light-filled and noble rose. . . .

I grabbed the hymnal and could barely turn the pages to see who had written it; all I could discover about the author was, "Johann Khuen, Munich, 1638". He had to have written this during the Thirty Years War. Had he heard somewhere about the Virgin of Guadalupe, "Who rises like daybreak over Paradise"? I turned around to look at the new organ. They had made it to blend perfectly with the architecture of the back wall of the church: two wooden towers highly decorated with golden fretting; next to them were two angels poised for instant flight. Two weeks earlier Father Claus had placed, directly in front of the oval of the main window a baroque-style Madonna that had been gathering dust in the rectory's storage area. It had been recently gilded and, back-lit, projected a tenuous silhouette downward over the nave of the church. Her gown was silver, her open mantle blue, with a crescent-moon under her feet; she was surrounded by rays blazing like flames from the sun.

William of Ockham had been buried in this very cloister. Once May devotions were over, I asked Father Claus if he would come to our house so we could talk about William of Ockham. He was not only a great medieval theologian but was the secret protagonist of Humberto Eco's *Name of the Rose*, which had fascinated many readers and left them with the insight that the Middle Ages was much more than a period of darkness. In fact, William of Ockham was one of the central figures in the so-called "dispute about universals", the controversy about conceptual images, about proto-ideas or proto-images, both as ideal types and as conceptual reproductions of reality. I had heard some talk about this, usually with the additional comment that it had been as important to the development of the modern world as had been the theory of relativity. I had heard about it but had never understood either the debate about universals or the theory of universals itself.

Many years before, when I was still a professor of history, a colleague, a very good painter in a very realistic style, referred to these ideas. I asked him one day what kept him from painting some local girl as the Madonna. Would this not be an awesome challenge for a painter of the modern era? We were standing at the entrance of the school, enjoying the sunshine and smoking. He gave me an amused look and observed dryly: "Do you really think I could or would want to go back in time to the dispute about universals? At least this debate has been decided." I was trying not to look completely blank, so I did not dare ask him what he meant. This was the last time we saw each other. Three weeks later he lost control of his car on a curve and crashed into a tree by the side of the road. Perhaps this is why I could not let go of the question and kept looking for an answer, without success. And so far I had not gotten an exhaustive explanation on this topic. Now I wanted finally to understand what this argument about universals was really about. I begged Father Claus to try to bring along Father Raynald, an experienced old professor of the former Franciscan college, who now was in charge of the old library.

"No, William of Ockham was not buried here", said the guardian, a tall man with lively eyes and a Roman profile. "He was buried in the choir of the old church of Saint Anthony, next to the royal residence—where the opera house now stands. One night in 1862, during the Bavarian secularization of Church property, the church of Saint Anthony was secretly leveled and, with it, William of Ockham's tomb. Why? Because in the opinion of the enlightened Bavarians, mendicant religious orders with their spirituality and their libraries did nothing but spread superstition among the people when they took them under spiritual charge. Ockham's bones, if they are still buried, are lying under the opera-house stage." In any event, they could not be found within the eight coffins, full of bones, remitted to the Franciscans at the beginning of the 1960s, when the old Franciscan cemetery was discovered in the process of building a parking garage for the opera house. "But

perhaps Ockham's bones were also saved and are in the
ossuary underneath Saint Anna's. No one knows." Father
Claus smiled roguishly. However, he was delighted to visit
us together with Father Raynald. A little later, after vespers,
the guardian of the friary and his old teacher came to our
house and climbed the stairs—Claus with a large cloak over
his brown habit, Raynald with a brown raincoat over
his.

Father Claus was a preacher of many talents. I already
knew that he like his Franciscan brothers in Munich did
not think much of the events at Medjugorje. He was not
impressed by the fact that his Bosnian Franciscan brothers
were playing a central role in interpreting events there. Tra-
ditionally, not even the bishop of that part of the formerly
Ottoman Balkans had the importance that the Franciscans
had had there for centuries.

Now I discovered that neither of these two highly educated scholars had yet heard anything about the history of
the Marian image of Mexico, even though Franciscans had
from the start played an essential role in these events. At
the beginning, the mission in Mexico was almost completely in their hands, even under Zumárraga's successor,
Bishop Alonso de Montúfar, a Dominican. They were completely unaware of my "millennium history". But they understood much more about philosophy and theology.

We had not even begun on our pasta when I asked them
about the philosophy of conceptual images and about what
had actually been so significant in the debate about universals. "Could you explain this business to me so that I can
finally understand how it could be as important for our
world as the Copernican revolution?" Father Claus looked
at his teacher; Father Raynald cleared his throat, took another
sip and proceeded to give us a short lecture while the pasta
got cold.

"So," he began quietly, "the universals controversy in a nutshell!" This was a dispute among the Scholastic theologians of the fourteenth century, who were totally preoccupied with where universal ideas came from and to what reality they corresponded. "This is how they put the question: Do universal ideas express the way a thing really is, or are they only labels, mere names—in Latin, *nomina*—that attach the things more or less extrinsically to their appellation. Following Saint Augustine's lead, the Middle Ages had accepted Plato's teaching, according to which, behind all manifestations or external phenomena, there can be found proto-models, quasi-heavenly concepts or ideas, of which all manifestations and external phenomena are copies, their images reflected or reproduced in three-dimensional objects or phenomena. So there is an idea of Tree (an idea that subsists independently) behind every particular tree; an idea of Oak behind every particular oak tree; and so on. A corresponding approach is found in Islam, which in many ways still retains the point of view of antiquity as it speaks of 'the mother of the book' or 'the mother of all battles', concepts or ideas that in the East are never interpreted ironically. This way of seeing things is especially important for the Eastern Church and for an understanding of her images. In the East, images are always understood as copies of the original heavenly images. If we do not keep this in mind, we will never come to understand icons. Icons always refer directly to the saint in heaven: icons are like a vision of the saint seen through a window or in a mirror. Every icon of Mary refers immediately to Mary there, in the heavenly world. Likewise, every icon of Jesus refers directly to him. The icon is not just a copy referring to some distant archetype or original image in heaven; rather, it makes the archetype somehow present in the copy. This explains the great reverence paid to icons in the Eastern Church. They refer, not simply to the person of whom they are a copy, but to the archetype or original reality whom the copy or reproduction makes present. The original reality itself sends its splendor into the copy. This is why, in the great iconoclastic struggle, the images were defended passionately against those who considered all images blasphemous graven images. In the East all images are valued as mirrors reflecting the original image or reality or as copies of it."

In the West, during the Middle Ages, however, those called "nominalists"—among whom Ockham certainly played the most prominent role—called into question this connection and relation between the archetype and its copy or image in the three-dimensional world, leaving Plato's world view behind. "They insisted that one had to approach each thing and phenomenon in its individuality. God had not created the world either by an archetypal image or reality or according to some matrix of realities or according to some mother-image of created realities; finally, God continues creating life, not according to worn-out models, but always in a completely new way. Everything must be examined and viewed in its individuality, as what it is in itself." Thus, there can be no such thing as conceptual reproductions or images of things. Each thing—and especially every human being—is a distinct entity. The nominalists also questioned whether there was a "heavenly" kingdom of realities or archetypal images, eternal and unchanging concepts or ideas of which our world and our experience are but imperfect copies. So, neither could we posit archetypal realities or images that God would use as presumptive models and by means of which he would create the world. This is the way Plato had presented the question, and many Christian theologians followed him. The nominalists insisted that this would restrict God's freedom in a way not acceptable to Christians.

Father Raynald's eyes were lightning bolts. "According to the nominalists, God did not have to subject himself to any laws or order. On the contrary, any order to be found in this world exists thanks to God's freedom. For this reason the positive ordering of this world could have been totally different. God himself is not subject to the order he created for the world, though he usually does so subject himself, because his free will created the order. It follows that he also has the freedom to intervene in this order as he wishes in order to perform miracles. I do not have to apologize that William of Ockham's vision of the world has opened an enormous possibility of miracles and miraculous phenomena that other visions of the cosmos have to treat as nonexistent—'according to which it should not or could not exist'. On the contrary, according to the nominalists, everything is possible. This is what preserves God's sovereign liberty. In contrast with the gods of antiquity, with their foreseeable and predictable ways of acting, the God of the nominalists can intervene at any time in the world; he can break his laws and act in surprising and unforeseeable ways, as we see the God of the Bible acting now and then in history. The God of the Bible, the God of Abraham, Isaac, Jacob and Jesus, is completely free and therefore not dependent on anything—on any model, exemplary image or archetypal reality or image. Ordinarily he subjects himself to the laws he created, though clearly because he is moved from a desire to limit himself. He is not forced to do so. He is completely free."

I objected. "Are you implying with this that the controversy about archetypal realities and images, both physical and conceptual things, opened the gates to the freedom of modern man? Are you saying that we have this controversy over physical and conceptual images to thank for our freedom?"

He continued. "In a certain sense, yes, this was the decisive point of the whole debate! For during this quarrel the human being kept seeing himself as created in the image of God, as the Bible asserts. For this reason, any ideas to which man gave rise in such a cultural milieu would have radical consequences for his understanding of himself. This was the revolutionary nucleus of the controversy. Thus, this new jumping-off point led rapidly to a new view of nature and its phenomena. Each thing—and especially every human being—was no longer seen as an imperfect copy of a divine original; rather, it suddenly stood completely for itself. Since then, above all else, things are no longer "commodities". From an archetypal image one could make as many copies as one wished of things identical in what they are, though differing in details. But if there is no original and eternal archetype, the individual thing and individual person immediately acquire a totally new dignity. There is only the individual being; there is no universal being. This had to be one of the fundamental principles of medieval nominalism. The individual irrupted into the world! It was also the decisive breakthrough in the process of stripping all phenomena of mystery and taboos. From this point on, one could engage any phenomenon without danger of damaging or offending against some heavenly original. With respect to conscience, this sea change gave experience a rank and standing it had never enjoyed in Plato's world view. This principle was one of the most important reversals in the evolution of modern natural sciences. But in painting, the ultimate consequence of this way of thinking led directly to abstract painting, to images seen as new and individual creations. From that moment in history, it was no longer necessary to reproduce or copy anything." Exhausted, Father Raynald paused.

Father Claus broke into the lecture: Of course, things cannot be divided up as neatly as we have done here at table. For example, we have to point out that William of Ockham was not so radical. He is classified as a conceptualist. In some way he found a middle path. According to him, certainly, God was completely free. Nevertheless, he created and redeemed the world precisely as he did and not otherwise—even if he could have revealed himself in some other way if he had wanted to. This would be an immense field for reflection. For even if the nominalists had by and large prevailed in this controversy, both ways of thinking would—as in any great controversy—have in a certain way lasted into our time, continuing to be in conflict. For example, Father Claus went on with a malicious smile, Cardinal Ratzinger [now Pope Benedict XVI], as custodian of Catholic orthodoxy in Rome, is frankly a classical Platonist. "As I see it, whenever this guardian of orthodoxy touches on any problem, he always and with full clarity sees the whole heavenly system behind it and can explain it better than the person who raised the question or, better said, even before someone asks the question. Only with great difficulty can this visionary understanding be disturbed by reports about different individual cases."

Finally, I asked the two Franciscans what they would expect to happen if in our time images were suddenly discovered that were both archetypal realities or images and their copies? One hundred years ago a scientific study in Turin led some investigators to say that the image on the Shroud is a reflection or glimmer of another dimension of reality, the shadow of the lamb, so to speak. What would happen if this same kind of claim were brought forth in the case of the image in Mexico when it was proved to be an *acheiropoietos*, a miraculous image that had not been painted by human hand? And what can we make of those twelve icons of Mary universally held to be painted by the evangelist Luke, like that very ancient miraculous image of

Częstochowa, to which, for centuries, people have flocked from all over Poland. Perhaps in such a case, should not the debate about universals take some new direction? Or how could the question even be raised today, if it is true that the controversy about universals gave rise to the modern age? What would happen if, amid the successive, ever-growing floods of images of the modern age, we were suddenly faced with the discovery that, in our world also, there are authentic and living images? What would happen if—in the unforeseen flood of our epoch's new language of images and signs—it became evident that, in Turin and Mexico, there are "things" in which archetype, copy and image coincided in a single "event", not as a copy or forgery, but as something authentic and complete in itself? Then, at least within Christendom, could we not come to understand that we could hope for in the new millennium a new and definitive Copernican revolution, with a whole new orientation toward the universe? Or have I just drunk one too many?

Both Franciscans looked at me as indulgently as if I had just informed them of a Marian apparition I had personally had the day before in Munich's English Park.

CHAPTER TEN

MAIL FORWARDED

From the apocalyptic city to the apocalyptic Madonna, from brilliant gems to glimmering colored flowers and the beating heart of a bird. In relation to this, a 1986 letter from someone in the beyond.

Very early in the morning, ten days later, I made the final corrections to a manuscript that I had been working on for almost ten years. I printed the final pages one last time, put them in an envelope and ran downstairs to the flower shop on the corner to buy a bouquet of roses for my editor and to deliver the packet to the publisher in person. My aims were ambitious: to recount, yet again, the essential forces for change in the history of Europe up to the end of the last millennium.

I had been fascinated for almost two decades by the discovery that the vision of the heavenly Jerusalem in the book of Revelation was the predominant theme of the history of the Judeo-Christian world: a vision of a redeemed society coming to earth from God. By good means or bad, amid unprecedented happiness and terrifying suffering, the nations of Europe had pursued this ideal for an immensely long time. And, of course, even today, this history is not finished and is still bound to the dream of a peaceful and just world, in which "the foundations of the wall of the city were adorned with every jewel; the first was jasper, the second sapphire, the third agate, the fourth emerald, the fifth onyx, the sixth carnelian, the seventh chrysolite, the eighth beryl, the ninth topaz, the tenth chrysoprase, the eleventh jacinth, the twelfth amethyst. And the twelve gates were twelve pearls, each of the gates made of a single pearl" (Rev 21:19–21).

The glimmering concept of brilliant gemstones had become the keynote of my life, and I was bringing it, packaged, to my publisher. *Old Europe in Search of the Heavenly City*. I announced my arrival with exultant whistling. However, I still had questions. Was it not unusual that at precisely this moment, for the first time, my memories of the apocalyptic city were suffused with bird trills and feathers, with the blossoms of the "Castilian roses" of an apocalyptic Madonna? What could all this mean? Could it be one and the same history? Or its continuation and the translation of the language of the Old World into that of the New, but now brought to perfection, not with minerals and precious stones, but with the living fabric of nature, made from the hearts of birds and of blossoms, not as an image or idea, but as the very breath and trills of the birds, no longer as a city, but as a person in whom whole peoples find their home. I handed in the envelope with the manuscript to the secretary at the publisher's office. I warbled like a bird on my way home. Between the Isar River and the Thierschplatz, the city of Munich lay radiant.

In my mailbox I found an unstamped, hand-delivered letter from a young man I had not heard from for years. I opened the letter as I climbed the stairs and began reading it before I got to my door. He had sent me a photocopy of a poem he had just found by chance, he said; it had been dedicated to me, thirteen years before, by a friend, three years before her death. The poem had been all but forgotten all this time. Hedwig Fornander, the author, was an unknown Swiss poet, with blue eyes and deep voice. She had a genius for foreign languages; she was single, chaste as a nun, with the passion of a convert. As was I, she was a lover of the heavenly Jerusalem. In her later life she had spent very solitary years in

Rome, before falling ill with cancer in Munich. To this day, her modest laughter rings in my ears. I can still see how, on a dark night in 1986, I held out my hand to steady her. Her fingers were cold, moist with sweat, and she could barely hang on to my hand. A few weeks before this I had moved with my family from Offenbach to Munich, also because of her. A couple of days later she wrote and sent to me the poem that I now suddenly held again in my hand, as if it had come from some other epoch, in the letters of her old-style typewriter, with a note written in a sharp hand at the bottom of the page: "For Paul".

It was entitled, "Apparition of Mary"; the first words were "Go seek her."

Go seek her, the Glorious One
From east to west, from north to south
To see if by chance she has left some sign
If by chance someone has seen her on the way.

Here everywhere is a foreign land
Here all roads are lost on the horizon.
You have to travel through triple-dense woods
You have to travel through the valley of forgetting
You have to travel through water
That frees you from all that disturbs you.

Look, there she is, the Glorious One
More beautiful than ever
Shining in the splendor of her people
In the light-filled circle of humanity
She is greeting you
She, whose you are.

Below that was written "8/30/1986", and nothing more, not even her name. Back then, with a shy smile, she had come to show it to me personally at my office. The punctuation was off, but every word was chiseled in stone. At that time had she understood what she was writing? The one sure thing was that I had never dared dream that the poem would find me a second time. Now I read it again, this time from bottom to top, to the conclusion: "Go seek her!" I almost burst with joy as I went out on the balcony, letter in hand, and looked down on the Thierschplatz. School was out. Streams of children were flooding the streetcar stops or were running underground to the Metro, and adolescents under the trees by the fountains were smoking stolen cigarettes.

CHAPTER ELEVEN

A MODERN PAINTING

A news flash in Frankfurt; an extraordinary task for the feast of the Visitation of Mary, the feast of the first Magnificat, and a telephone call like a lightning bolt in a cloudless sky.

"Thomas, what in your opinion is the most important event of the last millennium?" I asked my editor-in-chief in Frankfurt, shortly after the episode of the poem, as we ate in our favorite Italian restaurant. For in those days, even though my book on the heavenly Jerusalem seemed wonderful, I made my living, not as a book author, but as a journalist for the weekly magazine of the *Frankfurter Allgemeine* newspaper, whose editor-in-chief was Thomas Schröder. The year previous I had researched the Shroud of Turin for him. "The most important event up until now?" He looked at me thoughtfully. Certainly he knew this was a trick question. As usual, I had come to Frankfurt to discuss ideas to be developed in the magazine, only, this time, things were different. This weekly magazine published articles only on stories, not on novels or books. By phone he had instructed me to bring him at least five ideas for possible stories, three possible interviews and at least one personal profile. Yet the current mood and atmosphere were more miserable than ever now, and, from one issue to another, the ads to which the magazine owed its existence were diminishing; rumors were flying in every office. But things remained the same between Thomas Schröder and me, at least when we left the office and got into the car to go eat.

"Tell me. What do you think was the most important and most significant event of the last millennium?" I repeated my question as I took a drink and turned my deadpan face to my spaghetti. We had already discussed my suggestions for stories, and he had been unenthusiastic. Once again, we did not have enough money for great investigative pieces; we could barely cover the cost of travel within Germany. For this reason, first of all, he had scotched a story on the apocalyptic plain of Armageddon in Israel. The same for stories on Istanbul or Saint Catherine's monastery at the foot of Djebel Musa on the Sinai Peninsula ("a Christian ark in the sea of Islam"). Also too expensive were a double interview with Yasser Arafat and Benjamin "Bibi" Netanyahu and a report on the "Saint Petersburg Blues", for which I wanted to be accommodated for a week in the Hotel Astoria on the bank of the Neva in the former Leningrad. He thought a comparison between the Qur'an and the Torah would be cheap enough, but perhaps too boring for our coddled readers. "In spite of everything, we have to offer people something with content", I said to him, "especially now on the eve of the year 2000! Our readers are fed up with airy-fairy media babble. They want to read something real, something big and exciting. We need to give our magazine more weight for the sophisticated reader. We need to remember, once again, what makes us and has made us invincible: reports of great scope and great intensity and penetrating reporting."

He agreed, but "What can we do? Money, Paul, blessed money! It's not coming in. One after another, the people who take out ads are running away." This is why I had not put Mexico on the list of stories I wanted to do. At the time, a transatlantic flight was unthinkable. The decade between 1980 and 1990 was definitively over. And at that moment no other low-budget projects suggested themselves to me. Something, perhaps, on the new European borders? Traveling in my car, staying in cheap hotels along the Holland border, as if we were making a road movie along the lower Rhine? I could get there, and relatives could put me up. He shook his head, no. I had given myself time to drink a glass of wine and to pause in proposing ideas, before I again put to him the question about the most important event of the second millennium.

"I would say Gutenberg and printing. Do you want to check out Mainz?" he asked.

"No way", I laughed. "You're expert in art—what would you say about this picture?" As if slapping down a wild card, I whipped out a paperback on the *Morenita* that I had been rereading on the Metro, covered the title with a napkin and put a photo of a detail of the head of the Virgin next to his glass. Thomas Schröder pushed his plate aside, adjusted his glasses and, chin in hand, examined it carefully. "This is a modern painting, probably from the first half of the twentieth century", he finally answered, "by a painter completely familiar with the history of Western art from the Gothic period." "Not bad, Thomas, but now, if you will permit me, I would like to tell you something about this painting." He fixed his curious eyes on me.

"The modern age began with this image. It has changed both the weight and the balance of the earth", I began. He raised his eyebrows. I took another sip of wine. "Don't you want to know how?"

Thomas Schröder was, preeminently, a free spirit, and, as with all free spirits, his journalist's curiosity always raised him above all dogmas. His job had sent him to get to know Saint Petersburg, Lisbon, New Orleans and Tokyo, to name only four ports. So to tell him and to go into raptures now about the Madonna was, in some ways, the

most natural thing in the world. "While you were snatch-
ing eight million Christians from Rome and the Madonna
and delivering them to Luther in Wittenberg, and the Turks
were cutting the Balkans off from Christianity, the following was happening on the other side of the world with
this image."

Thomas Schröder placed his silverware on his plate as I
related, not the whole story, but at least as much as I knew
about it at the time. I explained that it might help him
to imagine the situation after the conquest of Mexico as
similar to that in postwar Yugoslavia. For, after every victorious campaign, there usually arises the question of
legitimation. This is why we now have to introduce democracy in the Balkans. Back then it was clear that the conquered Amerindians—who were too numerous for all to
be murdered—had to become Christians. There was only
one difficulty: the Mexicans did not want to play the game.
Nothing could persuade them to become Christians. This
is why they had learned to know the Spaniards well. By
November 1512, a law had been passed in Burgos that
allowed the forced conversion of the Amerindians. But this
strategy came to nothing. There was no hope. My boss
ordered another bottle of wine.

"Thus in a certain way the modern age began with an
apparition. This is what the image next to your plate is
saying. In 1531, in North America, Mary revealed herself
to an Amerindian to whom she left this image", I continued. "This was an irruption of what is foreign into history,
such as had not been seen since the emperor Constantine
converted to Christianity in the fourth century. Africa never
became Christian, much less Asia. Imagine if the Amerindians had become Muslims just to spite the Spaniards! For
they were not so ignorant that they would not have quickly
become aware of the struggles for dominance among the

religions of the Old World. On the contrary, they had an eminently intelligent and educated elite, people very alert in observing the Spaniards and their background. But after the apparition at Guadalupe, amid an immense number of daily baptisms, Mexico very quickly became Christian. But this is not all. After the christianization of the Mexicans, as if at a single stroke, Mexico became the model of christianization for all Latin America, as far as Tierra de Fuego. From this time on, Latin America became one of us. That we can speak of the West as a unity is very much based on the fact that this region of the earth was joined to Western culture in a fantastic way. In this way the course of the world was changed. America would be totally different if this immensely important event had not occurred, an event that we are only now beginning to discover."

By now I knew that there was no lack of earlier stories of apparitions. Nevertheless, the vision of Guadalupe marked a genuine leap in time: "Generally, we consider apparitions to be medieval phenomena. But the apparitions of Mary are, above all, modern phenomena. We might even say that with this image the modern age began. From this perspective, you are absolutely right in your observation that this is a modern painting."

I had not yet told Thomas Schröder that the stars on the mantle of the Virgin Mary were like a star map of the day of the apparition in Mexico, December 12, 1531, when he put his glasses back on and interrupted me: "It's perfectly clear, Paul. You will make this trip. We are going to publish the story." This came completely out of the blue, so to speak, as trips to far-distant places were in the magazine's far-distant past. "This will be our masterpiece", I told him. "We've spent twenty years of our time, our imagination, our money to secure the best pictures and photos in the world. I swear that this story will become the culmination of all our stories. It will be judged as "the mother of all images".

"Dear Thomas", I wrote the next day from Munich. "I have already told you how much I enjoyed our lunch together. But I want to repeat it again briefly here. So we certainly and decidedly need greater weight in the magazine if we want to stay current with other publications and with our own vision! For this reason I would like to leave as soon as possible for the New World, to research the story of the incredibly unknown image of Our Lady of Guadalupe in Mexico, which will surely come to be one of the most striking stories in the flood of German publications. I tell you that this story will be a blockbuster. Of course I will try to make sure that the project will be as economical as possible: cheap air fares, cheap hotels, etc., but let's do everything we can to begin as quickly as possible. To expedite this, I am including the travel application. View it with generous eyes."

Perhaps I was not entirely sure about the project. Perhaps, too, my curiosity had simply become too great. As the story ought to have been the crowning story in the issue that marked the new millennium, I now wanted to go to Guadalupe as soon as possible, preferably for a Marian feast. The closest was the Visitation of Mary, July 2. In the city of Siena, Tuscany, I had once experienced how the city virtually stood on its head on that day. Would it be any different in Mexico City? This Marian feast, introduced in 1263 by the Franciscans, celebrates the visit of the pregnant Mary to her much older cousin Elizabeth, also miraculously pregnant. Elizabeth is the mother of John the Baptist.

At this point I looked up the passage in the Bible. It is in this encounter that Luke's Gospel gives us the *Magnificat*, the hymn Mary intoned when Elizabeth went out to meet her on the Judean hills:

My soul magnifies the Lord,
and my spirit rejoices in God my Savior,
for he has regarded the low estate of his handmaiden.
For behold, henceforth all generations will call me blessed;
for he who is mighty has done great things for me,
and holy is his name.
And his mercy is on those who fear him
from generation to generation.
He has shown strength with his arm,
he has scattered the proud in the imagination of their hearts,
he has put down the mighty from their thrones,
and exalted those of low degree;
he has filled the hungry with good things,
and the rich he has sent empty away.
He has helped his servant Israel,
in remembrance of his mercy,
as he spoke to our fathers,
to Abraham and to his posterity for ever. (Lk 1:46–55)

It is the Song of Songs of revolution, a Mother's song of longing for a complete change in the way things are, longing for justice, longing for marvelous things, longing for mercy—a song sung every day as evening praise in innumerable convents all over the world.

With the help of Ramona, the faithful soul in the editorial office in Frankfurt, I booked a flight and a hotel in the heart of Mexico City, close to the cathedral.

Everything was working out marvelously. I would soon fly to Mexico. Life was wonderful. My book was published and looked fantastic. We celebrated after work with the best Italian wine in town. I was the luckiest man in the world. The next morning I telephoned Thomas Schröder to tell him a joke my nephew had told me the night before. "Wait a minute and hold the joke", he said. "First I have to tell you something that is no joke. The publisher of the magazine was just with us in the editorial office. The magazine is being discontinued! It's the end! It's over! The last issue will come out June 25."

CHAPTER TWELVE

LEAVING FOR THE NEW WORLD

A pink slip arrives at the right time; a brief excursus on the shape of Europe. Leaving for the New World and two small bottles of wine at a window seat under the dome of the sky and above the clouds.

A week later in Frankfurt I learned that the termination of the magazine had also brought the termination of my wonderful job with one of the best publications in Germany, in its best year ever, precisely on the fiftieth anniversary of the newspaper's inception. I learned that my termination date was slated for December 31, 1999—in spite of everything, a wonderful, quasi-cosmic date. Unfortunately, the decision was irreversible. Until then, I was released from work. I was fifty-one, on the street without a job like my son Jakob. Not literally, of course. I had a house, a car, a bed, a few tables and chairs and a desk on which, as the fruit of eighteen years at the newspaper, lay a just-published book on the vision of the heavenly Jerusalem in Europe. I had, as well, an airline ticket, reservations for one of the hotels on the Zócalo Plaza of Mexico City and a plan to write a report about the Virgin for the new millennium. I really wanted to do this, and so she did not let any sadness enter the project, to which she was adding her own plan for something completely new, as I had suspected.

Before the week was out, the editorial office called with a request that I turn in the airline ticket. What would happen to my great story if I could not even make it my last? There was only one thing I could not do—become sad. I was sure about one thing: I was not giving up my ticket. I

had never been to Mexico. I was going to travel there, even
without a formal assignment, even if they would not pay
for my travel expenses. I suddenly remembered that they
had given me six months to research the story on the Virgin, more time than ever before. Rapidly I saw how the
article would automatically turn itself into a book, which I
could read even as I wrote it. At the same time I began to
see images of the Virgin everywhere. And, just as suddenly,
I discovered that no other image but that of Mary, under
thousands of forms, had so shaped the Western world. What
image has so formed Europe as her face [in German, the
word for the noun "image" (*Bild*) and the word for the
verb "to form" (*bilden*) are of the same root]? In the Afra
chapel in Landshut I saw a Gothic painting in which Saint
Bernard was being fed by a great gush of milk from the
breast of the Mother of God. "What is this trying to say?"
I asked the sacristan. "That she personally has nourished
him," he answered me with a wink, "so that he could sing
about her as beautifully as he has done."

The night before I left for Mexico, we had a visit from
our elderly pastor, Kreft, from Offenbach, a man I knew
prayed a rosary every morning, as my childhood pastor had.
"What does the last glorious mystery actually mean?" I asked.
"What does 'blessed is the fruit of your womb, Jesus, who
has crowned you in heaven' mean? How is it to be understood?" He looked at me astonished and answered me with
his soft Mainz accent: "Oh! The rosary and its mysteries do
not exist to be understood. It is a prayer for contemplation,
not for understanding."

The next morning I was seated in the plane. It was June
29, 1999, the feast of Peter and Paul, my name day. At 10:15,
in my window seat, I began to write the first notes for the
book, at first in the form of a travel diary. One thing was
evident: my career as a journalist had come to an end. I was

already too old for the job and needed to find some other way to support myself. So I began.

"The Air France plane to Paris turns its wheels into position and takes off. We go in search of the milk that had nourished Saint Bernard and made his voice strong and peaceful. By a sudden, primitive blow, my last business trip has become my first, brand-new pilgrimage. I polish off all the butter with my bread, I drink the little bottle of champagne, a little bottle of red wine, and then another. I eat and drink everything my doctor at home has forbidden. On this name day I don't want to do anything that will prolong my life! I look at the clouds under us and at my wristwatch. It is 4:30 P.M., European Central Time. I look at the bright swath of sky along the horizon and crane upward to this mysterious and dark cosmos, on this luminous June day. Who are we? Who am I? Where have I come from and where am I going? What are human beings; what is the world? Only what our poets have said, they who invent everything? Not a single one of them knows, even by hearsay, the story that moves the universe, the story that I am now tracking down or presuming to tell. What is the explanation of this sensational event and of the fact that, even after more than four hundred years, it has yet to penetrate European consciousness? Or, perhaps, the story was once known and was simply forgotten? After all, I am familiar with enough beautiful works on the subject. But how could it be that no one has organized the elements of the story into the novel of the millennium, with deeds even more incredible than Don Quixote's heroic feats, more ingenious than Grimmelshausen's *Simplicissimus* and more earthshaking than *The Brothers Karamazov*? More powerful than Herman Melville's *Moby Dick*. Why has there been no Franz Werfel to draft *The Song of Juan Diego*? Why has Gabriel García Márquez not appropriated such powerful literary material? And why have the great painters of

Europe not assimilated the themes contained in this 'mother of all images', particularly when you consider what else they often deal with?" I fell asleep.

Columbus' three-month journey took me twelve hours. When I awoke I saw how isolated clouds were reflected in the depths of the ocean as dull, dark stains on the brilliant waves. Suddenly a few emerald stains appeared in the deep blue. Were we already in the Caribbean? The jets propelling the jumbo shuddered gently behind the window. For a long time, there was only a dense bank of clouds under us. The shadow of the plane passed rapidly over the clouds like the shadow of a flying dragon. Then splendid clarity, the sea in currents of silver. Over us, three swaths of clouds, one after the other, climbing like three ships in full sail before the wind. Until 1:30 A.M., European Central Time, the sky grew more and more luminous over the Gulf of Mexico. At 1:35 we flew over the coastline. On the right, a river was emptying into the sea; next to it, a lake; before it, a flashing fire whose absurdly long plume of smoke insinuated itself over the continent. *Adelante!* Completely awake in the splendor of this night, at 6:45 P.M., local time! I looked at the green mountains and the passes which Cortés had conquered in two years with his five hundred men, and I remembered how as a child I had devoured a library book about those burned ships, about the *noche triste*, about the hoarse thundering of leather drums and the captain's cry, *Adelante*, Onward! At 2:06 A.M., European Central Time, after we had circled the gigantic city surrounded by mountains for twenty minutes, the plane put down on the runway. Here I continued celebrating my name day. It was a bright night, at 7:07 P.M., local time. A rainbow embraced the airport.

CHAPTER THIRTEEN

AN EIGHTEENTH-CENTURY
OPINION

The Labyrinth of Solitude, Mexico City in a fog of jet lag and "the coming together of splendors in the marvelous image of Our Lady of Guadalupe in Mexico", as analyzed according to the rules of painting by Miguel Cabrera in 1756.

Arrival in an extended time warp. When I finally stow my suitcases in the taxi, Mexico City overwhelms me with surprise in the half-light of electrically charged exhaustion. About twenty million people live in the endless environs of Mexico City. The taxi driver makes a correction: twenty-five million. To most, the exact number in so great a city is a matter of indifference. Nothing I had read led me to expect an idyllic situation in the country. On the contrary, violence and an inexplicable death wish are rooted deep in the Mexican soul along with an almost common obsession on that account. Torture is still practiced. The injustice among mestizos, Amerindians and whites cries to heaven. In recent years, the border town of Juárez has seen around 250 unsolved murders of women, perhaps shot to harvest their still-warm organs for sale in the United States. Five hundred other women have disappeared. Poverty, violence and crime debase and stigmatize the birthplace of machismo. Perhaps the only fruitful branches of native industry are the trafficking in drugs, white slavery and pornography. As we drive across the capital, businesses are already closed. I am reminded of *The Labyrinth of Solitude*, by which Octavio Paz inserted Mexico into world literature and from which I still retain scarcely more than this metaphor.

The old Grand Hotel, where the taxi driver leaves me, has lost its splendor. Its location on the great square, the Zócalo, bears witness to its ancient distinction, as do its high prices and its marquee of colored glass, dating from 1899. The building is just off the great plaza in front of the cathedral, which is already closed. The church that contains the image of the Virgin Mary is forty-five minutes away by Metro, with three transfers, a passerby tells me—and it is already too late to go. A longtime Mexican friend tells me by phone from New York that "now no one can wander around the center of town, and don't take a taxi—it is really dangerous." There is no hot water; one has to make arrangements to make a telephone call. Drums beaten under my windows do not let me rest. Circles of Aztecs dance and leap by a blazing fire. In the darkness the gods again become lords of Tenochtitlán. A night spent roasting under nylon sheets and on plastic pillows, a night of sweating and restlessness. There is no air conditioner. I am too exhausted even to think of sleeping. I turn on my bed lamp again and unpack a book I brought to read on the trip: thirty photocopies I made hurriedly before leaving home, because the original is too expensive to pack between my pants and my shirts. It is a thin, yellowed book of only thirty pages in large format, from 1756, of which there are only two copies in the world, available by Internet. These facsimiles of the original were published in 1946 on paper so woody, brittle and fragile that it seems to be at least three hundred years old. As I had to trim some pages with a paper cutter I noted that the typeface was similar to that of the *Nican Mopohua* of 1649. But it was written, not in Nahuatl, but in old-fashioned Spanish, even though the author was an Amerindian.

Don Miguel Cabrera, a native of Oaxaca, Mexico, was considered the most renowned New World painter of his day. He had arrived in the capital at age twenty-four; the earliest of his surviving works dates from 1741, when he was forty-six. In 1753 he founded the first painting academy in Mexico. The Cathedral Chapter considered no other painter but Miguel Cabrera when they wanted to have a true copy of the *Morenita*, María of Guadalupe, made for Pope Benedict XIV, to persuade him to include a feast of the Virgin of Guadalupe in the liturgical calendar. No one had made better copies of the miraculous portrait of the Virgin Mary, so this copy was to be a masterpiece. To make his work possible, without the obstacle of the glass in the frame, he had access to the image, day and night, so as to study it undisturbed: cloth, colors and technique. For as far back as 1666, some painters had asserted that the picture did not have a primer coat, which is necessary for any painting on a normal canvas.

For his studies, Miguel Cabrera brought seven painters with him and soon discovered that it was impossible to make a true copy of the original. They could only make paintings or portraits, as of a tree, a cloud or a living person. For this reason, Cabrera promptly painted three masterpieces, so as to be able to send the best to the Pope. As he worked, he came up with some ideas that he later summarized in the thin book I held, to which he gave it the singular title *An American Marvel and a Collection of Marvels in the Wondrous Image of Our Lady of Guadalupe of Mexico, Analyzed According to the Art of Painting.*

By my hotel, the cathedral clock sounded. I forgot to count the strokes because it was as if the story were beginning again. Under a richly figured coat of arms, Cabrera begins his text as if it were a letter: "Most reverend Lord, justice requires me to return to Your Reverence what is due you, to dedicate this small work to Your Reverence, both because of the exaltedness of the subject and as the fruit of my labors, to which you, my Lord, have a right." The introduction is a courtly bow in written form in which the painter in the end places "these useless observations" under the patronage of the archbishop, "so that they may somewhere along the way report truly about the singular skill manifested in this painting, unknown until now by the best artists". The introduction is signed: "At the residence of Your Reverence, August 12, 1756. B.L.P. of Your Reverence, and Your Reverence's most trustworthy and faithful servant. Miguel Cabrera." Where the abbreviation B.L.P. can only mean "Besa los pies"—I kiss your feet.

"I call this work the wonder of America," continues Cabrera's report,

> because our America was chosen by our most exalted Queen to receive the marvels of her portrait. I have also called it a "collection of singular marvels", because it seems to me that in this miraculous painting, not one, but many marvels compete with each other.... In the first chapter, I deal with the consistency of the cloth and the colors; in the second, I explain what I know about the cloth on which the holy image was painted. In the third chapter, I speak of the lack of a primer coat that one observes in this heavenly painting. In the fourth chapter, I speak of the superior painting; in the fifth, of the four painting techniques used in this accumulation of various marvels. Then, in the sixth chapter, I discuss that splendid gold work in this image of the Virgin; in the seventh chapter, I will try to respond to various objections (if any be made), and finally, in the eighth chapter, I will draw a conclusion about the task you confided to me.

Since I already knew about points one to three, I wanted to skim them rapidly; however, I got caught already in the first chapter by Cabrera's report on his research. I paused, interrupting my reading, and then simply read along farther:

> The great age, more than 225 years, of this admirable painting of our Lady of Guadalupe, and the adverse climatic conditions all this time in the part of Mexico in which the shrine is located, where the Virgin Mary is venerated by the New World, have caused me to reflect. The valleys around the former great lake are rich in salt, the air is humid and full of salt particles, all of which, together with a mild climate, lead, as we see, to the falling apart of buildings and the disintegration even of iron by oxidation. What is sure is that these climatic conditions have not militated against or compromised the fabric.... The hand-woven agave cloth on which the Queen of Angels has been painted consists of two identical pieces. They were sewn together with a very thin cotton thread incapable of resisting any violent stress. Nevertheless, this fine thread has resisted, for two hundred years, all natural forces, above all, the weight and tension of the two pieces of cloth themselves, which are substantially heavier and stronger than the weak cotton thread.

But the climate has not been the only danger to the image. Over the centuries, an unending procession of innumerable devotional objects have been pressed to the cloth, to be taken home as relics that touched the Virgin. "In 1753, I myself witnessed how the glass was opened and how not only rosaries and religious medals were touched to the cloth, but also, by my estimate, more than five hundred images." But above all, the fibers of the tilma are "the worst possible material a mortal could choose from which to produce such a sublime and masterly image." What Cabrera was most astonished by was the flexibility and fluidity of the cloth, which, in spite of its rough surface, felt like silk when touched. He had retested this repeatedly. No similar cloth had this characteristic. As far back as 1666, the Jesuit

Francisco de Florencia affirmed under oath that the reverse of the cloth, seen against the light, revealed "a complete reflection of the image in full color, which proves that there is no primer coat." Cabrera himself repeated this experiment at various times, always with the same result. Here, there was simply nothing of the preparations with which every painter begins his work.

The fourth chapter says: "I cannot express my astonishment. The excellent and charming symmetry of the image, the harmony of parts and whole make this a marvel that takes away the breath of the viewer, even if he knows only the rudiments of painting." By more modern art criteria put forward in *Albert Dürer, the Great Observer of Nature*, taking the measure of the Virgin, whose proportions are "eight and two-thirds times the length of her face", the subject is "a young woman, fourteen or fifteen years old, fully realized". More surprising to the painter than the age of the Madonna is the technique used in painting.

> In nature, we call a creature composed of four types of animals a monster. And frankly, in art, we call deformed a painting in which four distinct pictorial styles unite on a single canvas. Nevertheless, this is what can be observed cohering marvelously in the painting of Our Lady of Guadalupe. And what a mortal artist cannot do, not only because of lack of harmony but also because of a show of impossibly bad taste, is precisely what we find represented on this canvas so charmingly that it would be impossible to exaggerate what the eyes of the viewer see. This is the art of painting such as it has never before been seen. It seems to be applied with a heavenly brush, as if the painting combined in itself, to the highest degree, not only everything good in painting but also the four painting techniques: one with oil, one with tempera, the third with watercolor and the fourth with egg tempera. It appears that in this portrait

of the Princess of Guadalupe, the head and hands are in oil; the bottom part of her robe and the angel as well as the clouds surrounding her are in tempera; the cloak is in watercolor. But the area where the rays fall seem to be egg tempera as in fresco painting. These techniques are so different that they each require a different base. But I have already said that there is no such primer coat for any of these four media.

On the other hand, in many places the gold appears to be gold dust, which the merest breath could disperse, just like the gold "that nature places on a butterfly's wings", which adheres to our fingertips at the slightest touch. Nevertheless, with reference to this image of the Madonna, the feeling and experience operate in the opposite way. "Here, as I touched it, I could feel how the gold fused with the fibers of the cloth. It felt as if the gilding process had taken place simultaneously with the weaving. You can see each individual gold thread, sometimes in lines as fine as a hair, something never before seen in any painting—and all this with a mastery so complete and so extraordinary that it cannot be perceived except up close."

The objection that this painting goes against that "accepted rule of art, according to which there must be a single source of light in a picture" should be granted. This painting has as many sources of light as rays of the sun around the Virgin Mary, "so that, in the lack of focus regarding the light source, we see the supreme artistic skill in the making of the painting. For here, although the light comes from precisely opposite directions, the result is that the work exhibits what in painting is called 'a good position', that is, a balanced harmony of luminosity and darkness." It was already very, very late when Miguel Cabrera addressed those who asserted that the colors in the painting were fading, "because today we see that the color of the mantle is neither blue nor green, but exhibits elements of both, and that, after all,

it had to have been blue originally." He referred these critics briefly to the image of the angel at the Virgin's feet.
"For the angel reveals in his wings a blue so fresh and bright
that it looks freshly painted. But if the colors of the wings
have not faded, so the colors of the sacred cloak have, to be
sure, not behaved any differently. The mantle had to have
been painted exactly the dark greenish-blue as we see today."

I do not know when I fell asleep. At five in the morning a
band of musicians came down the street. The photocopies
had fallen from my hand and were scattered on the floor
next to the bed. Through the curtains I could make out a
full but waning moon. But then a thrilling burst of chirp-
ing finished waking me up. At dawn, in the hotel's inside
patio, the night coverings of an immense aviary are removed
and the birds begin to sing.

With coffee, a wonderful view from the roof terrace, under
an unclouded sky above the huge square of the plaza. So
this was the famous Zócalo. An immense sun shimmered
behind a huge Mexican flag, which flew from a gigantic
flagpole: an eagle standing on a cactus, devouring a serpent.
Occasionally the wind caught the huge flag. I had never in
my life seen a flag so enormous. This had been the center
of ancient Tenochtitlán: the pyramids of the last Aztec
emperor, Montezuma, the great sacrificial altars of volcanic
rock, as if stained with dried blood. Before going into the
city I ordered another coffee so that I could read the last
chapter of the report by Miguel Cabrera, the rococo painter.

It did not add much new information. At least four times
he genuflected before the idea that only a careful personal
visual examination—and not erudite theorizing without first-
hand knowledge—could answer, spontaneously and clearly,
all the questions and doubts about the image of the Virgin
that he had heard in the course of his life. He concludes: "I

confess frankly that writing this report has been difficult, the same kind of difficulty a writer with no art background would have painting a picture. And just as it is incomprehensible to me that a person who knew nothing of color would try to paint something and be paid for it, so I am baffled and exhausted trying to write this poor report. But my explanations correspond exactly with the truth." Nonetheless, when he, as writer of this balanced report, approaches the face of the Virgin, he reverts to being a painter, as can be seen in this report:

> Her lovable face is neither narrow nor broad. In it, beauty, sweetness and plasticity vie with each other. Eyes, nose and mouth are so finely delineated that, taking nothing from their individuality, they contribute such a beauty to the whole composition that the viewer's heart breaks. The forehead is very well proportioned, her black hair giving her a special beauty.... The eyebrows are thin and well-arched. Her downward glance is tender as a dove; and the joy and deep reverence that overcome one on seeing her are completely inexplicable. The nose is beautiful and marvelously in harmony with the other parts of the face. The mouth is wonderful, and the lips very sweet. By chance or by mysterious providence, the lower lip rests on a break or knot in the agave fabric, which gives the impression of being higher. Because of this, her face is graced with a special charm— she appears to be smiling. Her jaw line fits with all this beauty and wondrousness. The cheeks are lightly rosy, a little darker than the tone of a pearl. The neck is rounded, thin and perfect.

Cabrera interpreted the pose of the angel at Mary's feet as if it had just ended its flight. Then, in his eulogy, he soars higher and higher, like an eagle, losing himself in exalted praise: "Though I need not say it, nevertheless I affirm that this work surpasses anything that artists have dared to attempt." With this miracle, the "all-powerful Princess" wanted to honor the Amerindians, who "knew no other writing or phonetics or literary conventions besides symbols or painted pictographs. Moreover, in her maternal compassion, she wanted also to honor in those kingdoms both painters and the art of painting. At a single blow, with this portrait, she has introduced painters to four different painting media and has simultaneously provided them the basis for a holy pride."

I had to laugh. This is what I also wanted for myself and the art of journalism: "a basis for holy pride" in our profession, even though I, together with my sharp-witted colleagues, were just beginning, a quarter of a century later, to be aware of what the painter Cabrera had discovered back in 1756.

CHAPTER FOURTEEN

IN THE SHADE OF THE MOTHER

Morning in Mexico City. A case full of skeletons; open doors in the Palace of the School of Medicine; a girl in the ring dance of the eagle; the refraction of light on feathers; an unfathomable smile on the Virgin's face.

A very elegant bald man at the next table had overheard my laugh. He turned to me with curious eyebrows and entered into conversation. He was the chief of staff in the ear, nose and throat department of a large clinic in Mexico City. Waiting for his wife, he held forth with brief lectures on what was going on around me: about this sector of the city, about the city, about the land of Mexico, about its history and about the world. He was most impressed that someone would have traveled all the way from Germany simply for the Virgin of Guadalupe, all the more because I was a mature man, a journalist and, above all, German. He had never heard the like. "Are you asking if I have ever personally visited the *Morenita*? Of course not", he replied, perplexed. All that is known about the image is that country people and fools believe in it. Besides, he knows for a fact that it is nothing but a copy of another painting that was nothing but some kind of forgery. He is a Catholic and proud of having become an agnostic. A charming man, very intelligent, with odd ideas. How was Mexico conquered? Very simple. The Aztecs surrendered to the Spaniards out of conviction because their own culture had reached a dead end. And it is a fact that, later, there arose a culture without racial discrimination. There is no other explanation. I surely had to visit him, he added, as his wife entered the fifth-floor café. He, too, was a painter, and I would be astonished at what he had created on canvas, as if by magic, while he lived in Paris. But it was time for him to go.

It was right here that the conquistadors had placed the center of the new city. Trash blew through the streets; small fires had been lit on the street corners. Against the wall right in front of me stood a family singing something achingly sad. None of the passersby listened. A thousand children were jumping over holes in the pavement. Everywhere there were short policemen with Amerindian features. Despite their dilapidated state, many old flat-roofed buildings still bore witness, behind their crumbling façades, to their former magnificence. Here was the first printery in America; there, the oldest royal armory; there, the oldest conservatory. The modern plan of the city, like a chessboard, had a view of distant mountains in every direction. In the ancient center of the metropolis of millions of people, the side streets, patios and churches seemed almost provincial. Roosters crowing in the center of Mexico City. The mass of people was immense, the center of the city one great bazaar. Next to the impressive cathedral there were new excavations of an ancient complex of pyramids, littered with rubble. Between the cathedral and these ruined pyramids, bonfires had been lit. Men and girls danced ecstatically in ring dances. The plaza was surrounded by the primitive staccato of muffled drums and the rattle of the ankle bells of the Amerindians stamping rhythmically on the ground. In front of the entrance to the cathedral, a young girl detached herself from the crowd of the curious and inserted herself among the dancers; she danced in concentric circles, moving toward the center until it seemed that she was simply floating in the air: a young, eagle-like girl, who, lost in herself, circled ever higher. I watched her carefully until a

sudden gust of rain drove me from the plaza. It was the
rainy season—the worst time to visit Mexico City, as I soon
discovered. A storm broke. The feast of the Visitation [for-
merly celebrated on July 2] is not celebrated here, the feast
of the *Magnificat* for which I had selected early July as my
date of departure. No one I asked had ever heard of it.

The rain had driven me into the museum behind the
pyramid. Just beyond the entrance, to the right, the visitor
is faced with a wall full of skulls. The god of death must
have been the lord of this plaza. Not one single god, but
uncounted gods and idols. It is difficult to recall so many
faces in obsidian and other semi-precious stones, not to mention their names. In the neighboring church the only one
still suffering is Christ on the Cross—but in a style more
frighteningly realistic than can be found anywhere in Europe.

Meanwhile it had stopped raining. I wanted to go to Tepeyac
Hill, but all afternoon I could not pull myself away from the
center of this city constructed of rust-colored volcanic rock.
I let myself be carried along. I followed the colonial Spanish
façades and the domes of churches, until at the intersection
of Republic of Venezuela and Republic of Brazil Streets, in
the palace of the School of Medicine, I found myself standing in front of an old, dissected and preserved Amerindian
man and four sixteen-week human fetuses with distinctly
pensive expressions on their faces, swimming together in
a solution. All the doors of the palace were open. I found
myself alone in these enormous spaces. Was all this some
dream? When I found myself in the street again, it seemed
as if the Amerindians in front of the cathedral had not interrupted their dance for a minute. Only the young girl had
disappeared. Next to the cathedral rises the building in which,
in December 1531, before Bishop Zumárraga, the miracle
of the roses was worked as Juan Diego unfolded his tilma.
The building was closed.

The journey from the center of the city to the shrine of the Virgin of Guadalupe—which back then Juan Diego made on foot along a path—now takes half an hour by the Metro or three-quarters of an hour by taxi. I took a cab. There was not much to see, as it was raining again. Finally, the new basilica came into view and, by its side, the ancient baroque basilica, now half in ruins. The new basilica, a concrete tent shaped like the cone of a volcano, rises over the Avenida Montiel in a neighborhood of low, architecturally insignificant buildings. Everything was gray.

A camp composed of yellow plastic awnings and booths nestled along the lattice fence that surrounded the shrine, along the pavement and staircases. The unlicensed market crept and spread into every open nook and cranny on blankets that could be rolled up quickly when one of the many policemen appeared. Along the pavement were arranged hundreds of food stalls and small iron grills for making tortillas and small sweet cakes. But suddenly a grate blocked the way of this colorful, noisy and ever-moving mass of buyers and sellers to the restricted area of the basilica. On the other side was the plaza, all at once totally empty.

Entering the circular church was an experience like that of Turin. Although I had traveled so many thousands of miles to see the image of the Virgin, it caught me by surprise that she could be seen even from the threshold of the open door. The image came out to meet me. Mass was being celebrated at the main altar. The marble benches to the left and right of the altar sank into a mass of flowers. On the floor, one bouquet of flowers was piled next to another: gladioli, roses, asters—a dazzle of blossoms. But I had eyes only for the pale image of the Madonna in its massive frame of gold and silver roses hanging on the back wall above the altar.

"Father, I thank you that you have hidden these things from the wise and learned and have revealed them to simple people" (Mt 11:25) was the Gospel being proclaimed just as I entered the Church. I moved along the back wall of the hall and was astonished to see that the image of the Madonna really did glimmer and shine differently, depending on the visual angle. Seen from the left entrance, the rays of the sun behind her looked golden; seen from the right entrance, they were grayish—and not spectacular from any point of view. The colors refracted light as do iridescent bird feathers and beetles, I had read in Callahan's 1979 research. He was right. The colors changed before one's eyes, depending on where one stood. Was this some kind of camouflage? Was this the reason the image remained unknown in large parts of the world?

In a shrine along the back wall, I saw a fantastically twisted crucifix resting on a cushion designed to fit it. It was *El Cristo del Atentado* (Christ of the Attempt), as the card beside it said. On November 14, 1921, in an attempted dynamiting of the image of the Virgin, a charge had been placed in a vase among the flowers directly below the image and had been detonated. The violence of the explosion had twisted the crucifix into its present shape. All the windows of the ancient basilica had been reduced to slivers. But the painting remained intact. The attempt had not left even a single scratch on the glass. The cross alone continues to bear witness to this act of treachery.

A pamphlet next to the shrine related other curious things that the image had undergone. In 1791, twenty years after the image was placed in a new gold frame, the workmen cleaning the gold inadvertently spilled a few drops of saltpeter on the image. These drops should have damaged the image, as, normally, when this acid comes in contact with vegetable or animal proteins it breaks down the cellular structure. In this case, nothing happened. The liquid simply evaporated on the surface of the image without leaving the slightest trace. At this time it had also been observed that the fabric bore no traces of either dust or insects. Not until 1936 did Professor Richard Kuhn of the Kaiser Wilhelm Institute in Heidelberg and later winner of the Nobel prize in chemistry discover that the two threads of the tilma he had removed for study, one red, the other yellow, showed no trace of either organic or mineral colors. We can exclude synthetic colors, which were not developed until three hundred years after the formation of the image. In 1946, the cloth was put under a microscope for the first time. This confirmed the conclusions made ten years earlier and verified unequivocally that the image on the tilma is not a painting because there are no brush strokes. A new examination made in 1954 by the Mexican physician Professor Francisco Rivera confirmed this conclusion.

I returned the pamphlet to its rack. Who could verify all this?

In the front part of the basilica, next to the altar, high up, there was a modern crucifix on which the torso of the Crucified was draped with the same star-strewn mantle as appears in the image of the Virgin Mary hanging just ten yards beyond it, on the left. As with the man on the Shroud of Turin, this crucifix also showed the nails in the wrists rather than in the palms of the hands. And, as in the Shroud, the thumbs are invisible; there are four fingers visible in the Virgin's praying hands, but no thumbs.

At the altar, the priests, in festive vestments, were celebrating one high Mass after another, without interruption. A priest passed through the congregation sprinkling the pilgrims with holy water from a silver urn. I got a stream of water from an aspergillum full in the face; for the Mexican altar servers and singers—and for me—nothing could have been funnier.

An elegant marble ramp takes the many pilgrims down to another floor, behind the sanctuary, directly below the image, where three short moving walkways carry the people below the Virgin Mary; there is also a return walkway. The opinion of various visitors to Mexico, none of whom could tell me the story of the image, was that these walkways were an intelligent solution to keep the masses of pilgrims flowing. I remained standing next to the walkway closest to the Virgin, looking up. Light fell from above through a crown of windows in the cone of the cement tent, into the shaft where the image was hung on the back wall. Here, the rays around Mary were again of glittering gold. But how could this be? The colors were completely different from those in the reproductions. All that appeared delicate, tender—the pink and old rose, green, gold—now gleamed like pink copper, rosy bronze, like dawn itself. They were the colors of paradise. Before me, completely pale, was the dark Virgin. *Am I, your Mother, not here?* she said to each visitor in an inscription written in gold behind me. *Am I not shading you?* The face she inclined toward me withdrew from my curious and searching eyes. Everything was tranquil, very peaceful. She looked down on me with the same inscrutable expression I had observed that very morning in the School of Medicine in the faces of those unborn fetuses. But then why was I weeping?

CHAPTER FIFTEEN

THE SPEAKING EAGLE AND THE WOMAN WHO CONQUERS THE SERPENT

The anniversary of the Night of Sadness: in a parish in a Mexico City suburb, Don Mario Rojas Sánchez deciphers the image of Mary as if it were a codex; he interprets flowering jasmine, serpents, northern and southern firmaments.

Don Mario finally answered the telephone, with ancient Mexican courtesy: "At your service." After the first encounter, I had visited María of Guadalupe several times and spent hours contemplating her. However, from that first afternoon I had begun my search for answers from local people who had studied the image of the Virgin for years. People like Don Mario. Once, he had just gone out, they informed me; another time, he was at church; another time, they said he would return soon; another time, no one answered. I spent one entire morning noisily dialing his number on an old rotary phone in my hotel room, while from the bed I watched the incessant rain of the first day of July through faded curtains.

At midnight, July 1, 1520, the Night of Sadness had begun for the Spanish conquistadors, as they were about to abandon Tenochtitlán secretly, because, even after several massacres aimed at the ruling class, they still had not secured complete control of the city. The Aztec emperor, Montezuma, had died at the hands of his subjects under a hailstorm of rocks, and all pretenders to the throne had also died.

The Spaniards had treacherously decimated them. But later this Night of Sadness became a sheer catastrophe for the invaders. The Amerindians made a surprise attack as the Spaniards fled by night through the narrow streets bordering the canals; they attacked by war canoe, as rapid as arrows. "Like a plague of locusts" they fell on the routed. The war howls assaulted all the senses. The night engulfed the Spaniards in an abyss and, even more, their Tlaxcaltecan allies. Chaos laid them waste. Cortés wept in rage and despair. But the next morning it is reported that he said: "Onward, we have all we need!" Everyone was wounded, most gravely, only a few not seriously. They had lost hundreds of their troops and thousands of their Amerindian allies. The luckier ones died during the night; the less lucky were taken alive by the Aztecs. While the Spaniards hurried to escape faster, they heard, from the apex of the Great Pyramid behind them, the thunder of the horrible background music of people drumming and rattling conch horns that accompanied their comrades, prisoners, being dragged violently up the stairs to the priests who were offering them in sacrifice. Soon their heads and those of their horses would be strung like pearls, one by one, in a skillful display of skulls like that I had seen in the museum. Cortés had been able to save only four hundred men and thirty horses. More of the wounded died every day. Nonetheless, one year later, in August 1521, he returned with fresh reinforcements, destroyed the city and definitively wiped out the Aztecs. "Onward, we have all we need!"

It had begun to rain early in the morning, as if the air were simply dissolving in a fine mist, a combination of steam and water. But now, suddenly, a hundred years worth of rain deluged this part of the city. From the terrace I had observed how, simultaneously, the sun continued shining on the nearby hills. Mexico was evaporating. The climate was truly ghastly for the preservation of any unprotected image. Add to this modern industrial pollution and long-term emissions from millions of unfiltered smokestacks and tail pipes—together with all the soot that centuries of candles in honor of the Virgin had put into the atmosphere. If what should have happened had happened, then that pale image I had seen for the first time the day before should have been coal-black. During the same period of time the frescos of the Sistine Chapel had become so dull that they were scarcely recognizable. In the book by Smith and Callahan, who had examined the image of the Virgin of Guadalupe in 1979, I had read that the ultraviolet light coming from candles fades most colors, organic or inorganic. The color blue, especially, disappears almost completely under ultraviolet light. Nevertheless, I myself had seen that the image imprinted on the tilma had clearly resisted this environment without suffering any damage.

But the person who could best inform me about these important concerns had to be Don Mario Rojas Sánchez. He had dedicated his whole life to the study of the image. Years before, in 1978, he had published a translation of the *Nican Mopohua* from Nahuatl to Spanish, now considered to be the definitive translation. By profession, however, he was neither a scholar nor a translator, but rather a pastor of Our Lady of Mount Carmel, a remote suburban parish in Cuauhtémoc.

Meanwhile, I was encountering the *Morenita* on all sides: in the taxi, at the newsstand, in every bar. Among the bookstores of the metropolis, I discovered stores that specialized in the Virgin of Guadalupe. As I browsed though the books, Don Mario's name kept recurring. The address that I had written down was so incomplete and incorrect that it was a wonder that the taxi driver could find it. In my wallet I carried two photos showing Don Mario with a rectangular piece of agave cloth like that used as a tilma in the past and how it could be knotted on the left shoulder to serve as a mantle. Don Mario had to have been about seventy-five years old at the time, and I had heard that he was a kind-hearted man of God.

That is how he sounded on the telephone. Of course, I could visit him whenever I wished. Why not right now? Since he never had time, he had to use bits of time, if it was important, if I would not mind accepting the little bit he had. Of course, if I could see my way clear to taking a cab, it would cost about 140 pesos to get from the basilica to his small, modern parish church up in the northern part of the city where the cliffs of the Sierra Madre climb even higher into the firmament and where the City of Mexico becomes the cosmos and the airport and landing strip of heaven; seven thousand feet above sea level, on the shore of this ocean of twenty million human beings.

In the rectory next to the small church, Lourdes, the housekeeper, was waiting for me. Don Mario entered the room still wearing the alb in which he had just celebrated Mass. He immediately got so involved in conversation that he forgot to take it off. He was short, compassionate, over-flowing with mischief, humor and wit. His roguish eyes reminded me of some Irish pastor, his Amerindian grand-father notwithstanding. "You never can tell about the laws of heredity", he laughed, without missing a beat in the con-versation about his much-praised translation. But I had to be careful, because there are always unsuspected pitfalls in translating from one culture to another. Of course, he still spoke Nahuatl. Once a year he celebrated Mass in Nahuatl for the old folks, who still prefer it to Spanish. "Afterward, they all come up to me and hug me, and then, all is good for another year."

All the doors and windows of the house were open. The smell of roasted chiles came from the kitchen, and I got hungry. But with his first word, Don Mario forgot about lunch. "What about the colors? Yes, you are right about them. Painters like ours would have laid the colors on differently, with more intensity and vigor. There are many examples in the magnificent paintings of Mary both in Europe and in America. What is spectacular here is precisely the non-spectacular, the incredible restraint." He laughed briefly: "Our Virgin is painted with the blood of roses. Here Mary has appeared as a true monstrance; she does not wish to draw our attention to herself, but rather wants to reveal her Son to us. This is the most important thing, this is the central message of the image. It is nothing more than what is in the Bible. With her motherly eyes, she orients our gaze toward her Son."

"To her Son? Where is he? Are you referring to the small angel at her feet? If not, she is absolutely alone in the painting."

"Not so. A while back a gynecologist examined the face and determined by the blotches that she is pregnant. This was nothing new to the Aztecs. They had already inferred this from the way that the purple sash is tied across her waist. Her pregnancy causes the sash to shift up and rest above her convex womb. There is music in her. She is clothed with the glory of the heavens. The ancient Mexicans quickly saw this. For them, this image was a manuscript, a codex, *sui generis*. In one stroke, she has translated the gospel into the Amerindian language. As in the famous Aztec stone calendar, now in the Anthropological Museum, this image contains no unnecessary embellishment or line. Are you at all familiar with the celebrated stone calendar? You must have a look at it if you want to be able to learn something about María of Guadalupe. But wait a moment."

He went out. I began to look over his bookcase; I paged through the *Confessions* of Saint Augustine. I looked at the embroidered pictures hanging on his turquoise walls: pine forests, waterfalls. Just then he returned, without the alb, in street clothes, with three or four folders under his arm, two rolled-up images and a large reproduction of the Aztec stone calendar on poster board. "Come, come!" We went into the next room, where he unrolled a print of the image of the Virgin Mary in the original size on a table. He stood to one side like a teacher. "Yes, this is a manuscript, a codex. However, more important than anything else is the tiny, isolated four-petaled flower right in the center. The Aztecs recognized it immediately. It is a jasmine flower, the Amerindian symbol of the sun, just as we find it here at the center of the Aztec calendar. Do you see it?" Suddenly he held in his hand a small extendible pointer and moved it from one point of the picture to the other. "For the Amerindians the image as a whole was a brand-new Aztec calendar, which proclaimed: 'The most holy Virgin bears or carries within herself the sun, that is, God.'"

"Look there!" He paged through his notebook until he found a small, dried white flower, similar to the drawing on the Madonna's dress. "Don't you love it?" He stood, went to the telephone, called a neighbor and asked her to cut him a small sprig of jasmine and bring it over.

As he hung up, I asked: "Is it true, then, that the stars on her mantle correspond to the constellations of stars over Mexico in December 1531?"

"Yes, of course. But that is not all. And—as with everything in the image—it is not a simple fact. It takes an even more subtle, more beautiful turn." He returned to the table, on which the housekeeper had placed two cups of hot water, Nescafe and a little dish of honey, and proceeded to chart out the marks on the calendar stone on the enormous photocopy worn out with use. "Look, do you see there the two serpents that surround and compass the whole? Today, you would scarcely find a single Mexican who knows that these two serpents are also represented on the five-peso coin. And, naturally, these serpents are also found in the image of the Virgin."

"Serpents? In the image of the Virgin? Where?" Don Mario began to laugh. With both thumbs and forefingers he made two circles like eye glasses, turned around, swung his hands forward and put on his "glasses". "Of course, you have to look with Amerindian eyes. We just have to put on our glasses upside down, like the Aztecs. For the Amerindians, the two serpents were the northern and southern firmaments, the northern and southern constellations. The head of the serpent is resting in the east, its feet in the west. Here are the serpents: look how here, to the left is Ursa Major, and here, at the right, the Southern Cross, both inverted. Here, the cosmos encircles the sun at the center. This was the constellation of stars over Mexico in December 1531, but not as we would have seen it, but rather as if we were seeing it from the other side. In this mantle there is imprinted a view of the earth from the other side of the cosmos. And now I have to show you something that I personally have discovered."

He leafed back and forth through his folder until he suddenly produced a sheet with a detailed enlargement of the jasmine flower on the mantle of the Madonna. "On the original, the jasmine flower is perhaps the size of a fingertip. However, look carefully." He handed me a magnifying glass. At that moment the neighbor came in and handed me a sprig of fragrant freshly cut jasmine, with two buds and one opened blossom. I thanked her, took the magnifying glass, bent over the enlargement, looking at the heart of the flower, and I saw an open eye on one side, a small nose beneath, a small mouth above a jaw line. I dropped the magnifying glass. "This isn't possible!"

"Yes, yes", he laughed again, and, winking, he wrinkled his face. "A child, isn't it? His eyes are still closed. He has just awakened and is blinking as a baby does whom his mother has just roused. The right eye is still closed. In this image everything is a beginning, a new start, a birth." Don Mario described the image exactly as I had just seen it through the magnifying glass, and he laughed mischievously.

I asked him: "So, there are no changes in the picture?" He winked: "Only a little on the head. In the first years they often tried to improve the masterpiece. Neither Spaniards nor Amerindians could imagine the Virgin Mary without a crown. So they tried to paint a crown, but nothing of it remains."

I insisted: "Then what about the retouching that some scientists today claim to have discovered by means of infrared light?"

"I do not believe it, and for a simple reason. You see, complete unanimity prevails among all the investigators that the basis for the image's existence is inexplicable: not only its origin and production, but also its coloration and depth, etc. This is a work of God—and this is not just my opinion. There is a great deal of evidence for this. I'm sure you have already heard about how the image escaped the dynamite attack unscathed. Other attempts also failed. Don't you think, then, that the Creator of this image could frustrate and has frustrated other attempts against his masterpiece? In short, a few ill-conceived retouches? I do not have the least doubt. And with specific reference to these retouches, Miguel Cabrera, in the eighteenth century, calls attention to the fact that—against all the conventions of painting—the image demonstrates four different painting techniques. But does this conflict with the fact that it is God's style and work? Did he not permit the Gospel to be produced in four versions? And by this means, is the image not more beautiful, mysterious and profound? Does it conflict with the fact that we find here, in the deepest layer, a Jewish girl from Galilee and, in its final, the Queen of the Apocalypse—and all together in a single indivisible person? Or take another example: Does the fact that in recent centuries we have discovered the hand of more authors and more strata in the Gospels perhaps not make them more the work of God? Or does it make them less? I say no. And so it is, too, with the image of the *Morenita*, the most holy Virgin."

And how did he explain that for a century not a single document mentioned the image, not even the many documents of Bishop Zumárraga? How could he explain this enigmatic Guadalupan silence?

"So you have read this, too", he observed appreciatively, like a teacher pleased with a good question from his pupil. "What does this mean? For that, let me now ask you: What does it mean that Paul, who surely knew Mary in Jerusalem and who wrote more than any evangelist, never mentions her by name in any of his numerous, famous letters? Not a single word! Only once he says 'born of a woman'. That's it. Does this mean that Mary never existed?" Now he laughed even more cheerfully.

"But what about the putto at the Madonna's feet? Isn't it remarkably like a small figure of an angel that Raphael, around twenty years earlier, had painted at the feet of the Madonna of the Sistine Chapel? Hasn't this figure, at least, been copied?" I kept on questioning him.

"The putto, you say? But, that is no putto. It is the widower Juan Diego, of course, presented as an eternal child. His Amerindian name, Cuauhtlatoatzin, means "he speaks like the eagle." In spite of this, people are always asking about the "little man" or "the angel" at the Madonna's feet. But simply look at the eagle's wings behind his shoulders." At these words, Don Mario lifted his own shoulders. "Note that the wings are spread for flight. He is still in the nest, but he will soon take flight." In his blinking and fluttering, suddenly the ancient Amerindian took shape in him. He himself was an angel, a small eagle, like the small figure at the feet of the *Santísima Virgen*, as he habitually referred to Mary. At once, also, his old man's face became completely young. In front of the window, a chick strutted diagonally across the patio of the rectory.

Lourdes called Don Mario to eat. But first he wanted to accompany me through the small garden in front of the rectory and through the mile-long labyrinth of streets to the highway. "Have you already seen the image?" he asked me. "Yes? Then do not believe that you have seen it. No one who gazes wholeheartedly at the most holy Virgin is ever done contemplating her. And yet the image is only captured face to face, not in photos or prints. She does not let herself be reproduced. This image is totally personal. This is the only explanation for the pilgrimages to Tepeyac Hill. Human beings want and have to return to her, because it is there that she bends down to them from heaven."

On the way I asked him: "And what about Abbot Schulemburg, who is personally unable to believe any more in the existence of Juan Diego?"

"Poor fellow!" he answered with pity, as though the abbot had really lost his wits, while he kept searching through his tattered notebook for phone numbers he could give me (all of them no longer in service, I later discovered), and telling me without a pause about his great love: "The image of the most holy Virgin is really a translation of the Bible into the pictographic writing of the Aztecs, without unnecessary embellishments. As the great sign of the Virgin appeared to the seer John, "the eagle of Patmos", only as a bright vision bathed in the light of the sun, with the moon under her feet and crowned with stars, so also she appeared to this John, Juan Diego, 'the eagle of Tepeyac', but in her full reality as Queen of Heaven, clothed in the sun, with the moon as her footstool, adorned with forty-six stars. As María of Guadalupe, on Tepeyac Hill, the Virgin of John's Apocalypse truly entered history! Juan Diego became a second John." He added, slyly: "For us, at least, he naturally, in some ways, remains the first."

Reaching the main road, Don Mario hailed a crowded minibus out from the flow of traffic to take me to the next Metro stop. Then he gave me a quick blessing before I jumped aboard the bus. "At your service."

The passengers wedged me in, first on the cross-town bus, then on the Metro, where I watched the blossoms of the sprig of jasmine wither before my eyes, those flowers that brought back the memory of the Queen of the Flowers. From Don Mario, I had also learned that the combination of vowels and consonants in the name Guadalupe is impossible to Nahuatl. "So it is impossible that she could be called Guadalupe, a meaningless sound in Nahuatl. The Aztec word that is phonetically closest to Guadalupe is *Coatlaxopeuh*, which means: 'she conquers the serpent.' It is probable that the most holy Virgin so named herself. Others think that the original word should be understood as 'she comes from the East.' The word 'Guadalupe' can only be a Spanish corruption, a mis-hearing or a misinterpretation. It was clear that the Spaniards could only have understood it as Guadalupe, and nothing but Guadalupe. They loved their Spanish homeland and were mad about the Black Virgin of the village of Guadalupe, among the mountains and hills of Extremadura, southwest of Madrid. Together with the Virgin of the Pillar, in Saragossa, and the shrine of Saint James of Compostela, the Madonna of Guadalupe attracted most of the pilgrims of the Iberian Peninsula. She was the patroness of sailors and the conquistadors. Almost none of them had failed to say good-bye to her before beginning their Atlantic crossing. So when they heard the word *Coatlaxopeuh* from the mouth of the 'Speaking Eagle', they all, to a man, heard 'Guadalupe' and understood 'Guadalupe'. They simply could not imagine anything else. They would have quickly pointed out to Juan Diego that he must have heard incorrectly. So it remained. Confusion and misunderstanding asserted themselves."

I seemed to be seeing Don Mario again amid the crowd in front of me, like a young eagle, dancing, rising from his patio to the heavens. "In the end, of course, the most holy Virgin tramples the serpent's head. She triumphs over evil by her tenderness and goodness, whether we call her María of Guadalupe or María *Coatlaxopeuh*."

CHAPTER SIXTEEN

MAN-MADE MODEL OF A
DIVINE ORIGINAL

A brief tour of Spain. Toward the "River of Love" in the Guadalupe mountains and a slightly cross-eyed Black Madonna gazing at a man-made model of the Mexican divine original.

With its outlying neighborhoods, Guadalupe, Hidalgo, has a very different configuration from the Guadalupe in the mountains of Extremadura, a minuscule region in southern Spain, about which Don Mario had told me. A month after my trip to Mexico, my wife and I were able to visit the tiny royal city, with a name so musical that the Spaniards thought they had heard it even on the lips of the Mexican *Morenita*.

After our arrival from Germany, we drove nearly a whole day, by car, in torrid heat from Saragossa, through Chinchón, Aranjuez and Toledo to the ancient place of pilgrimage, which lies in an impassable area, remote from all highways. Finally, late in the afternoon, on a foothill of the Guadalupe range, the compound of the Franciscan monastery rose up to the heavens like an imposing crown before our very eyes. The houses of the town huddled tightly against the shrine.

The abbey church bells were calling people to vespers. The temperature remained around 102°, and everything was dry and gritty. But the tiny city was drunk with excitement, for the bulls were running freely through the crowd. The streets boiled with people. The night before, no youth had closed his eyes. Now, as the afternoon drew to a close, at the entryway to the Basilica of Our Lady of Guadalupe, they finally faced the bulls. In front of the staircase the main plaza had been covered in sand, like an open bullring. One lone bull remained behind. The whole crowd roared. Fear-filled pleas for help and sharp cries of secret pleasure rose in waves at each movement of its horns. Many had taken refuge in the entrance halls of their houses and from the upper stories tossed flowers at the enraged beast. Bloody froth drooled from its mouth. At once a circle was cleared around the bull. From somewhere nearby, a youth had gotten a chair and placed it on the sand. He sat down on its backrest, balancing himself with his feet, and snapped his fingers like castanets in the direct line of vision of the colossus that breathed with difficulty, as if waiting for something. When the youth extended his arms right in front of the inclined horns, the bull pawed suddenly and attempted to attack him. Then the youth made one great leap over the bull and landed on the other side of the furious animal, which had hurled the chair about ten yards farther into the arena.

I held my breath. This was not a duel between a lone bullfighter with cape and sword and a contending thousand-pound animal. Here the whole town was facing a monster, as when, in the shadows of prehistory, the whole group went up against a mammoth. Now, from among the enthusiastic crowd, six, seven youngsters in jeans and sneakers ran toward the aroused victim, one grabbing it by the horns, another delivering a single death stab with a dagger, next to the fountain in the center of the plaza.

The fountain was as ancient as the abbey church, but its skillfully carved shell-shaped basin had not always been there. Originally, centuries ago, this decoration had rested in the choir of the church of the Marian shrine. It was the ancient baptismal font of the town, in which, on July 29, 1496,

Christopher Columbus had baptized the first Amerindians of the New World. It had been a gift to "Our Lady of Guadalupe", the "Queen of Mercy", whose dark image had been venerated there from the fourteenth century. Millions of people have seen themselves reflected in her eyes.

At the head of the grand staircase, the filigree façade of the monastery is a masterpiece of medieval architecture. Columbus had often come here as a pilgrim, before and after his voyages of discovery. Hernán Cortés also came at various times, after visiting his mother in Medellín. In 1528, in gratitude for the reckless but successful conquest of Mexico, he brought to the Virgin of Guadalupe a gold scorpion taken from Montezuma's treasury. After him came Francisco Pizarro, conqueror of the Incas; Francisco de Orellana, the first to cross the Andes and navigate the Amazon to its mouth; Hernando de Soto, discoverer of the Mississippi; and many others. Saint John of the Cross took the dark Madonna in his arms. The monastery chronicles list pages and pages of those who came to be blessed here before leaving for parts unknown or who were thanking the Mother of God for a happy return—including Pope John Paul II, who came to worship at the shrine on November 4, 1982.

All came to a display case above the main altar where the image of the *Virgin of Guadalupe*, with a child on her lap, is enthroned. It is totally dissimilar to the image in Mexico, except, perhaps, for the color of her skin, although the color of this Madonna is darker, like that of a Sudanese. The ancient carving in cedar wood is a marvelous image, Egyptian in feel. Or, perhaps, better, Byzantine. It is about a foot and a half high, a classic representation of the Mother of God, of which many were produced in the Mediterranean area after the Council of Ephesus in 431. She is seated erect on a stylized gold throne; her dress is blue, her mantle red, and she has a veil on her head. The child Jesus is seated straight up on her lap as on a chair.

But the visitor to the church sees nothing of this. The space is as magnificently decorated as if it were in competition with the Basilica of Saint Mary Major in Rome. And the Virgin Mary herself is so weighed down with robes of gold and purple brocade that all that appears is her face with its large eyes, the head of her Son, and one hand holding a scepter. Everything about it is strange. A double strand of pearls calls attention to her immobile face. A crown laden with jewels forms an arch on her forehead. Slightly cross-eyed, the dark Virgin Mary looks fixedly at each person who kneels before her. The benches in front of her are never empty. From all of Spain, women and men come to view her quietly or tenderly ask for her intercession. Even on this day on which the bulls had put the town into turmoil.

The Arab name of the monastery, the town and the mountain range is derived from a small stream of water below, on the border of that place, which the Arabs called Guadalupe. To date, scholars do not agree on whether this means "hidden water" or "river of love" or something else. What is certain is that this whole region is dominated by this image, whose "discovery" is the stuff of fourteenth-century legends, which can be summarized as follows:

After the evangelist Luke had sculpted or carved the image in Jerusalem, with Mary as his living model, the image arrived in Byzantium. Here it had to remain hidden, until the future Pope Gregory I the Great took it to Rome and venerated it in his household chapel. The Pope gave it to Leandro, who would soon become archbishop of Seville. Saint Isidore brought it by ship to Spain, with miracles accompanying it everywhere: a plague was halted, a frightening storm was calmed, and yet another plague was wiped out before her.

Wherever she went, she was the Mother of Mercy. By 711, when, in the last defensive battle against the Moors, King Rodrigo bled to death in the Andalusian "River of Forgetting", the image was highly venerated throughout the kingdom of the Visigoths, which already then was famous for its Marian fervor and from whence arose the future Marian zeal of the Spaniards. To keep the image from falling into Arab hands, the priests took it north with them in their flight before the armies of the caliphs and buried it, together with a bell and a document, in a cave in the mountainous region of Villuercas, near the rivulet that the Arabs later named Guadalupe. This happened just before a great part of Europe came under Muslim influence.

About six hundred years passed. Then it happened that a shepherd lost a cow in the neighborhood of the rivulet. He looked for it for three days in the mountains and stands of holm-oak. He followed the stream to its source until he found the cow, but it was dead. It had entered the cave in which the statue had been hidden and had been killed in a fall. He was astonished that it had been neither wounded nor attacked by a wolf. Then he set about cutting the cow up. He had just started to butcher it, with a butcher's cross-shaped cut in the breast, when the animal stood up, alive. The shepherd, frightened and confused, fell back. Suddenly, "Our Lady, the holy Virgin Mary" appeared to him and said, "Do not fear, I am the Mother of God. The salvation of the human race came through me. I have borne the Savior. Take the cow and return it to the herd. Then go home and tell the priests and all the people to come back here with you. Here they need to dig and find a statue of me." But she also commanded that the statue not be moved to any other location and that a chapel be built around it. "In time a church will be raised here: a unique house . . . in which every poor person who comes should receive a daily meal."

The rest of the story is predictable. Mary disappeared. The shepherd did what she asked and so reaped the first taunts from other shepherds. But they believed him when he showed them the cow's cross-shaped scar. He then set out for Cáceres, to tell his family about what had happened. His wife came out to meet him weeping, telling him: "Your son is dead." He replied: "Don't cry or worry. I am going to dedicate him to Holy María of Guadalupe, so that she will awaken him, and I will promise him to her as her servant." At this moment the son woke from the sleep of death and said: "Father, let's go to Holy María of Guadalupe."

With this kind of miraculous confirmation, the shepherd fared better than did Juan Diego in Mexico when he first went to Bishop Zumárraga. In the shepherd's case, the ecclesiastical authorities doubted for only a while—probably due to the Virgin's promise that, "because of the many miracles I will do on sea and land, many people from many places will come to see me in this place, which I will make into something significant." Then the churchmen traveled back with him and a large crowd to dig up the statue at the spot indicated. They found a tomb-like cave and, within it, a rock on which stood the Madonna, with a bell by her side." Then they built a small building of unmortared stone, unseasoned wood and cork roofing, for, as everyone knows, there are many cork oaks in the region." Thus began the shrine of Guadalupe.

But was this the real reason? Is this the only reason that this Marian shrine was set up in such an isolated place—to attract pilgrims and exploit them? On our travels toward the shrine, we had spent a night in the main plaza of the ancient city of Saragossa, by the side of the enormous Marian cathedral. In it there is a column that has been touched and kissed for centuries, a column against which Mary had supported herself when, in 40 A.D.—seven years after her Son's death and before her own—she visited the city, not as an apparition, but "in human flesh". Naturally, the claim is incredible, even though the church of the Virgin of the Pillar became the mother of all churches dedicated to the Virgin in Spain. Nevertheless, when we exited the cathedral, there was a stairway right in front of us leading to an archeological park exhibiting the excavations of Roman Saragossa, the ancient Caesaraugusta. These excavations resembled the Roman columns excavated beneath the Damascus Gate in Jerusalem. The Roman Empire had established a unique trading zone from Jordan to Spain. Within this zone there was a Mediterranean network of roads similar to the modern network of highways in Europe. Moreover, nowhere else but on the sea were long voyages so easily undertaken in the ancient world, and no other mode of transport was faster than shipping.

After Saragossa, we rested in Calayatud, beside the main highway. This seems to be still as Moorish a city as Fès in Morocco. Along the city wall, on a rocky promontory, there is a small church where the Virgin of the Rock is venerated, a black Virgin, which was found, also, with a bell. At the entrance, the housekeeper was chatting with the pastor before starting to clean the church. "Of course our Virgin performs miracles", he replied to our question. "She fills every request that is made to her. Except one should not ask for money."

In our luggage we had Richard Nebel's wonderfully erudite book *Santa María Tonantzin, Virgen de Guadalupe*, in which we had read that in Spain a large number of similar Madonnas had been rediscovered. In the province of Jaén, apart from Señora de la Peña, there was Señora de Cabeza; in Valencia, Señora del Puche; in Alava, Señora del Aránzazu; and many more. Many of these were dark-skinned; many were found with a bell, especially in caves into which animals had broken.

A whole crown of pearls could be fashioned from these images, from the Virgen de la Antigua, in Seville, to the "Virgin of the Grain Market", in Madrid. Beyond Barcelona is the famous black Madonna of Montserrat. The legends, saturated with miracles, became entwined between the twelfth and fourteenth centuries, nearly all following the same outline: The discoverer is a lowly person; at first the Church authorities do not believe him; miracles have to be performed to establish his credibility. A chapel is built. Pilgrimages begin.

But, on the other hand, there are also many documents that vouch for the fact that not a few of the sculptures were already being venerated in Spain before the Arabs arrived. The Muslims had great reverence for Mary as the Mother of the prophet Jesus, but, because of the strict prohibition of images in the Qur'an, they hated all her images. For this reason, during the Islamic dominion of Spain, veneration of the images of Mary went underground. Expecting a crackdown by the caliphs, Christians buried images and statues of Mary "in valleys, mountains and other places". And for this reason, after the victorious Christian reconquest, "many legends unfolded in the reconquered territories about the discovery of images of Mary under miraculous circumstances. They spoke of images well hidden and secured before the Moorish invasion, which, when found later, became miraculous images, a focus for the devotion of the people of the corresponding regions."

I could scarcely believe my eyes. Like Jews, who according to rabbinic law, are obliged to preserve from desecration the smallest piece of parchment, papyrus or paper on which the name of God appears, even partially, so Christians in Spain protected the images of Mary from falling into Muslim hands—the Virgin in whom, they believed, the Old Testament Word became man. Perhaps this is why the modern story that most resembles that of the cow in Spanish Guadalupe is the unprecedented 1947 account of the shepherd in the Judean desert whose goat had become lost in a ravine by the Dead Sea and had fallen into a cave. There, two thousand years before, part of the library of the Qumran desert monastery had been hidden in pottery jars, which is now the greatest treasure of the Museum of Israel in Jerusalem. Just as, during the final conquest of the Promised Land, Jews rediscovered their ancient writings on parchment scrolls, so, eight hundred years earlier Spanish Christians came across, most significantly, the images of Mary.

It is difficult to leave Guadalupe behind. This tiny place is enchanting. One last time before leaving, I entered the church and used binoculars to examine every detail of the jewel-framed face of our Lady above the main altar, which was heavily laden with gold. One last time I studied the mysterious transparency of her gaze, noting exactly how she gazed simultaneously at me and above me—beyond me. I followed her gaze, turned and put the binoculars down. Across from the miraculous image that the pilgrims seek out, hangs an ancient image of the Mexican María of Guadalupe, unadorned, almost hidden in shadow, high up in the choir enclosure. But there the *Morenita* is represented, not in painting, but in carved wood. There she is not pregnant, but carries her naked child in one arm. Otherwise, she is surrounded by the sun and its rays; she is wearing a starry mantle; a black moon is under her feet. Behind the Gothic Madonna, two small figures of angels are lifting a curtain, as in Raphael's painting. A thick, almond-shaped cloud mass surrounds the figure. She wears the same pink-gold robe as in Mexico. Even little Diego emerges under her feet from the clouds. A thick layer of dust covers the masterpiece. The handful of Franciscan priests do not have time to care for all their treasures. The Child's left arm is broken.

But without doubt it was the *Morenita*, with her marvelously compassionate eyes, as if she were simply a Virgin from the lower Rhine like those I had known in my country. And, in fact, this Lady of the Conception is the work of a Guillemín Digante, William of Ghent, a Flemish sculptor, as I discovered at the monastery door, thanks to Father Antonio, a barrel of a man with eyes as round as balls, who sold me a book with faded pictures that corroborated his assertions.

"When was this image placed here?" I asked.

"It has been hanging there since 1499", he answered with a satisfied smile. "No one knows when the Madonna was carved."

"But this is impossible!" I answered; "the image of the Virgin in Mexico has existed only since 1531. So this copy cannot have appeared before!"

Laughter brightened Father Antonio's whole face: "Before? Before? Of course before! Which one has to be the copy? The one here is the original that Hernán Cortés had seen before the conquest of Mexico. So how could it be a copy? This work is the model. She is the archetype!"

CHAPTER SEVENTEEN

TREE OF TEARS AND HELP FROM HEAVEN

Visiting Our Lady of Divine Succor, a look at the Aztec stone sun calendar and an hour with Don José Luis Guerrero, who speaks about the miracle that bloomed for the Spaniards within the miracle of the Morenita.

I had indeed already seen a copy of the Spanish Madonna of Guadalupe in Mexico. It took me almost a whole day to reach her at the top of a hill behind the "Tree of Tears", where Cortés rallied his forces for the first time after the "Night of Sadness". The final station of Line 2 of the Metro is Cuatro Caminos. I wasted another hour in the immense crush of foot traffic in the bus terminal, looking for the right taxi, a blue federal cab, as my destination lay outside the city limits: Nuestra Señora de los Remedios—Our Lady of Succor. A tiny, friendly Aztec finally guided me to the shrine. Children were jumping around everywhere on the hill where she is venerated and were watching me from nearly every nook and cranny of the walls. Every hill on the perimeter of Mexico City is a sign that, in Aztec times, it lay on the shore of an immense lagoon that then surrounded and defended the city. The hill of Our Lady of Succor is on the far side of an axis, with Tepeyac to the north. The Virgin is childlike in her beauty, dressed up luxuriously, about three spans high, and the Child on her lap, perhaps one span. She was wrapped in a mantle of golden and turquoise color when I saw her. The historian Hugh

Thomas relates that when Cortés conquered the nearby Cholula, in the eastern part of the city, he installed an image of the Sevillian Virgin of Succor, with her Sienese smile and golden cloak. Without delay, he set it up in a case at the apex of the Great Pyramid, which, with its 120 steps, was the highest pyramid in the world. Cortés made sure that such Marian images were set up on Montezuma's bloody altars as soon as these had been taken and destroyed. The Aztecs were beside themselves, because they were forced to contemplate how these Madonnas with Child had dethroned their powerful gods. For their part, the old Spanish soldiers loved these Marian images tenderly and on every liturgical pretext dressed them up in a variety of ceremonial robes, just as little girls love and dress their dolls.

Sixteen ceremonial outfits of our Mother of God of Divine Succor—all embroidered with pearls and gems—are stored in a wardrobe in the sacristy. It is believed that after the trauma of the Night of Sadness, Juan Rodriguez de Villafuerte, one of the Captain General's officials and later governor of the depopulated Tenochtitlán, had brought them in thanksgiving for having survived. The tiny Lady of Succor—made of wood, pearls and brocade—had already conquered the gods of Mexico, before ever María of Guadalupe appeared in order to win over the people who, until very recently, had allowed beating hearts to be ripped out as sacrificial offerings to their gods. It is believed that here, on this hill, Antonio Valeriano, the author of the *Nican Mopohua*, set up the first small chapel to Our Lady of Succor. Even today, from her shining case of gold and crystal, with her childlike wide-open doll's eyes, she can gaze at the city through the open door.

On the Metro, I strained to remember William of Ockham, Father Raynald and his explanation of model images

and copy images. What Europeans seek in vain to *understand*, here in Mexico, truly seems to have been *pondered*
for centuries. A blind man was feeling his way along the
central aisle of the Metro car; singing monotonously and
tapping his cane, he lurched along, straight into an old Amerindian, who welcomed him with open arms and started
guiding him around himself, as if he were light as a feather.
The Metro stopped at the Tlatelolco station, which is surrounded by a neighborhood with blocks of apartment buildings such as one might find on the outskirts of Moscow or
Vladivostok at the height of Soviet modernity. At the center, among the unadorned buildings, there is an Aztec temple excavated in the 1940s. To the side, like a fortress, rises
the most ancient church in Mexico, with its immense black
baptismal font, in which, says a hand-written notice, the
Amerindian Cuauhtlatoatzin, a Chichimecan, was baptized
and given the name Juan Diego. Here he was catechized.
Contiguous with the church, the college of Bishop Zumárraga still stands, the place where Bernardino de Sahagún
wrote his chronicle and Antonio Valeriano studied Latin
and Greek, taught philosophy and wrote the first draft of
the *Nican Mopohua*. Is it possible that on this very spot Juan
Diego told him all that he had experienced? The church
encloses an enormous, austere space, in which to the rear,
left, there hangs nothing but a particularly beautiful painting of the *Morenita*.

At the time of the Spanish conquest, Tlatelolco was a
suburb of Tenochtitlán and the largest commercial center
of Mexico. All the references to places in the *Nican Mopohua* can still be found on the Mexico City map and in the
network of Metro stations, which, back in Germany, I had
been so persistently advised not to take. In the past few
days I had spent at least twenty hours on the Metro. I loved
the Metro, where I encountered daily the flesh-and-blood

faces that just that morning I had viewed carved in stone in the Anthropological Museum: the same noses, eyes, lips; all the features of every Spanish strain: Iberians, Visigoths, Asturians, Galicians, Catalans, Berbers, Arabs, Jews, along with ancient Texans, Californians and Floridians. There is probably no better place than the Metro to observe the broad reality of Mexico.

In the Anthropological Museum I wanted to examine closely the Stone of the Sun, or calendar stone, to which Don Mario had referred. It is displayed as if it were the museum's high altar, and it is perfectly lighted. In 1497, Axayácatl, the sixth Aztec emperor, had it carved from a single block of stone to honor the sun god. When the Spaniards conquered Tenochtitlán, they dislodged the stone and threw it in the dust from the main temple to the main plaza, the precise location of my hotel in the modern Zócalo. But since veneration continued, they finally buried it. It was not rediscovered for many centuries. It is an enormous wheel, at least four yards wide. And as I approached it, I became aware that, from the center of the stone, the eyes of the sun god were examining me!—the precise spot where Don Mario had magnified the eyes of the jasmine flower on Mary's mantle. I heard Don Mario's words again: "We just have to put on our glasses upside down like the Aztecs." But how could I have done so? "The warriors of the eagle are servants of the sun and of the powers that rule the world: day and night, sun and moon, good and bad, north and south", I read on a sign. What did that mean? At the Insurgentes station of the Metro, in the Reforma district, I left the labyrinth of the Metro to meet Don José Luís Guerrero on Durango Street; Don Mario had given me his address. I had already consulted his book *Flor y Canto* (Flower and song), many times, as the epitome of Aztec culture. For this monsignor had also written a book, which he quickly

handed me, when, for the scheduled meeting, we arrived
at one of the buildings that housed the archdiocesan offices:
a cement block with security bolts on each elevator. The
sixth-floor room was furnished with almost no decoration.
It had a view of part of the skyline from waist-high windows that, through Mexico City's milky mist of smog,
allowed an unobstructed view of neighboring offices.

Don José Luís was an imposing man in a slightly worn
suit, with a large head and full and updrawn lips. He would
soon be assigned to the basilica, but at present he was serv-
ing at a small chapel in the city's ocean of houses. He
breathed with difficulty because of congestion, and he spoke
English fluently. Frequently our conversation was interrupted by the telephone, which he had to answer in an
adjoining room. In spite of having a full calendar, this very
busy churchman had found time for me. For this reason I
asked him not to talk about his book, but only about what,
for him, after so many years of concentrated work on the
Virgin, seemed the most important thing about the apparitions. He did not need to be begged. "What people discover in her eyes and in the colors does not interest me at
all. The stars in her mantle or the flowers on her robe—
who cares? Also the unmanufactured colors—all these enig-
mas can remain enigmatic, as far as I'm concerned. All that
leaves me cold", Don José Luís Guerrero asserted yet again
and moved toward the window. "All that is just trivia", he
affirmed, extending his arms. "But that here, five hundred
years ago, out of nowhere another world, a new world,
found its way here, into Mexico—that overwhelms me. For
me, the theology of this apparition is much more important for our day than all the reflections in her eyes! Why?
Just take a good look at the world! The Balkans or Africa
or the Near East! Think about Israel and Palestine! What is
going on there is not just murder, it is suicide. They are all

going to perish if they do not grasp what has happened here."

I told him briefly about my visit to Bosnia. "You see? That is exactly what I think. Compassion and mercy were just as alien to the Aztecs as to the ancient Greeks. They simply were not acquainted with it. But the Spaniards were even worse than the Serbs, and not in Mexico alone. Between 1492 and 1530 they had completely annihilated the Amerindians in the Caribbean Islands. In that same era, because of doctrinal disputes, they devastated Germany. Later, under Philip II, they cruelly oppressed the Low Countries. The Duke of Alba's massacres have never been forgotten. After the victory over the Moors, the Spaniards became the terror of Europe. In May 1527, in papal Rome, Charles V's mercenary lancers carried out a massacre unlike anything the Eternal City had ever seen. The Sack of Rome horrified the West. There an out-of-control Spanish and German military, each and every one a Christian, poured out their fury. It is scarcely possible to imagine worse missionaries. In the wars against the Moors, the same Spaniards became half-Muslim. Needless to say, there were many upright Muslims among them and also Jews. They called themselves Christians, but in reality they were Muslims." He breathed with difficulty. "In any event, the Spaniards were incapable of evangelizing the Aztecs. They had proven this already on the Caribbean Islands. Another thing: How would they go about evangelizing? Forcing love is rape. Selling or misusing love is prostitution. In a word, the situation was hopeless."

Another call came through in the next room. He disappeared for a while, but when he returned he picked up the conversation in mid-sentence: "Here, then, a Jewish girl suddenly appears in an Eastern costume, with an Arab name and mestizo features, whose father was Spanish and whose mother was Amerindian, and she becomes the soul of Mexico.

Then, immediately everything changes. There has never been a greater message of peace. The answer rises up: "Only united in solidarity can we survive under the same sun."

He did not quite convince me that the Virgin Mary looked mestiza, but I hesitated to interrupt his Marian fervor. He fixed me with his huge eyes and spread his fingers: "You absolutely need to understand something else: among the Amerindians, the mothers were supremely important, as the fathers generally died young, in war or on the altar of sacrifice. Also, among the Spaniards, there were great women missionaries, though shut away in convents. If Jesus had come to Mexico in person, the Amerindians would not have been particularly impressed—either by his miracles or his wounds or even his blood. They had already seen too much blood and too many wounds. But the encounter with the Mother of Jesus was something completely different. From the first moment, her apparition drew them to her. They were completely taken by her. For this reason, as far back as 1648, Miguel Sánchez, B.A., wrote boldly: 'Just as Israel was chosen by God to give rise to Jesus Christ, so God has chosen Mexico to reveal the Virgin of Guadalupe.'"

Don José Luís was already around sixty, a professor of canon law. But his real passion was the explanation of the fifth gospel, the Amerindian gospel of Guadalupe. "Truly, the Amerindians were profoundly religious. They were worth being saved. But, as in no other nation, their redemption came through the Virgin Mary. More than anyone, she showed the Aztecs the way to the true God, a way that the Spaniards had brutally slammed shut.

"Imagine. Immediately after her apparition, both military cultures, people who before were seeking to annihilate each other, literally began to embrace each other like lovers before this picture! Look around—in the plazas, in the streets, everywhere! There are no more Spaniards or Amerindians. From that moment there was a radical new beginning: the Mexicans have been shaped into a new people. Here they have totally blended into an infinite variety of shades. Never, before or after, anywhere, has anything similar occurred. Contemporary sources report that the Franciscans were busy all day long, baptizing innumerable people. Most of the time, they baptized people two by two, from sunrise to sunset, without pause. This was one thing. The other is even more incredible. In Europe, during this same period, the Spaniards were lopping off heads in defense of the faith—as can still be noted in the Moorish heads displayed on the shield of Aragon. Here they suddenly intermingled with the most savage Amerindians. This really was a miracle. Immediately after the Guadalupe event, the two peoples, who before were so alien to each other, fused like bride and groom. Compared to the alienation that had been here, the Israelis and Palestinians are like brothers and sisters, kissing cousins. This kind of fusion of peoples has happened nowhere else, not even between neighboring peoples like Poles and Russians. Just a short time before, the idea of "pure blood" had arisen in Spain, so as to be able also to expel converted Jews, not only from high office, but from the very land itself. As late as 1492, the year that Columbus discovered America, the Spaniards had expelled from the country all Jews and all Moors, so as to create one of the world's first pure-race nation-states. 'Ethnic cleansing' was not an invention of the Serbs."

He took a drink of water and went on: "From then on, European medical books treated mestizos as an isolated genetic curiosity. But here, there are no isolated cases; rather, the Mexicans had become a mestizo people. Look around! Never have there been seen greater contrasts and oppositions: religions, races, skin colors, cultures. Here Mexicans, Lebanese, Jews, Germans, Spaniards, Amerindians have been changed to Guadalupans, regardless of origin. In its own way the narrative of the *Nican Mopohua* is also a mestizo creation! It is neither Spanish nor Aztec, but an integral work of art, a mixture of both cultures, a dialogue between two cultures, unique unto itself. Nor should anyone dare say that the christianization of Mexico was not solid and authentic, a tenuous façade hiding a pagan core. People who assert this have no idea of what either ancient paganism or the Christianity of the day was like in Mexico. Evangelization went very deep, with colossal speed, for both Aztec and Spaniard. Eight conquistadors of Hernan Cortés' inner circle became churchmen, Franciscan, Dominican or hermit. No one campaigned as passionately and boldly for the rights and defense of the Aztecs as did the mendicant orders. Among these was Las Casas, who became the preacher to and advocate of the Aztecs, taking his case about the precarious and devastating situation as far as the court of Charles V in Spain. Nor has anyone gone so deeply into Aztec culture.

And the same thing happened in reverse. Soon the Aztecs were singing Gregorian chant and writing Masses and hymns. They learned musical notation as easily as the catechism and the Bible, through which the history of Israel and far-distant Palestine reached them. These very Aztecs soon began building innumerable churches, convents and schools throughout the land—one church more beautiful than the next, as we see in those that have been preserved to our day. Shortly after the apparitions of the Virgin Mary, the Imperial Academy of Tlatelolco, the Indian College of Santiago, was producing indigenous intellectuals of the caliber of Europeans. The polished Latin of these Aztecs was admired even in Spain, not to mention their musical and impeccable Spanish. It is believed that Antonio Valeriano was the nephew of the emperor Montezuma. A letter written by Montezuma's great-grandson in 1587 has been preserved. Addressed to his imperial relatives, by way of conclusion, he hopes for these "dear ladies" that "the Holy Spirit might take up his dwelling in their hearts."

Here Don José Luís paused a moment and smiled: "Surely, the Holy Spirit has done this. The Holy Spirit has come to have, in Mexico, his true joy—once the Virgin Mary opened the doors of Aztec hearts."

After the unheard-of clash of civilizations, Mexico also experienced an even more unheard-of marriage and reconciliation of cultures. As he said, Mexico became the model for Central and South America, that is, for a good half of the members of today's Church. "And I swear: Here there are many problems and tremendous tensions facing poor and rich, Church and State; but one problem we do not have is racism like that in other countries. Differences in skin color play a less important role than in other places. The idea of this people is totally opposed to the concept of an ethnically pure nation. It is much more ancient, much more humane, and much more charged with a future. Mexicans are truly a model people, a people of the Mother of God, even though you look at me so skeptically. Mexico is a Marian nation. This is the greatest miracle of the apparitions. It was this image, not the Spaniards, that, after 1531, led the Amerindians to Western culture. At the most disheartening and desperate moment of their history, the Aztecs were transformed into a people of the Virgin Mary, into a new people! And into a model for others, Brazil for example, where—through Mary's intervention—the process of fusion was repeated, even between black and whites. Nonetheless, I have not the slightest doubt that the most important part of the story is still ahead. In a few years, in the United States, Hispanics will be predominant! Only then will the universal significance of the story of Guadalupe come clear." His breathing again became labored.

I asked him how he personally invoked the Virgin Mary. He did not pause for thought: "Mother! or Dearest Virgin! But before all, Mother. She is our Mother. Thus, sometimes, also *Madrecita*, Mama. Sometimes *Morenita*. Most pilgrims go to Lourdes because of some ailment or pain, to Fatima, for reasons of faith. But here, everyone comes to see the Mother! Have you ever seen the tears flowing before this image? That is what I am trying to say."

As a good-bye, he escorted me to the elevator and yet again exhorted me earnestly: "If Europe does not come to understand what happened here soon, we will have to endure yet another catastrophe. If Israelis and Palestinians do not understand what has happened here, we will have to suffer their mutual suicide, drawing the whole world into the abyss with them."

What is the significance of this precisely at a time when the peace process is moving toward its final and decisive phase, its peaceful culmination? "I tell you, the Israelis and Palestinians cannot know how to extricate themselves from this mutual suicide unless they understand that here, for five hundred years, a totally new way was opened, in which whole peoples have room to live in peace, side by side, together", he added. But I still did not understand his point.

By now we were standing in the corridor by the elevator, where he stayed with me. He smiled: "Just wait. Strange things happen once a person begins to approach the *Madrecita*." The elevator door opened, and I shook his hand and entered. Before the automatic door closed he blessed me and my work. He moved his hand top to bottom, left to right. This gesture of blessing with the cross was my last glimpse of him.

CHAPTER EIGHTEEN

DAY OF WRATH AT MARY'S BIRTHPLACE

With the "letter from heaven" from Berlin to Munich, then to Jerusalem; the image of the Morenita *on Mount Zion, a Marian door in the wall of the city and a day of wrath in the place of her birth.*

I returned to Germany. But I soon set out again for Italy, to do more research for this book. While I was on the way, my eldest daughter, Maria, called to tell me that someone with an unintelligible name had phoned. Perhaps I could phone Berlin? Berlin? Whom did I know in Berlin? After my book on the Heavenly City was published, I had sent an advance copy to a long-time colleague, a young journalist, who, in the meantime, had become editor-in-chief of the newspaper WELT. Perhaps Mathias Döpfner wanted an interview and a review of the book for the paper? Yes, Maria said, the caller was someone from the WELT.

I called the paper. A kind secretary wanted to know if by any chance I would be coming to Berlin sometime and if it would be possible to meet with Dr. Döpfner. I checked my calendar. I still had some European trips to make because of the *Morenita*. I proposed Friday, August 13. That would be perfect, Mrs. Neubert answered, on the other end of the line; she would reserve a table at the Borchardt.

I had last seen Mathias Döpfner ten years before in Munich, shortly after the fall of the Berlin wall. But I recognized him through the enormous window of the restaurant as he crossed the street. One would search long and in vain to find a better colleague in Germany. At our last meeting he was a head taller than I; now he seemed to have grown even more. Of course he knew about the discontinuation of the magazine of the *Frankfurter Allgemeine Zeitung*, in which, many years ago, we had articles appearing in some of the same issues, and he wanted to know what I was doing now. I ordered a steak and thought about the *Morenita*. Had I not already put aside my work at the paper forever? "Do you perhaps want to write a book?" I evaded answering. Maybe I should tell him about my new book, which in some curious way seemed to be writing itself (like the log book of a voyage whose destination was a new puzzle to me every day)? But there was still a great deal to talk about. How had he been since last we met? It was clear that he had become every inch an editor-in-chief, assured and purposeful. "What could you be tempted to do for us?" he asked unexpectedly.

I hesitated. Eight years earlier I had been fired up to go as a correspondent to Jerusalem. I was about the same age as the State of Israel. As I recall, I had taken part in the rebirth of the Jewish nation and the Zionist conquest of the land with admiration and sympathy. Was I thinking out loud? "Yes, that is what we will do: Jerusalem!" So said Mathias Döpfner and shook on it. We ordered two glasses of red wine and clinked a toast: For Jerusalem. And for peace.

If possible, I was to report for work as Jerusalem correspondent by January 1, 2000. My return flight to Munich departed at 5:40 P.M. from Tegel airport in Berlin. I asked the cabdriver to pause briefly once more at the zoo station. I wanted to buy a pure Cohiba to celebrate the day's events later, breaking my seven-year stretch of no smoking. Once past the security checkpoint, sitting on a plastic chair in the waiting room, I held the Havana under my nose to sniff it a little. Through the windows of the terminal I saw my plane, of the German BA line, which at that moment was being refueled. It was called "Letter from Heaven".

The following weeks and months of good-byes flew by in a flash. In Mexico I had bought myself a copy of the portrait of the Virgin of Guadalupe on silk. In Munich I framed it and hung it on the wall among our old pictures. Now my first concern was to put the notes I had taken about the *Morenita* into moving boxes.

On November 21 we flew to Tel Aviv to look for a house in the Promised Land. A pilgrim sitting next to me on the plane told me that that very day marked the celebration of "the feast of Our Lady of Jerusalem". In our search for a house in the city, we made inquiries, not just to friends and real estate agents, but also to the German Benedictines of the Abbey of Holy Mary of Zion. It was wishful thinking that, of course, came to nothing.

But there in the crypt of the Abbey's church on the very first day of residence in the Holy Land, we came across a life-size mosaic of the *Morenita*, the Virgin of Guadalupe, a gift of the "people of Mexico" to this sacred place where, from antiquity, the death of Mary had been venerated. The next day, not far from there, we found suitable accommodations in an ancient Palestinian house facing the Damascus Gate, at the very navel of the world.

It was wonderful to be in Jerusalem, even in January-February. Pale blue, flowering rosemary covered the foothills of Mount Zion. Here, too, roses bloomed in winter. Our first trips in search of information took us through valleys of flowering almond to Nablus, then to Jenin and Nazareth, then down to the Lake of Gennesaret, and then back through Bethlehem, home to Jerusalem. A hummingbird was flitting from flower to flower outside our window. After every rainstorm, the pomegranate bush extended its red leaves and buds against the limpid blue of the sky. Once spring arrived, sometimes even before daybreak, I could not lie in bed. The muezzin's call echoed throughout the city; the song-birds offered a full-throated concert under our window. Then I would go out to the street, barefoot, to watch the dawn light up the city skyline. Brilliant sunrise, red to gold.

For me, Jerusalem is a unique vision. Even King Solomon had sung in the Song of Songs about this light and the rosy glow: "Who is this that looks forth like the dawn, fair as the moon, bright as the sun ... ?" (Song 6:10). "Behold you are beautiful, my love, behold, you are beautiful! Your eyes are doves behind your veil. Your hair is like a flock of goats, moving down the slopes of Gilead" (Song 4:1). This place is unlike any other on earth.

The city's most ancient name, "Salem", derives from the ancient Near Eastern goddess of the dawn. And where else is the dawn more beautiful and more translucent than here, as it climbs from the Judean desert and breaks over the Mount of Olives? It is the same light that inspired the prophets. Everything seems to have been right here from time immemorial: the rays of the sun, the stones, the wind, the human beings; also the injustice and the longing to overcome it. And in the year 2000 it seemed that this longing was finally going to come to fruition. The final stage in the Olso negotiations forecast that this year, finally, Jerusalem would become the capital of all the Holy Land, an event so promising to the rest of the world. Shalom, Salaam! For my first report, I was to accompany the Pope on his Holy Land trip. On him converged the great hope of the people living there, surrounding him like a halo. It seemed as if a new dawn had broken.

But what I saw more clearly, day by day, from Bethlehem to Nazareth, from the coast to the desert, was something completely different: This land is not only a topographical gem in the eastern Mediterranean; it is also a unique artistic icon, as Father Raynald had explained in Munich. Heaven is reflected in this land. Here, suddenly, a shower of childhood images flashed through my mind, moving from memory into actuality. Jerusalem was an overpowering lesson on their meaning. All the world's spires point here, like the needles of a compass. Here was incarnated the life-sized reality represented by thousands and thousands of paintings, frescoes and mosaics in innumerable churches all over the world: Golgotha, the Temple courtyard, the Mount of Olives. What were monumental images in the Gothic, Renaissance and baroque eras, however, was here only stone: here, this happened; there, that. Everything can be touched. Did I really feel more at home here than perhaps anywhere else in my life, in any other place? What other city in the world was more real? The streets, the hills, the stones, even the sky? Everything was shouting ceaselessly the one word, *here, here, here*! Finally, what are images? "I don't know", a Russian hermit on the Mount of Olives told me. "I only know what icons are: they are windows open to eternity. That is why the Church struggled so passionately during the iconoclastic controversy in support of them. For this reason, in our chaotic age, icons have to do battle for the Christian world."

"But doesn't the first of the Ten Commandments from Sinai forbid making images of God? Why do Christians not comply as do Jews or even Muslims?" I pressed him.

"Yes, you are right, the first commandment forbids it. This is the same argument used now and again by those who attack images. It goes as far back as the iconoclastic controversy. But naturally, it is not absolutely true. Because the first commandment says : 'You shall not make for yourself a graven image, or any likeness of anything that is in heaven above, or that is in the earth beneath, or that is in the water under the earth' (Ex 20:4). The commandment says '*You*'! It is directed to men and women. But it does not say

'*I*'. God does not command himself not to make an image of himself. So anyone who takes Christianity at all seriously should not fall into such a misunderstanding of the first commandment. For Christians believe that God himself has created an image of himself in Christ. This is what has left his fingerprint on the world. If one does not believe this, one has ceased to be Christian. No one has to believe it; no one is forced to be Christian. But for the one who believes this, the world is completely transformed, beginning with the first commandment. For if God has made an archetypal image of himself, human beings are naturally permitted, in fact required, to recall the archetypal image by making copies of it. But we do not adore those images. By means of them, through them, as through a window, we are venerating the Creator again and again. All our images are the fruit of this opening into heaven."

We were seated on a stone bench in front of the church of Mary Magdalen. We were looking over the Kedron Valley, to the walls of the old city of Jerusalem; above them, the dome of golden stone. A marvelous view. I remembered some advice an old Jesuit had given me in Rome, years before: "If you want to understand something, you need to paint it, or at least draw it. Everything written is soon forgotten. Images are never forgotten."

Jerusalem is the resolution of images. This is true. Therefore, it was no miracle that, even in my new responsibilities as a foreign correspondent, I would soon discover the images and traces of Mary throughout the Promised Land, even though, unexpectedly, I had to postpone the final editing of my report on the *Morenita* indefinitely. For, no matter how disputed the boundaries of ancient Palestine and modern Israel are, with their inhabitants long at enmity, beyond all these borders, the hills and valleys unarguably constitute the authentic land of Mary.

In the Old City, in the House of Mark the Evangelist, venerated from ancient times and now the episcopal see of the Aramaic-speaking Christians, I discovered a jet-black image of the Madonna and Child, painted on deerskin "by Saint Luke". Only photographs taken with a flashbulb allow us to see that the picture is a truly marvelous and surely very ancient portrait of Mary. My guess that it could be a Byzantine painting was roundly rejected by the archpriest of the church: Saint Luke in person painted it. Many miracles had taken place before this image; only a month before someone had left his crutches behind.

In the carving on the main altar, dating from the seventeenth century, I discovered a medallion of the *Morenita*, the Virgin María of Mexico, surrounded by rays of the sun, wearing a mantle covered with stars. Guadalupe? Here no one had as much as heard of the title. But why not? If there is one place in the world where everything speaks of Mary's life and death, that place is Jerusalem, even, perhaps, this very house. In any case, somewhere in this neighborhood, the first Christian community in the history of the world had gathered.

Below the Holocaust Memorial, Yad Vashem, on the slope, we soon came to the town of Ain Karim, which Christians have venerated for generations as the place "in the hill country of Judea" where the pregnant Mary greeted her pregnant cousin Elizabeth. In the apse of the church we found a painting of Mary coming over the hills to meet us as the Mother of the *Magnificat*.

In the fall, my colleague Alan Posener called me from Berlin, asking me if I could write something about the feast of the Birth of Mary, September 8. The year before, Posener, a Shakespeare scholar, had written a brief, colorful biography of Mary as the woman "who had most influenced world history". This was the first time I became aware that, in

England, the witch hunts had begun at the precise time when the veneration of Mary broke down in the West. He now said: "As long as you are living in Jerusalem, wouldn't you like to research her birth a little, in honor of this feast? She comes from there, after all."

Was Mary, Miryam, the Galilean girl, not supposed to be from Nazareth in Galilee? The birth of Mary? I needed to ask Bargil Pixner, an elderly Benedictine monk living on Mount Zion, the best-informed expert on local traditions in Jerusalem. So that same afternoon, at the entrance of the abbey, the monk told me deliberately: "There are historical sources from the second century that speak in detail about Mary's birth in Jerusalem, especially in what is called the Protogospel of James, which is clearly highly embellished with legends. Nothing similar has been found in Nazareth. It is also interesting that the Church's liturgical calendar, which, except in the case of Christ, only marks the saints' death as their feast, makes two exceptions: the birth of John the Baptist, Jesus' desert-dwelling precursor, June 24, and the birth of Mary, September 8." The liturgical calendar lists it as "The Birth of Our Most Holy Lady, Mother of God and Ever-Virgin Mary". For a long time it had been acknowledged as one of the twelve principal feasts of the liturgical year. By the sixth century, in Constantinople, it was celebrated on September 8 as "the beginning of salvation history". Later on, calculations were made so that the date of the feast of the Immaculate Conception, December 8, would be related to the date of her birth. But most important, this is the date, in 543, on which, in Jerusalem, the "new Marian church" was consecrated alongside the destroyed Temple—"there where she was born", as the ancient sources say. "Go look at it", he advised; "the house is in the Old City, by Saint Stephen's Gate, which is why, from time immemorial, the Muslims call it Bab Maryam, 'the Gate of the Lady Mary'."

1. Full view of the miraculous image of our Lady of Guadalupe, imprinted on old agave cloth, which had been the mantle of Juan Diego. The image is venerated on the outskirts of Mexico City.

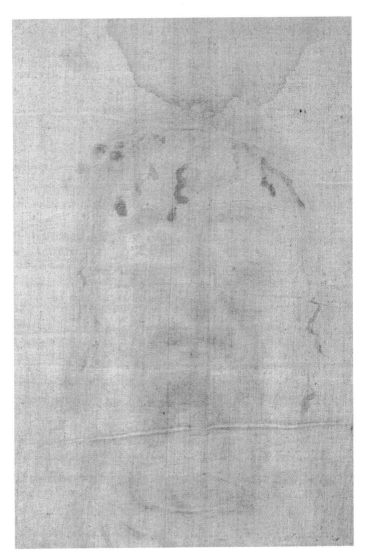

2. Image of the face on the Shroud of Turin. This is the most ancient image "not painted by human hand", *acheiropoietos* in Greek, considered the "mother of all icons".

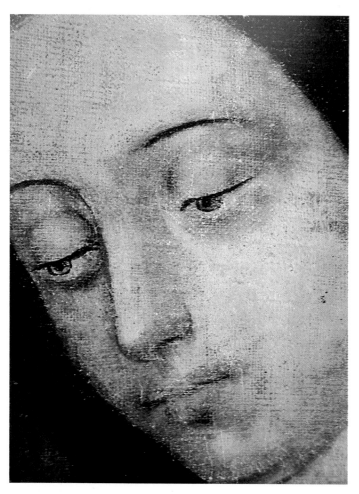

3. Detail of the apocalyptic Madonna of Guadalupe, which, since its apparition in Mexico in the sixteenth century, is also venerated as *acheiropoietos*, that is, as "not painted by human hand".

4. Portrait of Mary preserved in the "house of Mark" (cf. Acts 12:12), belonging to the Aramaean Christian community in the Old City of Jerusalem, attributed to the evangelist Luke. Of undetermined antiquity.

5.   A portrait found in the Egyptian oasis of El Faiyûm, as an example of Hellenistic portraiture in the first century, A.D. Archeological Museum of Florence.

6. Entrance to the Crusader church of Saint Anne in Jerusalem, venerated from earliest times as the place of Mary's birth. In 543, the feast of the Birth of Mary was introduced here.

7. Entrance to the "tomb of Mary" in the Garden of Gethsemane. This site corresponds to Judeo-Christian reports about the most ancient account of the end of Mary's earthly life (*Transitus Mariae*) preserved in the Vatican.

8. Site of the birth of Jesus in Bethlehem. HIC DE VIRGINE MARIA JESUS CHRISTUS NATUS EST is written above the star: "Here Jesus Christ was born of the Virgin Mary."

9. Support for the cross on the crest of Golgotha, where Jesus at about age thirty-three, died before his Mother's eyes. In 1988, the stone ring was discovered by the archaeologist Theo Mitropoulos.

10. Place of the Last Supper and the initial feast of Pentecost, in Jerusalem, built upon dressed stones from the destroyed Temple in Jerusalem. At its base can be seen the bell tower of the Abbey of Hagia Maria on Mount Zion. Here Mary lived and, according to some traditions, ended her earthly life.

11. Flight of steps leading from "Mary's tomb". This construct, from the period of the Crusades, is in the Garden of Gethsemane in a cemetery dating from Judeo-Christian times.

12.   The Assumption of Mary by Giulio Pippi (1499–1546), called Giulio Romano, and by Gianfrancesco Penni (1488–1528). Gallery of the Vatican Museums.

13.   The empty final resting place of Mary in Jerusalem, shaped like a trough. Not until 1999 was it discovered that it is carved out of bedrock, as reported in the narrative *Transitus Mariae*.

14. Don Mario Rojas Sánchez of Mexico, the most distinguished translator of the *Nican Mopohua* from Nahuatl to Spanish. He wears an agave tilma. The image of the Virgin is preserved on similar fabric.

15. The Benedictine monk Bargil Pixner (1921–2002) on the shore of the Lake of Gennesaret, where he excavated Bethsaida, hometown of the apostles Peter, James, John and Andrew.

16. Miraculous image of Our Lady of Guadalupe in Spain, to which the apparition in Mexico owes its name, thanks to a linguistic confusion with the Amerindian *Coatlaxopeuh*.

17.   The naval battle of Lepanto, October 7, 1571. Ignatius Danti (1536–1586) painted this picture of the Christian defense against the expansion and the military power of the Ottoman Muslims.

18.   Crystal sarcophagus of Pius V in the right front chapel in the Basilica of Saint Mary Major in Rome. This pope raised the joint European resistance to the Ottoman Turkish superpower.

19. First copy of the miraculous image of Guadalupe to reach Europe. Admiral Andrea Doria carried it with him to Lepanto as the standard of the Christian fleet. Today it hangs in Aveto, near Genoa.

20. The "Dormition" of the Mother of God in the crypt of Hagia Maria Abbey on Mount Zion; the abbey of the German Benedictines in Jerusalem has a mosaic of María of Guadalupe in original scale.

21. Modern mosaic in the Guadalupe chapel in the crypt of the Basilica of Saint Peter in Rome. It is directly under the center of the cupola, adjoining the tomb of Saint Peter, on the left-hand side.

22. "Stone from the house of Mary" in the foundation of the bell tower of Hagia Maria Abbey on Mount Zion, in Jerusalem. Natives of Jerusalem particularly called the architect's attention to this during the construction of the basilica.

23. The mysterious small "angel" under the Madonna's feet in the miraculous image of Our Lady of Guadalupe in Mexico.

The vignette at the end of page 237 is from Miguel Cabrera's "An American Marvel and Collection of Rare Marvels". See Select Bibliography.

It is only a fifteen-minute walk from Mount Zion to Mary's Gate. I set right off. At the entrance, a Greek inscription indicates that this is where Mary was born. The entrance takes one to a lower basement and from there to a ramp going lower; a solitary custodian first showed me the house of Joachim and Anne, Mary's parents, and below this, the place of Mary's birth: two wonderfully cool caves. The custodian flipped the light switch next to a little basket of shekels, coins and dollars. In front of a small font, he anointed our foreheads with oil, placed a candle in our hands and let us admire the spaciousness of this ancient crypt. It was one of those crypts excavated from rock, like those which even today are used here and about the Mediterranean as summer housing.

"Alas, you were with the Greek Orthodox", Bargil Pixner said the next day, laughing. "This house is second-rate. The original site is under the Church of Saint Anne, the next building down. There is where Mary's mother lived, next to the Sheep Pool, which some think is the site of the most ancient church dedicated to Mary in Jerusalem. But the church was christened Saint Anne only after the Persians destroyed the first church dedicated to Mary and it was rebuilt. Later the Crusaders, who always had the surest intuition for authentic traditions, built today's church over the place.

I went back again. At the neighboring house there was an alley leading to a portal with a small, narrow door. Behind it was a garden within which stood a fortress-like church, belonging to the White Fathers of France. Today, the house of Mary's birth stands in the middle of Jerusalem, in the free zone inside the walls of the Old City, immediately next to the Temple Mount, whose controversial sovereignty still presents the world with an insoluble challenge. In the nineteenth century, in gratitude for its friendly help during the Crimean War, the Sublime Porte ceded this scrap of land to the French. The Church of Saint Anne resembles the most beautiful Romanesque churches in Europe. The acoustics are magnificent, both in the main body and in the crypt, in which the bare rock has again emerged on one of the walls. Therefore, this grotto must have been the birthplace of the *Morenita*. Miryam was a seven-month baby, the ancient texts say; they also say that her parents quickly took her to the Temple, which was nearby. It is not known with any certainty if Mary was born thirteen or sixteen years before her Son, but it is certain that she was born while Herod was still reconstructing the Temple across the street. This would include all that is still visible: the Wailing Wall, Huldah Gate, along with many large stones in the foundation. At the time of Mary's birth, right in front of her parents' home was the site of the greatest construction project in the Near East. The hammering and chiseling at their front door was almost constant. As a child, Mary had the Temple Mount always before her eyes. However, when the feast of her birth was introduced into the calendar, the Temple had lain in ruins for over four hundred years, just as the Romans had left it after they destroyed it in A.D. 70. The most ancient reports by pilgrims say that the Jews, during their new exile, returned every year to weep over the rubble that the Christians did not want to touch. So then, with this feast and the first church dedicated to Mary next to this ruined site, Christians declared that God no longer lived in the Temple. The first witnesses to this were the rubble and the devastation itself. In this little Jewish girl, God had found his definitive home, they affirmed back then. God no longer dwelled, as before, in the stone tablets of the Ten Commandments or in the Holy of Holies of the old Temple. God dwelled in his Word made flesh, his human Word. From that time Christians venerated the daughter of Joachim and Anne as their new Temple Mount.

Three weeks after my article about Mary's birth had been published in the WELT, the street in front of the Church of the Nativity was reduced to rubble. The Temple Mount, in an elemental explosion of violence, had been transformed into a crater vomiting rocks. Like a flock of gulls before a storm, pebbles and fragments of rock were raining down from the northern wall of the Temple square. Fragments were ricocheting through the air; one of them grazed my temple. Blood was flowing down my cheek. Five thousand young men opposite Mary's birthplace stood and jumped on the wall surrounding the Temple complex and the Al-Aqsa Mosque—just as, eleven years earlier, the Germans had scaled the Berlin wall. But here, behind rolls of barbed wire, with raised fists, they started a full-bodied roar: "Allahu akbar! Allahu akbar! God is great! God is greater! Long live the Mosque of Al-Aqsa!" From the cover over Mary's Gate, Israeli soldiers lunged forward, shooting into the rubble. The reverberation of these shots was muted in the narrow alley. The police station in the arch of Mary's Gate was taken by storm. The interior was devastated, the surroundings were full of the acrid bite of tear gas. An official was bellowing orders through a megaphone. Deafening screams. Ambulances rushed to the Temple square. The Al-Aqsa intifada had begun, the battle for control of the ancient Jewish Temple Mount, on which, for the last fourteen hundred years, the most illustrious Islamic shrine had been built upon the ruins of the ancient Jewish Temple. I seemed to be witnessing the beginning of the third world war.

Only a few days before, on the eve of the Jewish New Year 5761 [2001], I had been present there when the retired Israeli General Sharon brought in over a thousand Israeli policemen to proclaim a "message of peace" and open a way into "the holiest Jewish site" and make sure that "there would be freedom to pray and freedom of access to everyone, especially to Jews." Of course, from then on access was forbidden not only to Jews in general but also to all Muslims living outside the city. So now, after Friday prayer, stones were being hurled not only at the Wailing Wall but also at all four walls surrounding the "Illustrious Quarter". By nightfall, all the streets around the Holy Mount were covered in pebbles and fragments of rock. The whole world knows that in Jerusalem the most ancient mountain of human destiny is an eschatological volcano. On this day, a "Day of Wrath", it had again erupted and was smoking and belching.

CHAPTER NINETEEN

CLOUDS OF VIOLENCE
OVER BETHLEHEM

"Mary of the Unburnable Bush", fire and smoke over Mary's land: a
burst of fire from the Paradise Hotel; first breath in a cave in Bethlehem;
Jerusalem's fright and an image of the Morenita *in an empty tomb.*

Before dawn, at five o'clock, the call of the muezzin arose
like a lamentation in the night sky, spiraling up through the
Old City. Was he singing more piercingly than usual? Was
that some other voice? Out of the darkness of the sky, he
was answered by the whirling of a helicopter. The city became
electric. At the Damascus Gate a couple of youths were warm-
ing their hands at a fire made from produce boxes. And they
were looking very attentively up Sultan Süleyman Street toward
the New Gate. Two hundred yards farther up, the street was
hermetically sealed. There, before the juncture with Para-
chutists Street, the silhouettes of twelve stationary horsemen
squeezed together under a handful of palm trees. "This is
dangerous", said the man in the tobacco store, and he pulled
down the metal shutter he had just raised. A little child in
pajamas kept jumping in and out among the parked cars. In
front of a mocha café, old men in burnooses sipped their
coffee as if it were a medication. Behind a truck, nine men
huddled in a circle and devoured their breakfast, which they
had spread on a newspaper—sardines, humus, bread, water,
onions—taking turns dipping their hands into the bowl.

Somewhere nearby, Stephen, the first Christian martyr,
had been stoned. Could Saul of Tarsus have stood just ahead,

there by the palms, now a taxi stand, guarding the cloaks of the sweating stone-throwers? Or, even better, did this occur on the other side of the city, near Mary's Gate? And Mary? Along what streets in this labyrinth did she hurry? A ribbon of red glowed above the city wall and over the Mount of Olives; in a few minutes it became larger and more intense, a brilliant and transparent brightness.

"Tomorrow, don't even think of coming to the Old City! Stay home and bar the door!" all our acquaintances were saying in undertones. All the entrances to the West Bank were blocked. Even before dawn, Jerusalem looked like a fortress under siege. Police and army units were stationed before all seven gates of the city. The young men of the Holy Land encountered there were filled with silent hatred, some with bulletproof vests, helmets and automatic guns, others in short-sleeved shirts and sandals. "No good can come of this", said a businessman behind the Jaffa Gate. "Of the eighty people killed last week, 80 percent were under sixteen years old. With that, eighty families have been filled with hatred that will last for yet another generation."— "The battle will end only when they run out of stones", said the baker across the way. "How can this go on, if our children are dying every day? Armored tanks and helicopters can't shoot at people who throw stones." Not only had a volcano exploded, so had injustice, hatred and the desperation of lost generations.

On November 9, 2000, in the east, on the street to Bethlehem, on the lower left, I watched a small cloud rising from the town of Beit Sahur into the clean blue sky. This was the general area of the countryside where the shepherds had pitched camp—those shepherds who were the first to visit Mary after the birth of her Son (having seen a glow over Bethlehem and heard above the first Gloria sung). Afterward I heard a deafening explosion. A helicopter was circling overhead. In an abandoned chapel in the shepherds' field, the Franciscans had framed and hung a picture of the apocalyptic Madonna of Guadalupe in Mexico, the *Morenita*. I gave a shout, but no one answered, no one who could tell me what the explosion meant. The building seemed abandoned.

Around the next curve boys of Bethlehem were trying out the new game of throwing stones. On the return trip we met a teacher from Beit Sahur, whom the guards of the first blocked street no longer allowed to enter Jerusalem to visit his parents. He told us that the explosion had blown a car to bits. This happened right under his window; afterward, he could not calm the children down. Three helicopters had joined the attack. The car, a well-known vehicle in the city, belonged to Tansim combatants; the Israelis had recognized it and had destroyed it from the air, point blank, with an ultra-precise rocket. Besides killing the driver, they had wounded six others. The rocket had torn off the head of Hussein Abayad. "This cries for vengeance", the teacher said. "It is going to end badly!" It was a return to a strategy that the next day's papers were openly calling "political assassination". Later on it was called other things: "pinprick politics", "politics of planned extinction", "extrajudicial executions", and so on. But, names aside, every pinprick further inflamed the masses.

Less than a week later, the journalists were summoned to an urgent press conference, at eleven P.M., in the ISROTEL on Jaffa Street. After four Israelis had been shot by Palestinians, Major General Eitan announced the immediate sealing off of all the cities of region A in the West Bank. From this moment, only trucks carrying food and medicine could cross the Israeli control points around Ramallah, Hebron, Bethlehem, Nabulus or Dshenin. On that very day, three Palestinians had lost their lives to Israeli fire, two adolescents and a policeman. Again there were dozens of wounded. Violence was beginning to spiral more and more rapidly. The night before, the new Jericho Intercontinental Hotel had been attacked by Israeli tanks and troops. Only hours later, surprise attacks on Israeli civilian vehicles indicated that battle tactics had changed: the Palestinians were trying to force Israelis out of the occupied zones. A bold but dead-end enterprise. "The authorities of the Palestinian Self-Rule are completely responsible for these attacks", Major General Eitan had announced. Since these enemies attacked civilians, they certainly had to be labeled terrorists. "Therefore, we will take appropriate measures against them."

Through all this I began to recall Don José Luís Guerrero, in Mexico City, whose analysis I had not been able to follow at the time. Suddenly I heard his words resonating in my mind: "What the Palestinians are doing is suicide. What Israel is doing is suicide." Very soon I myself was confronted with the first suicide attempts and experienced, personally, how Israel intended to eliminate violence with a suicidal political strategy: night and day, cranes never ceased to swivel and shoot over the settlements in the occupied zones.

As the Palestinian youth were being blown to pieces on the commercial streets of Tel Aviv and Netanya, extravagantly huge, armed earth-movers brought down house after house in Bethlehem, Gaza and Hebron. That these were not "occupied" territories only means that they were "disputed" territories. In the middle of the Palestinian uprising, day by day, I saw rising on the heights of the hills of Palestine one new Jewish settlement after another: at first a couple of sheds fenced in with barbed wire, which, with the addition of an observation tower, became a free camp. This was not happening in Poland but in the hill country of Jerusalem. And a couple of hills farther on, there were "settlements" that had long since become complete cities, walled like ancient fortresses, on real estate that had belonged for centuries to ancient indigenous Palestinian families. At the same time one Palestinian town after another, one city after another had been cut off by blockades of all the streets, highways and paths, with fortifications spread over fields and olive orchards. I had to watch as a new map of Palestine was being drawn: new highways, new places, all built by Palestinians, were now without Palestinians. It was as if the ancient map, the ancient roads and the ancient places with all their inhabitants in Nabulus, Hebron, Bethlehem, had simply ceased to exist, as if all the Jewish settlements had not been raised in occupied land but had been rightfully conquered and held in peace. Very soon mountains of rubble rose from the pavement, obstructing the many junctions of this new traffic system on the West Bank in which many secondary roads were cut off from the primary corridors or were deliberately blocked with cement or stone barriers, with checkpoints at the entrance to Arab cities. Very soon they had built a thirty-mile-long trench around a city like Jericho, four yards deep and two wide, which would prevent a single donkey cart from entering or leaving the infernally hot city without being inspected. All in the name of the security of Israel, which each day was becoming more insecure.

All this time, on the street and in the newspapers, there was more and more open talk about resettlement of the population, as though this were the best solution to the problem. Moderates started to leave the country. Radicals remained. On walls, graffiti proclaimed for the first time: "Foreign press, Israel's enemy." Soon I saw Israelis lying torn to pieces along the streets of Jerusalem—and Palestinians' cities caged in and transformed into concentration camps. I met charming teenagers of both sexes in the cafés of Tel Aviv, in Beth El, gentle-eyed settlers and Madonna-like mothers of settlers in Hebron. In Gaza I saw children who seemed to be carrying ticking bombs on their chests in place of beating hearts. I saw trees blasted and houses destroyed.

One of my earliest memories returned to me. My father had taken me to a parade of the English occupying forces near our town. At the time, in the forests of my childhood, the victors were always holding maneuvers. We saw planes landing in the meadows, tanks that moved their guns and shot blanks. While my father talked to an officer, I had climbed into a jeep and began pressing buttons. Suddenly the engine turned over and the jeep took off. I nearly died of fright until, finally, a soldier jumped into the open vehicle and stopped it with a touch. In Israel an engine had been turned on, but no adult had jumped in to stop it. Zionism, which had called Jews back to their ancestral land and had, after nearly two thousand years, brought Israel back into the world, now, was eating into the West Bank of the Jordan like a war machine no one knew how to disarm, even though, for quite some time, it had landed and had moved inexorably inland. The violent conquest of the land could never be stopped, even in the midst of the new uprising, which, at the end of its strength and in despair, once again protested the occupation. No one was positioned to put out the fire and control the violence. In plain view of the whole world, a nineteenth-century ideology self-destructed in the twenty-first.

Thus, in the Holy Land, I became a witness to how the structural walls of the Near East were weakened like a house of cards. What the Balkans were for the First World War, this land suddenly seemed to be for the next apocalyptic struggle of peoples. Never before had I lived in a place so full of fascinating human beings, who so systematically and regularly broke the commandments one by one: do not kill, do not lie, do not covet the goods and possessions of your neighbor. The Holy Land had become the laboratory of the apocalypse.

"Violence and oppression! Violence and oppression!" The prophet Jeremiah's lamentation over Judea or Samaria could not be silenced. But no one listened. In the Torah there are thirty-six instances of the reminder: "You were in exile so that you might learn what it means to be an alien." Now I had become a witness of how suddenly both peoples had become aliens in their native land. The daily injustices cried to heaven. Nevertheless, both sides were convinced that they were right. Both were poisoned against peace for generations to come. Poisoned by their anguish, poisoned by betrayal, poisoned by accusations, poisoned by the network of spies and provocateurs—a poison that tore, unimpeded, into all families without exception. Every helicopter attack on the West Bank had been preceded by spying. Israel, made prisoner to a ludicrous cult of security, with ever new and ever more useless campaigns against King Terror. Palestine transformed into a land of prisons and concentration camps, with a system of cages that separated everyone from everyone, by means of a new map, with blocked highways, open graves, and defenses always newly built and always surrounded by barbed wire. One seed of violence after another polluted the land with each corpse laid in the earth.

It was as if after the massive assassination of European Jews, the curse of sheer evildoing had fallen on the land of Mary like a cloud, as if, overwhelmed by the exhausting desert winds that took from both peoples both breath and sight, leaving them to fall, groping, into the trap of totalitarian temptation. Two cruelly traumatized and neurotic peoples locked in hand-to-hand combat. Both sides would have to conduct a civil war against their own radical elements, though they want to demand such a struggle only of the other side. Every day, mistrust gazed at me from every pair of eyes I met. The world's worst counselor, anguish, ruled Mary's land. Here no one seemed to know the meaning of the words peace, tolerance, forgiveness, reconciliation. Nothing seems more absurd in the Holy Land than the idea of an intermingling of the two enemy nations.

On the afternoon of September 11, 2001, in a back room on the Via Dolorosa, I bought an antique Russian icon that represented Mary, not clothed with the sun, but in a burning bush, that bush burning but not consumed which appeared to Moses in the desert. We were just arriving home when our daughter Maria called from Munich, telling us to turn on the television. We saw a cloud of smoke rising over Manhattan from a tall tower. We had just sat down before the screen when it showed a plane appearing on the horizon, heading for the adjacent tower.

I was glued to the television set. I saw the first tower go down, and then the second. Then I jumped up and went out on the street to observe the impact on Jerusalem of the attack on New York and send a report to Berlin for editing. Our baker turned ghostly pale and dropped the bread he was wrapping, unable to say a single word. Fascinated, he and his employees watched the television set by the counter as it showed the images of the monstrous mushroom of dust over Manhattan, over and over. Yasser Arafat appeared, supported by two aides, trembling as he condemned the catastrophe on camera, speaking for the first time in English instead of Arabic: "God bless America! God bless America!" Arafat was scared to death. Dogs kept on barking and howling. Helicopters were flying low in the dusk, their rattling synchronizing with the mysterious comings and goings of police sirens, screaming near and far. On all streets, the blue light of military patrols and police enveloped the heartsick residents of Jerusalem—men, women, children. No one was in the mood for conversation. "It is the beginning of the end", said an Armenian physician at the Damascus Gate. "This means war—may God have mercy on us all!" "We were not the ones! We were not the ones! What sick mind could think that we could do anything like this?" a shoemaker muttered to himself. "This was done by the devil himself!" The barking and howling of the dogs went on and on, in rhythm with the beating hearts of those who met fearfully and viewed each other with suspicion, usually in silence. The twilight painted Jerusalem's walls gold, as if it needed to brighten them more splendidly that day.

I looked at the golden dome of the Mosque of Omar and noted that, if there is a building in the world that is the equivalent of the Twin Towers, it is this shrine. On the rock where Abraham did not sacrifice his son Isaac; where Jesus had written in the dust with his finger, the only writing he left behind; on which Herod had the last Jewish Temple built, while to one side, Mary was being born. Sweet God! "One thing is as sure as day and night," says Father Elias in a trembling voice, at the Church of the Holy Sepulchre, "whoever is behind this criminal attack is a mortal enemy, the worst enemy of the Palestinians—as well as of all the Israelis. No one can hate us more than the plotters behind this mass killing. This horror pierces the heart of the Holy Land. God have mercy on us all!" I hurried home by the deserted Salah e-Din Street, to write a quick report for Berlin.

At home, the television was still on. My wife and daughter were glued to the channel carrying BBC-World. But now I could see that, immediately after the burning of the towers, images suddenly appeared of jubilant Palestinians in Salah e-Din Street. A few children and two women were mugging for the camera. I could not believe my eyes. I had just come from there and had seen the street. Salah e-Din Street was in shock. That afternoon they could not have filmed a single smile, much less a jubilant celebration.

I went back there with my wife. The street was so life-less it seemed dead. In every window one could see the light of a television flickering upward. In all the shops people were sitting, glued to the spectacle. Mohammed came out to meet us on the pavement, disoriented; he was a young man from whom we often bought snacks. He had not seen either photographers or celebrating children or women waving flags in the street. He looked at us closely as if he doubted we were in our right mind.

I returned to my desk near the television and saw, while I was hastily writing my report, that the few reruns of the jubilant women and children on Salah e-Din Street were now on all channels around the world. I flipped desperately from channel to channel: from Israeli TV to German to Spanish to French to American to English; from CNN to CBS to BBC. Everywhere the same images appeared: Palestinians celebrating jubilantly. But they were certainly not Jerusalem Palestinians, who that afternoon were nowhere to be found and who were certainly not celebrating live alongside the burning towers in New York, towers that no longer existed.

Six weeks later, in Bethlehem, we encountered for the first time the specter of open war, not just a war of terrorism, counter-terrorism or counter-counter-terrorism. For some reason, at a checkpoint a tank had moved over to let our civilian Audi pass. Manger Street was dead. Bullet-riddled cars were parked diagonally on the curbs; flattened trash cans obstructed the road; the treads of tanks had torn up the pavement; there were many demolished cars, one completely crushed as if in a compacter. All exits were sealed with steel gates. A light pole was doubled over. Façades blackened with soot, windowpanes riddled by bullets, and fragments and empty shell casings all over the place. There was a ghostly silence. Emptiness, where ordinarily life throbbed in the deafening traffic.

It had to have been about here that Joseph (according to an unknown author about the year 200) turned to look at his bride, already well along in her pregnancy, as he led Mary to Bethlehem mounted on a donkey, "and he saw that she, resigned, looked around sadly. He thought to himself: 'Perhaps the child is kicking her.' When he turned around later, he saw her laughing. He asked her: 'What's going on, Mary? First you laugh, then you get sad.' Mary answered: 'I can see two peoples: one weeps and laments; the other is joyful and celebrates jubilantly.... Help me down from the donkey; the child is pushing and wants to come out.'"

I thought to myself: Would it be possible today to find at least one of these two peoples who could laugh, here where there are only two sad peoples? Both weep and lament. Suddenly the dead silence was broken by a burst of machine-gun fire coming from the Paradise Hotel, some fifty yards behind us. Then, in response to the firing behind our backs, came shots from Kalashnikov rifles just ahead of us. There were explosions and bursts on all sides, as if we were in the midst of fireworks. Bethlehem's Manger Street had become a combat zone. A stone's throw away from Abu Shanab, the shuttered restaurant where a week earlier we had eaten lamb, under the rain of bullets, an older couple called us into their doorway; the man's yellowish face was wet with sweat, and he carried a plastic bag. Would it be possible for us to take them with us? I was forcibly reminded of Father Claus of Munich: Need teaches us how to pray. At the corner farther on, a group of militia, dressed in black, were crouching on a staircase, automatic weapons at the ready. On Wednesday, Ahmed Abayad had been stabbed by settlers on his way home; on Thursday the Abayat family had lost three brothers in a bombing; on Friday young George Abu Eid and Abu Srour had been killed by stray bullets, as had Maryam Subai, a mother of six children. On the same day the pregnant Rihab

Nofal died together with her son in an ambulance that was not permitted to pass the checkpoint to get to the hospital. Also on Sunday, Aischa Odeh, a mother of eight, and the deaf-mute Mohammed Suleiman Baraka were killed. Sixteen dead since the previous Tuesday. Now the relatives of a seventeen-year-old altar boy were gathering in Shepherds Street; on Sunday morning, a high-velocity shot from Manger Square hit him while he was playing with his nephews.

My legs were shaking as I crossed Manger Square, approaching the fortress of the Church of the Nativity. There was not a soul present, except for a monk sleeping on the porch of the right wing behind a pile of candles that no one was buying. No one was in the Grotto of the Nativity, either, for a half hour, an hour, an eternity. No church in any ghost town could have been emptier. From the worn staircase a brilliant light penetrated the dusk of the deepest part of the church. A young, pregnant Palestinian climbed down the steps to the grotto and knelt before the star in the niche; she remained praying, placed her right index and middle fingers in an oil lamp and blessed herself. She silently scurried away to the left and up.

At twelve sharp, guided by some cosmic metronome, a delegation of Franciscans, the designated Guardians of the Holy Land, arrived with a Latin choir and descended to the lowest part of the church, where there is neither winter nor summer. Everything became marvelously silent. The shouting of the soldiers between Jerusalem and Bethlehem was muted here; so were the honking of cars caught in traffic congestion, the howling and shrieking of the police jeeps and ambulances, the hammering, excavating and grinding of the armies of construction workers, who, under armed guard, were rapidly completing the work of replacing checkpoints. Here there were no squealing brakes or explosions or grenades or horrified screams of fear. No shot could be heard, no roar of falling walls, no rattling of machine guns from the armed helicopters, no thundering of the F-16 bombers. There were no feverish teenagers, carrying live grenades into the dance clubs of the city under their shirts, above their beating hearts. Here everything was as and what it had always been. Today will not be the final word, said each stone here. The paradox was unbelievable. In spite of all the misery, in this alarming year, in the sacred sites of the Holy Land, a peace reigned that had not been experienced for decades. Here, Christians believe, God himself had entered the world so as to become a man. The burning bush of Sinai: here it became a young woman who gave birth by the power of the Most High. It was as if the *Morenita* were coming to meet me here, in the midst of all the horror that enveloped her country.

But where did she give birth to her son? "HIC DE VIRGINE MARIA JESUS CHRISTUS NATUS EST" were the words inscribed in a circle that surrounded a silver star sunk into the floor in the farthermost alcove. "Here Jesus Christ was born of the Virgin Mary." It lies at the far eastern side, in the farthermost corner of this rocky cave, like a womb. It was the last niche into which a woman in labor could withdraw. It is a recess eight hands wide. The oil lamps around it have turned it into the hottest spot of the cave. Ancient icons, sprinkled with oil, cover every inch of the far wall. Was it easy? How much light was there as her quiet whimpering and groaning echoed against the walls here? Or was the birth completely without pain to the young mother? The animals must have been able to sense the commotion, but they surely had remained quiet. Who cut the umbilical cord? Joseph, her bridegroom there in the shadows, he who was her shade and bridegroom? Could he have resembled Juan Diego? Did he speak to her with "my little one", or perhaps "smallest of my daughters, my baby, my child! My lady and queen!'"? And after her labor pains, had she addressed him as "Joey, Joseph, smallest of my sons!"?

I forgot the shooting outside. In this cave the memory of her dialogue with the Amerindian on Tepeyac Hill was suddenly overwhelming. And the idea that for her, surely, Juan Diego must have been a reflection of her husband; in the most tender dialogue we have from her, she must also have seen Joseph, her great love, in this Amerindian widower. In any event, she would have sighed and laughed, and the little one would have cried softly for the first time. The wonderful smell of a newborn would have mixed with the breath of the animals and with the soot of an oil lamp. Jesus was born. Mary had become a mother. All Jerusalem "danced for joy" in the fragrance of the smile of this young mother and of the new breath of this naked infant, says Luke. I had forgotten all the bullets that had been flying around us half an hour before, spraying the walls of houses with fragments. Truly, I had forgotten it all!

This was the era in which more and more evangelical free churches in the United States were sending their teenagers to Jerusalem, to have front-row seats for the end of the world and the Second Coming of the Lord in order to reinforce the beliefs of the apocalyptic Jews, who desired nothing more than to be able to build the third Temple in the Temple Square in place of the Mosque of Omar. One morning in the Old City, in front of the Church of the Holy Sepulchre, I heard unusually loud organ music playing. As I entered the open door and crossed the threshold, following the Gregorian chant, I saw to the left the Franciscans wearing especially festive robes gathered in front of Christ's empty tomb. They had just begun the celebration. Even the incense seemed special to the occasion. I have rarely smelled it so delicate. High in the church, the morning sun played through the columns as the waves of incense swirled into the cupola.

Along with the seven Franciscans and their two acolytes, an old woman from the Old City and I were the only believers there at the pink marble chapel. Meanwhile, behind the empty sepulchre, the Copts had started their celebration, with monotonous chants in ancient Egyptian. It was the feast of "Holy Mary Queen of the Holy Land", as I discovered through the Franciscan hymns, a feast celebrated only here, on October 25. Customarily, all the texts were sung in Latin; only the reading was in Italian. I heard: "un segno grandioso: una donna vestita di sole, con la luna sotto i suoi piedi"; a woman clothed with the sun, with the moon under her feet. It was the quotation about the apocalyptic Madonna taken from John's Book of Revelation.

Even after the first morning Mass, the room of the sepulchre remained empty, as in the days preceding and in subsequent days and weeks. The site of the Resurrection was abandoned, a site that in peaceful times was packed with lines of pilgrims and tourists snaking into the outer patio. Now I would have been able to remain in the room for hours, almost always alone, in this room that was the heart of Christianity. Once in a while a Russian nun looked in through the small door, or an Ethiopian with a look as deep as a well, kissed the marble slab that took the place of the slab on which Jesus was laid in the kingdom of the dead here on this spot. I spoke a quiet prayer and hurried out. Candles sputtered.

The rear of the narrow space where the Lord's head had lain was decorated with an icon of Mary Magdalen, Jesus' young friend, who, after his death, returned one more time, the first to arrive at the tomb to anoint him. So where was Mary his Mother? Was she still at home, prostrate with paralyzing grief, helpless with affliction, like any Jewish or Palestinian mother whose son had been ripped apart by a rocket or a bomb? Three days before, a stone's throw from here, her Son, dead and caked in blood, had lain in her lap. Christ's burial cloth, later called the Shroud of Turin, was found empty on this spot. Here it was soaked in blood and water. This spot was the photo lab that developed the life-size photo. There is no doubt that this was the site. The icon of Mary Magdalen can be opened like a window, so that one can touch the raw rock behind it, which stands out from the bedrock like the stump of a tooth after the destruction by Sultan Hakim. Except for this, everything else had been restored. Only the shape of the space remained the same. How could it not be incredible? The portable altar of the Franciscans still stood on the slab of the tomb. There was a crucifix on it, and, at the foot of the crucifix, a small silver Madonna was wringing her hands in the even smaller space at its base, as if it were the ventricle of ventricles of the heart. It is perhaps five centimeters high, but the robe and the mantle falling over her shoulders are the same as in Mexico.

At home I read again the biblical text of the day's reading, for the first time in its totality.

> And I will grant my two witnesses power to prophesy ... clothed in sackcloth.... When they have finished their testimony, the beast that ascends from the bottomless pit will make war upon them and conquer them and kill them, and their dead bodies will lie in the street of the great city which is allegorically called Sodom and Egypt, where their Lord was crucified.... At that hour there was a great earthquake, and a tenth of the city fell; seven thousand people were killed in the earthquake, and the rest were terrified and gave glory to the God of heaven.
>
> The second woe has passed; behold, the third woe is soon to come....
>
> Then God's temple in heaven was opened, and the ark of his covenant was seen within his temple; and there were

flashes of lightning, loud noises, peals of thunder, an earthquake, and heavy hail.

And a great sign appeared in heaven, a woman clothed
with the sun, with the moon under her feet, and on her
head a crown of twelve stars; she was with child and she
cried out in her pangs of birth, in anguish for delivery. (Rev
11:3—12:2)

I did not understand a single word, and every time I
tried to contemplate the "great sign", all I knew was that,
unlike this woman, the apocalyptic María of Guadalupe was
not crying out; rather, she was smiling at Juan Diego. Nor
was her head crowned with twelve stars; she was covered
with stars. But what did all this mean? It was only clear
that this question was simply not to be asked. This image
only allowed itself to be contemplated. In a footnote in the
Jerusalem Bible I read that "the great city" certainly referred
to Rome. The footnote to another translation thought that
it referred obviously to the earthly Jerusalem, which, at its
heart—perhaps right where we were living—had at this
moment become the most peaceful and tranquil place on
earth, without strangers, without pilgrims, without dangers, yet where, nevertheless, the work of a foreign correspondent was exhausted in reports about new attacks or
about "extensive and important military operations" in the
west, in the south, in the north or in the Gaza Strip.

By day I was digging up news; by night I wrote progres-
sively more skeptical commentary. Now and then, with a
few weeks in between, I wrote a page about the *Morenita*
in my notebook, amid the drone of flying warships that
plowed the night sky of Jerusalem and amid the explosions
of nail-filled bombs under the shirts of sweaty teenagers on
television or over on Jaffa Street, which I could hear from
my desk. There was scarcely a colleague who did not com-
plain about the sense of being burned out by the daily news

reports of further turns in the spiral of violence. Many of
them would have exchanged years of the their lives to be
transferred as soon as possible, preferably to Rome. Why?
"Rome is a dream, Jerusalem, a trap." Meanwhile, I was
convinced that only a dreamer could think it more likely
that Palestinians and Israelis would ever find the path to
peace on their own initiative than that the heavens would
open over the Mount of Olives in a new and final apparition of the Virgin and Queen of the Holy Land, finally
bringing peace to her land, bringing peace and reconciliation, as once—and hopefully once more—happened in
Mexico.

CHAPTER TWENTY

MARY'S LAST DWELLING PLACE

A two-year conversation in an ancient no-man's land; in the Church of the Holy Sepulchre in Jerusalem and in a cave in the Mount of Olives with Father Bargil Pixner—a lesson on images, dogmas, the Immaculate Conception and the Assumption of Mary above the heavens of Mexico.

If anything is true in what is recounted about her, Mary will have to intervene here. This land and this city cannot be a matter of indifference to her. To what piece of earth would she be more sorrowfully attached than to Mount Zion? From here, to the east and to the west, one must go downhill. Here Mary mourned her Son, here she died; here, today, the world is split precisely in two. From here she last saw the earth, over the hills back there and over the Silvan Valley farther on, where the wind over Jerusalem garbled the voices of the muezzins who, at this very moment, are praising, yet again, the greatness of God. Here stood the first houses of primitive Christianity. Here lived the same Mary who later appeared in Guadalupe, Lourdes or Fatima.

"Look at this", Father Pixner said to me, in one of our first meetings when I got to know him in his abbey; "those are the two stones." Thus began an ongoing conversation and an eternal friendship. He pointed out two large, bright ashlars of Jerusalem rock marked with a deeply carved cross, sunk slightly into the ground, to the left and right of the outer wall of the abbey bell tower. "This is Saint Mary's stone, and that is Saint Stephen's stone. When, in 1898 Emperor William II bought a vegetable garden near the

Room of the Last Supper so that monks could build an abbey here, some Ethiopians and Syrians came to ask: 'What will you do with the stones from Mary's house that are in the garden?' And they showed him two large, massive stones that lay there in the garden, venerated for centuries. They were these ashlars. It was said that one came from Mary's house, the other from Stephen's. Then the master builders took these ashlars and placed them in the foundation of the new bell tower, where now, anyone who wants to can touch them. Ethiopians still come regularly to caress them."

Over time, we spoke together often and at length, in a little cookshop by the Jaffa Gate, with a beer, with a mocha, as we walked through the city or took longer trips by car. In this violent city, the most politicized in the world, Bargil Pixner seemed free of aggression and as apolitical as a child. He loved to talk—and about scarcely anyone more than about Jesus, whose every footstep he had traced, and about Mary, Queen of the Holy Land. He had excavated Bethsaida, the birthplace of Peter, James, John and Andrew, along the north shore of the Lake of Gennesaret. He knew every tree in Galilee, even though he had been born in the southern Tyrol. He was approaching eighty. In Aramaic, the baptismal name of this Benedictine priest meant "son of joy". He had acquired it because of a misunderstanding of an Israeli city clerk, who misheard and misspelled his baptismal name, Virgil, a name he kept until he made his solemn profession here at age fifty. He went on to become a modern Heinrich Schliemann for Mount Zion, a scatterbrained genius who sometimes interwove the many languages he had mastered and spoke like a native. What was wonderful about his stories was that they came out without reservations like "perhaps", "probably", or as "it would be or would have to be". He was well-rounded and culturally astute, with a great talent for synthesis. What he most liked to talk about was life on Mount Zion in the first centuries of Christianity, but preferably without filters, as if he had been there.

In contrast, he was always laughing at my stories about the *Morenita* of Guadalupe. He had heard only incidental accounts about it and was skeptical. He did not believe in the marvelous story of her apparition, in spite of the mosaic of the Madonna in the crypt and the many Mexican pilgrims who kept coming to Jerusalem in the middle of the war to the abbey of Holy Mary of Mount Zion, which is also called the Basilica of Mary or Dormition Abbey. But he did believe strongly that she had lived here. For him, Mary was present, first and foremost, in Jerusalem.

"What do you mean, do I believe this? I love Mary. To love her, here in Jerusalem, I do not need an apparition. Here she speaks to me, above all, as a real historical person. Here she was alive. She was not some kind of phantasm or ghost. In spite of the many thousands of images of her—and in my opinion, also in spite of all her apparitions—she was and is only one single person. Not two, not three, not ten thousand. She was flesh and blood. And *Morenita! Morenita!* She is not a Mexican goddess. She is Mary. And there is only one Mary, always the same person, though she may have appeared many times."

"When did Mary die?"

"Around 48, 49, 50."

"On what do you base this?"

"This church is called 'The Church of the Dormition of Mary' because she died here. This comes from the most ancient traditions. The tradition affirms that this is the site where she lived after the Resurrection of Christ. Add to this the traditions of the Eastern Churches, especially the Syrian, Ethiopian and Greek, where all these stories live on. So very very probably she died here. That this happened around the years 48/49 or 49/50 I deduce from various observations. There is a very ancient story about her death, found in the Vatican. It is called *Transitus Mariae*; in English, the Translation of Mary. The narrative reflects many Judeo-Christian elements. So its origin lies in the most ancient period of the Church, addressed to those Jews who believed in Jesus and spoke Hebrew. It emphasizes that the apostles were present at Mary's death. But since most of them were scattered throughout the world, there was only one recorded event that could fix the date. That is the so-called council of the apostles in Jerusalem. That they could have met a second time somewhere else is neither mentioned anywhere in written records nor imaginable. And this council can be dated rather precisely."

"Mary died during the council of apostles in Jerusalem?"

"Yes, I believe so, or shortly before or after. Either John brought her from Ephesus to Jerusalem, or she was already residing here. In any event, John had to have been living with her, along with her family that had moved here from Nazareth. Surely she had related much of her life story. Some member of the family, I am sure, compiled these narratives into a *haggadah*. *Haggadahs* are narratives on biblical themes whose elements may have legendary properties, but whose basic foundation is historical. The evangelist Luke had to have come across these stories when, five years after the destruction of Jerusalem, he traveled from Antioch to Zion.

"So Luke came here in 75?"

"Perhaps even before. But surely after. In any event, he would then have come across this *haggadah*. It was written in Hebrew; if he himself had not mastered Hebrew, someone translated it into Greek. Thus the information about Mary was introduced into his Gospel, where we come across phrases like: 'Mary kept all these things in her heart; Mary reflected about what this might mean.' To my way of thinking, such a formula can mean only one thing, that she had been witness to the corresponding events. With this phrase, Luke wants us to understand that he is not writing about rumors or speculations, but is reporting on the Annunciation, the birth of Jesus in Bethlehem, the shepherds, the meeting between Elizabeth and Mary—all issuing from her. In this, Luke is clearly claiming the Mother of God as a co-author of the Gospel. For what Jesus had said to her, even as a young man, must surely have had a great impact on her. She is 'the memory of the Church', as the late pope kept asserting. So, in Luke's Gospel, Mary surfaces now and then. The story of Jesus' birth in Bethlehem comes from her, as do the stories of the old man Simeon in the Temple and of the twelve-year-old Jesus in the Temple. All these were originally Mary's stories. In any event, all that we know of her comes through Luke. And he had to have discovered all this here on Mount Zion."

"What about the portraits of Mary that antiquity attributed to Luke?"

"We need to say two things about this. First of all, it is a particularly valuable tradition; secondly, it is in no way an absurd idea. For Luke was a Greek. In Hellenistic times, especially in the eastern Roman Empire, portraiture flourished widely. There are portraits that are highly finished works of art as well as primitive portraits, indicating that portraiture was common to all social strata. About one hundred years earlier, in the oasis of El Faiyûm, in Egypt, an enormous number of contemporary first-century portraits were discovered; these were in fantastically good condition, though their quality was uneven. Among them there are masterpieces, together with sketches like hurried and fuzzy snapshots. In any event, they are all realistic portraits and extraordinary artifacts. This is just some background.

"However, we should not imagine that Luke personally sat at Mary's feet to paint her. For it is certain that he could

not have met her. But it is clear that for him, a Greek, portraits were not the exotic things that they would have been
for a Jew. As a physician, a student of nature, he would certainly have had a Greek's cultural attitude toward a portrait.
And the primitive community on Mount Zion would also
have included Greeks with a similar attitude toward portraits. So I can well imagine that a Greek convert close to
the Mother of God would come to paint her. This would
have been unthinkable in the Jewish circle around the Mother
of God. But from the Greek point of view, it seems very
natural to me. I imagine it would be as if you took a photo
of me as we sit here. So it seems very possible that the first
portrait of Mary came about in the same way. Thus Luke,
coming across not only the *haggadah* about Mary but also an
authentic portrait, naturally accepted it. Perhaps he later copied it or made several copies. In any event, these traditions
should not be dismissed out of hand. I have the greatest respect
for them because one thing is certain: no one would simply
have invented them. On the contrary, it is clearly absurd to
imagine that anyone would invent something in that way
and that others would believe it for centuries. But I can easily imagine that there was an original portrait of Mary painted
on wax, vellum, wood or papyrus—no knowing what. And,
to tell the truth, it would be a personal portrait of Mary, not
an idealization of the feminine, as in the representations of
the goddess Artemis. But that what Luke painted, according
to this tradition, has been preserved is another question. That
the portraits attributed to Luke came from his grandchildren
or great-grandchildren, and that these are copies of copies,
is also another question. But it is still surprising how and to
what degree Mary is always represented in images—since
many fewer written texts have come down to us about her
than about her Son, Jesus. In a very special way, Mary has
always spoken strongly through images, much more, perhaps,

than any other figure in world history. But here," Bargil Pixner said proudly before rising to return to the church for the choral office, "here, among us and in this place, she speaks in a different way."

"She speaks here as an unparalleled witness," he went on, "for she has lived here. Near here, she took part in the first feast of Pentecost. This was in the days when the apostles began to recognize in her features, better than in any image, the very face of the Son she bore. Now no longer among them, he continued to be reflected in his Mother's face. 'All were amazed and wondered' (Acts 2:7), Luke writes in his account of the events of Pentecost on Mount Zion. Why? What does this mean? Look up the text in the Bible. It means that on this precise spot where we are seated, in the presence of Mary, the barriers between Israel and non-Jews— between Jews and Parthians, Medes, Elamites and Romans, between Asians, Africans and Europeans—were all blown to bits. This marked an incredible revolution in world history. Almost immediately they began to do what before had seemed impossible; they began to eat in their homes with pagans, whom their culture declared unclean. This happened in Rome, in Corinth and in Syria, where, moreover, lords and slaves, men and women gathered at table. On this day, Judaism was opened up to all nations. Without this feast of Pentecost, the Ten Commandments would never have come down to us. I believe that this was the greatest revolution in world history. About twenty years later, this was brought to completion in the council of the apostles, here again, on this very spot, where Mary was also present and where she died. Perhaps she died of joy because she was able to experience this before finally being reunited to her Son.

"In any event, I believe she lived to see the dispute between Peter and Paul, which was finally decided unanimously by the apostles in such a way that in future the barriers between Jews and Gentiles had to disappear. No cultural wall would henceforth impede the union among nations. Perhaps with her death she sealed the incredible event of the overcoming of all barriers and sealed it once more for all time. Check the passage in Acts! If you visualize the historical background, you won't find anything more exciting in any novel.

"Moreover, Mary speaks to us here, not in images, but in her very existence and her death. When they were constructing this abbey a century ago, the excavations uncovered the foundations of an ancient church in whose western corner a chapel had been constructed specifically to commemorate Mary's death. She certainly died there. There is no other site that claims a more ancient tradition about her death. There is precisely where she died, there where our crypt was built, and, above it, our church and the monastery where we are now sitting. Of course, she speaks here in a very different way than at any other site, including Rome and Mexico. No painter, not even Raphael, has enabled her to speak thus. As in no other place, she speaks clearly down there in her tomb in the Garden of Olives. If you wish, early tomorrow I can show you, on Golgotha, how she makes sense even of a dogma here."—"On Golgotha? Of course I wish it. Which dogma?"—"The dogma of Mary's body and soul entering heaven." We agreed to meet at seven the next morning, in the Church of the Holy Sepulchre in the center of the Old City, the church the Greeks call the "Church of the Resurrection".

The next morning he stood punctually before the ancient door of the church built by the emperor Constantine over the rock on which Christ was crucified and over his nearby tomb. To the right, immediately behind the entrance, I followed Bargil up a steep staircase to the first floor. The Golgotha Chapel lies in permanent shadow. When we entered there were only two Jerusalem residents and an Ethiopian nun praying on a side bench to the right. Bargil went ahead and stood by the last column. In a display case before us was a rococo Sorrowful Virgin pierced with a sword. To her left was a Greek altar rising over heavy plate glass. Under this was a massive chunk of ash-colored limestone. It was barely illuminated and as naked and bald as a skull. It was the apex of Golgotha. Bargil moved a vase aside from the glass plate, turned on a small lamp behind the altar and pointed to a broken ring of stone in a hollow of the rock under the glass. "That is the place where the Lord was crucified."

Pixner continued in a low voice: "In Jesus' time this was the only piece of rock still standing in a quarry that was no longer useful for the construction of buildings; the Romans started using it for executions. Later, in 325, the architects of the first church cleared and leveled it on three sides until it could accommodate the new basilica which the pagan emperor Constantine had ordered built in honor of the Passion and Resurrection of Christ. They left untouched only the most elevated core of the central stone of the rocky hill. This is the place. The diameter of the stone ring indicates that we must imagine the vertical pole of the cross to have been a rough log, with the bark still on it, scarcely longer than nine feet. So, whoever was hanging on it died right at eye level of the closest spectators, and not at some lordly height. Rather, Jesus hung sinking toward the ground. You can see how small the area is. If Mary was with him, as the evangelist John says, she had to have been standing here. Here, within arm's reach, he hung, covered with blood, totally naked, as the Romans always crucified criminals. Here Mary heard, within intimate speaking distance, his last words and his last cries. She heard them when they drove nails into his wrists. Tortured to death, suffocated, he died within arm's reach of his Mother. To make sure, a Roman speared

him on the right side of his thorax. Blood and water spurted
out of his side, as a dying person's blood spills out. All this
right before her eyes. When the enormous nails were forced
from the wood and the bones of the sagging, inclined corpse,
it was done here. Here Mary held the bloodless and blood-
smeared body to herself. Here, as good as dead herself, she
saw his crusted lips turn blue. He was still bleeding from
hands and feet and especially from the wound in his breast.
Blood and water flowed over her clothing. Here she placed
him on the shroud and covered him with it. Here she saw
his dead and blood-smeared eyes. Who could imagine her
suffering? There, where you are standing, is the place where
the Sorrowful Mother stood. The *Pietà* that took place here
was not made of marble or made in Rome; it was made of
flesh and blood, living and then dead. Her pain joined her
to him as during her pregnancy." A group of Russian women
arrived and, standing before the rock, they intoned a tender, angelic song. Bargil gestured me to follow him down
some steps.

"This is what I was thinking about when I said that here,
the very place speaks of Mary; here we do not need apparitions", he said at the entrance. As we sat on an unfixed
column in the inner patio: "Here memories speak."

A Jerusalem morning spread over the rectangular patio
with blue brilliance. An immensely loud steel bell pealed
from the bell tower of the Greek-Orthodox church. The
roar and vibration of the last peal was suspended in the air
for minutes, shaking and vibrating between the walls of the
atrium for an eternity as if they did not want to fade away.

While the vibrations were lessening, Bargil said: "Can
you imagine how the mother of a condemned man feels
from the time of his death until her own? This Mother,
especially! I believe that from that moment her life seemed
like nothing but an exile, in which she longed only to go

home, to die as a unique victim of love." He became silent as if he were listening to the last peal of the bell.

"Basically, then," he continued, "it is from this that even the difficult idea of the Immaculate Conception arises, which almost no one understands today. That is, the idea that Mary, from the instant of her conception on, was chosen for all that she later suffered. Yes, she was foreordained for the kind of suffering that you have been considering here. So among all human beings—and the first Christians concluded this—Mary had to have been set apart from the beginning. Was this not clearly necessary? Nowhere can one understand the extent of God's demands on Mary as here on Golgotha. If it is true that Jesus is the Son of God, then it is simply incomprehensible that God, who allowed the Mother to suffer so greatly with her Son, would not glorify her in a way comparable to his, and, indeed, from the beginning. For the two were one flesh. Moreover, if Eve was created without original sin, would the Creator deny this privilege to Mary? No. If Jesus is God's Son, then, absolutely, God could not do otherwise! The ancient conviction about the Immaculate Conception is not so much about Mary herself; it is a verification that her Son Jesus was truly Son of God and not just another prophet. 'I am conceived without sin' means, above all, that 'my Son is Son of God, and with him a completely new history of the earth begins.' Are you asking why? Well, if God created Eve, the mother of all who live, without original sin, did he not have to create a new world for his Son? 'Conceived without sin' can only be understood as a seal of authenticity that what the apostles and evangelists later asserted was the truth. It means that he has broken the chain. It means that he has really been resurrected from among the dead.

"Nevertheless, the controversy within the Church went on for centuries, and when you tell me that Mary presented herself in Mexico as the Immaculate Conception, then this, after many centuries, is also an enormous appreciation of the participation of human reason in God's work of salvation. It is like a heavenly stamp of approval on a process of human knowledge pressing on to a logical conclusion. For the Immaculate Conception is not incomprehensible; on the contrary, it can be fathomed deeply by the human spirit, though, as always with men, amid controversy and conflict. So for centuries, the Church has been struggling with this. Many great theologians were against accepting the Immaculate Conception. Augustine was opposed. I think Bernard of Clairvaux, too. Only during the Middle Ages, after Anselm of Canterbury and Duns Scotus, did certainty about the Immaculate Conception gradually evolve, until finally, in modern times, from Lourdes to Fatima, Mary introduced herself as the Immaculate Conception—the meaning of which not one of the visionaries could have understood."

"But you wanted to explain the Assumption of Mary into heaven to me", I interrupted him, telling him the story of "the prison of Mary", at whose celebration my father and mother had first met.

"I'm leading up to it," he laughed mischievously, "for the Assumption is just a consequence of the same thought and observation. One more time: The dogma of the Immaculate Conception of Mary is basically neither more nor less than a consequence of all that Christians believe in. No one is obliged to believe in it. But if a Christian does not believe in the Immaculate Conception at the beginning of her life or in the Assumption into heaven at her death, then he need not believe in all the rest, especially that her Son is Son of God. This is the point of view of the Orthodox and Catholics, who have not lost sight of how closely united Mother and Son are, especially in suffering. But then it makes no sense that God can lift his Son, body and soul, out of the process of decomposition, while leaving the Mother—who suffered scarcely less—to fall into decay after death. This is why the Marian theologian of the Middle Ages, Duns Scotus, came up with the formula *potuit, decuit, ergo fecit*, which means: 'For God it was possible, it was appropriate, so he did it.' That is, God could have made it possible for Mary to be conceived sinless, without original sin; it was fitting that he do so; hence he did it. That is why, here in Jerusalem, there are two empty tombs and two feasts, the Ascension of Christ and the Assumption and Coronation of Mary in heaven. Here is where it has its origin. But the person who wants to get an idea of what Christ's tomb near Golgotha looked like needs to go see Mary's empty tomb. There is scarcely another site that sheds so much light. I have to show it to you."

He took me through the labyrinth of arched alleyways of the Old City to the Via Dolorosa, through Mary's Gate, to the Kedron Valley and down to the Garden of Gethsemane. There, in an empty field to the left of the highway, two short flights of steps led to the outer patio of an ancient crusader church; inside the entryway an enormous staircase went even farther down, into the earth itself, to Mary's tomb, as Bargil put it, a small, single room excavated from the rock. I asked him quietly, "But Gethsemane was an olive orchard, not a cemetery. How could there be tombs here? Are tombs built in a person's garden?"

"One of the Dead Sea Scrolls mentions that there was also a cemetery alongside Gethsemane." After saying a Hail Mary, he began again here below with a brief lecture. "The Copper Scroll is a document written by the Essenes; it also mentions Mount Zion, where they almost certainly had an enclave. Probably, this field down here was the property of someone associated with the Essenes. And probably the location provides another reason to look for Mary's tomb here.

The fact that Jesus passed his last night in the Garden of Gethsemane allows us to deduce that the garden belonged to a Jerusalem family who were friends of his. So does it not stand to reason that later the same family would also make a tomb available for his Mother in the same garden? In any event, the fact is that the tomb is located right beside the Garden of Olives.

"Around here also would have been buried James the Less, called 'the brother of the Lord', who in A.D. 62 was assassinated near the Temple roof; many, from earliest days, think he was the biological son of Mary's husband, Joseph, who was a widower when Mary married him. It is still not known where this tomb was located. But there is no doubt that Mary was buried here, as witnessed by the veneration of her tomb from the earliest days. The *Transitus* text, which is preserved in the Vatican, is the first to mention her burial. It also says that Thomas was not present at the burial. Because Thomas was the apostle who had doubted Christ's Resurrection until he could place his hand in the wound in Christ's side, some think it not credible that he alone arrived at Mary's deathbed too late—and consider the rest of the document unreliable. The story goes on to say that the tomb in which Mary was laid was trough-shaped. When Thomas arrived later, the tomb was reopened; leaving behind the round stone that had sealed the entrance and going through a small labyrinth, he came to the trough-shaped tomb where Mary was laid. Then Thomas said: 'There's no one here!' The belief that she had been taken into heaven was born right here."

"Is that the same narrative that relates that the tomb was full of roses?"

"I think so. But this would be a later addition. What is not an addition is that only two years ago they discovered that the tomb really was shaped like a trough. For Mary's tomb could be examined only once, in 1999, when there was a storm that brought torrential rain and flooded the whole complex. In this flood one of our professors nearly drowned. He had been praying down below and had fortunately just left when masses of water roared down the stairways. Images, icons, altars were all destroyed. Everything had to be cleared out and cleaned. In this major cleaning, it was discovered that Mary's empty sarcophagus had been cut from the rock in the shape of a trough and was rooted in the ground. Only two years ago! Before this, researchers had always put forward the thesis that, for one reason or another, the sarcophagus had been moved there. But from the very beginning it has been there, part of the very rock. Thus, for only a little while has it been known that the tomb corresponds to the most ancient text about Mary's burial. Only in recent times, have the Byzantines cut away and leveled the rock around Mary's tomb, as they did around that of Jesus, so that pilgrims might process completely around the tomb. That is why, today, the tomb stands totally isolated."

"But might it not be that someone placed this tomb here later just so that here again there would be something that corresponds to Jesus' tomb?"

"I do not believe so. Why would they have? A better starting point is the fact that, in first-century Jerusalem, people really did venerate two empty tombs. That Mary's tomb has become, today, a kind of model by which to contemplate that of Jesus—now largely destroyed—is beside the point. Simply put, more of Mary's tomb has been preserved than that of Jesus. Possibly this is related to the great veneration that the Muslims have for Mary. Look here: see, right next to Mary's tomb is a *mihrab*, a prayer niche oriented toward Mecca, where the Muslims come to pray. This is their shrine also."

We climbed a long staircase until we reached daylight and crossed the street in front of the Church of the Agony. Before it rises the walled crown of the Temple Mount, shining over the Kedron Valley in the evening twilight. Bargil went at such a uniformly slow and steady pace that he might have been walking the hills of Jerusalem for centuries. We went down into the valley; we climbed again to the Temple roof and followed the circular wall toward Mount Zion.

"You can trace from earliest days the belief that Mary, after her death, was received bodily into heaven", he continued as we walked. "That 'she was taken into heaven' has been believed by Christians from the beginning. Since no one has been closer to Jesus, so now, together with him, she has become an all-powerful suppliant. How could he not concern himself with what she asked? On earth, against his will and at her request, he performed the first miracle by changing water into wine at a wedding. How could he refuse her anything? This confidence goes back to the Church's very beginnings. All of this is the meaning of the Assumption of Mary into heaven as Queen of the Universe.

"There is still more that could perplex the great skeptics. From the beginning, Mary was the most exalted among the saints. Unlike the apostles and most of the martyrs, there are no earthly remains of Mary: not a bone, not a skull, not a molar, absolutely nothing. Never, anywhere has even a fingernail of hers been venerated, in spite of the enthusiasm with which people in other places, with regard to other saints, hunted down the tiniest fragment of material remains and sold them at the highest prices. Think about the bones of Peter, Paul, Philip, Bartholomew in Rome, John in Ephesus, Andrew in Patras, Matthias in Trieste; think about the almost complete skeleton of the evangelist Matthew in Salerno or of Luke in Padua. But nowhere is there venerated even a single hair of Mary! Not even forgers and crooks have dared offer a single relic.

"In any event, believers understood very quickly that the Assumption of Mary into heaven was the culminating fullness of the history of salvation. Look at European cathedrals. The most beautiful and most important images speak of this concretely, even from the outside, in the main entrance, as at Reims, or as the central mosaic in the apse of Saint Mary Major. In most of the ancient churches, the cross is not the main artistic theme, but the Coronation of Mary. The Assumption of Mary into heaven demonstrates that God, who had required that the Mother be only a step away during the execution of her Son, also insisted that she be the closest to him in his glory. What could be more obvious? Really, there is no feast more human and humanly understandable than the feast of Mary's Assumption."

So went the conversations with Bargil Pixner for two years or so, mostly in the evening after work, during a stroll around the city wall, alternating west and east; we went to visit him in the abbey around time for vespers. Had these two years of data-gathering not been two decisive years in the Holy Land and in the world? 2000 and 2001. How marvelously they had begun, these years that ended with so disheartening a prognosis! The detour signs that had sprung up would determine the course of history for a long time. Day by day, this was almost tangible in Jerusalem. One at a time, every day was etched on the retina like a film etched in fire. Very shortly before the Pope's arrival, we had arrived in the Holy Land; my work began with his trip. There is not much more to see, I thought then, when he again departed from the Holy Land. The afternoon before, right next to Mary's tomb, he had begun his good-byes.

Mary's tomb belongs to the Greeks and Armenians. Since the Latin Pope could not say good-bye to Jerusalem there, he did so next to it, in the Franciscan church in the Garden of Gethsemane, where Jerusalem Christians venerate the piece of rock on which Jesus had sweat blood. It was his last night. He knew what was about to descend on him. The soldier who would arrest him was already on his way out of the city. In the twilight, mountains of clouds rose up beyond the Kedron Valley, over the Temple.

One after another blue lights went on in the closed-off streets. With their searchlights, helicopters brushed the ancient olive trees in the garden where soldiers, armed to the teeth, were swarming. As the Pope was praying, none of this disturbed him any more than the silent electrical storm all around him. Head in hand, shoulders bent as if under the weight of the world, he remained kneeling before the naked rock, as if this were the innermost goal of his journey. He was aware only of the stone upon which Jesus had sweat blood. He prayed without ceasing in this chaos. As if this were his last promise: to carry back to Jerusalem his greeting and gratitude to Jesus and "the most illustrious daughter of Galilee", as he had referred the day before to the Mother of Jesus, in the hills rising over the Lake of Gennesaret. It was his Hail Mary.

Outside a little later, in the heavily guarded press bus, I asked Senhora Aura Maria Vistas Miguel of Lisbon: "What is your impression? Hasn't this visit of the Pope to Jerusalem been the high point of all his journeys?" This short-haired colleague with a perpetual smile had accompanied the Pope on all his trips, for Radio Renascença. It was March 25, 2000. In the morning she had been in Nazareth with the Pope for the solemn celebration of the archangel Gabriel's Annunciation of Mary's pregnancy. "Yes," she said and, after reflecting, "this trip is really something special. Jerusalem, Bethlehem, Nazareth, Capernaum—how could it not be?!" She flashed an even warmer smile. "Nevertheless, his last visit to Mexico moved me more. Mexicans do not have any of these places. Most are poor. But they have that image of the Virgin and imagination. When the Pope arrived over the city, millions of them were gathered in the streets to greet him by reflecting light from mirrors and pieces of glass from the roofs of that ocean of houses. No one could have organized anything like it. Who could have imagined it? No director could have set the scene or executed it! It was almost a minor miracle of the Madonna. It was absolutely marvelous."

CHAPTER TWENTY-ONE

MORNING STAR, STAR OF THE SEA

Re-encountering Aura, a trip from Zion to the Lake of Gennesaret; a star of the sea over the mountains of Carmel. The map of the Holy Land painted on an ancient skull; petrels above the bay of Lepanto and the "House of the Incarnation" in the Italian Marches.

On July 30, two years later, I met Aura again over Mexico City in the Pope's plane. The green, mountainous plateau was below us. We were coming from Guatemala; two days earlier we had been in Toronto; we had left Rome one week before. The next day, in the basilica of Tepeyac, the Pope was to canonize Juan Diego, the seer of María of Guadalupe; the day following he would return to Rome. Where was I? Was I still dreaming? Perhaps I would soon wake up? What was I seeing? I pressed my face to the window of the plane and remembered.

Leaving Jerusalem had been like being sucked into a tornado, which would, yet again, leave me free but would hurl me, with a great longing for tranquility, far into the eye of the storm. A few months earlier, in Berlin, Mathias Döpfner and his successor, Wolfram Weimer, my new editor, had asked me if I would not like to familiarize myself with the work of the Rome correspondent, to succeed the present correspondent, who was about to retire. Together, they were a winning team, two friends, both tall and impressive. But one cannot leave Jerusalem as one does other cities. Unlike other colleagues and in spite of the circumstances, I was sad having to quit in the middle of a war, which had really never penetrated to the innermost part of the city. In the past two years, right here, in the city's heart, I had experienced more peace than in any other place on earth—even though anyone would have thought me crazy had I mentioned it. Only two days before, Bargil Pixner had told me about a very ancient narrative flowing from the Jerusalem tradition, according to which Jesus had appeared to Mary on the day before she "fell asleep" to tell her that he would return the next day to take her with him. "After this, Mary took a bath", continued the old monk, "and put on her best clothes so as to go with her Son dressed for the celebration that would surely take place."

"I know the story in a Mexican variant. It says that Mary appeared one more time to the seer Juan Diego before his death, to tell him that she would soon return to take him. She wanted to have him completely by her side."

"But it is certain that one thing never happened in Mexico," Bargil said, "and I have to show it to you now."

He had gotten a key and flashlight from the abbey office. He took me to the basement of the outer patio of Dormition Abbey, where behind an abandoned installation of lavatories for pilgrims, he opened a grill. Behind it was a storage room crammed with books. "Excavating our monastery grounds, we found here part of the village where the first Christians lived. It was not a prosperous village", he said, already on the stairs. "There is a north-south street. To right and left there are hovels. Here we are right under the monastery storeroom."

He opened another door and asked me to lift up a grill in the floor. "Look at this," he laughed proudly, "this is a *mikva*, a Jewish ritual bath, that I have excavated. Do you see the steps leading down? Amid the rubble on one of the steps I found a coin dating from A.D. 68. So the whole area was probably still standing in 70, when the Roman destruction

of Jerusalem also pulled down and leveled this neighborhood on Mount Zion. We have many sources for this history. But do you see up ahead, the column next to the stair
with the curved handrail? Can you imagine what it could
be?" I could feel his satisfied smile, while he played the beam
of the flashlight on the column. "This is a kind of banister,
a column that could support the oldest women when they
wanted to go down into the bath."

Yes, if there is a place anywhere like an axis around which
the world turns, it is here. And if there is a neighborhood
anywhere that, more than any other, could claim to be where
Mary lived and died, it is here. Where can one discover or
uncover more about her? Sunday after Sunday, I returned
to the crypt (beside the hidden *mikva*) to see the life-size
mosaic of the *Morenita* who had greeted us upon our arrival.
Across from it was a mosaic of the *Salus Populi Romani*, the
Marian image of the *Protectress of the Roman People*, from
the Basilica of Saint Mary Major in Rome. Notwithstanding, in an initial fact-finding trip from Jerusalem to Rome,
traveling the Via Aurelia from the airport to the center of
the city, on the right, we were greeted by an enormous
medallion of the *Morenita* on a just-completed church. Was
I dreaming? No, definitely not. I saw it on the return trip
as well. In the center of Rome, in the crypt of the Basilica
of Saint Peter, immediately to the left of Peter's tomb, under
the dome, in the most prominent corner of the Eternal
City, I discovered a chapel of the Virgin of Guadalupe. As
in the Church of the Assumption on Mount Zion, a wonderful mosaic of the apparition had been installed, in gold,
rose, mauve, blue, bottle green, much more subtle than that
in Jerusalem. To the left, the scene of the miracle of the
roses, in silver-plated bronze; close by, to the right, the apparition of Mary amid the resplendence of the sun, on Tepeyac
Hill, in an aureola of multicolored hummingbirds. The

custodian told us that the chapel had been expressly commissioned by the Pope.

We spent our last days in Jerusalem in the Benedictine abbey by the Basilica of the Dormition, waiting for our ship. In February, I checked driving routes to the coast. Taking advantage of this last opportunity, Bargil Pixner asked us to take him along to the north shore of Gennesaret. Never before had there been such frequent roadblocks or such nervous young soldiers asking to see papers. The Judean desert had turned green. During those days flocks of birds migrating from Africa descended into the marshes of the Jordan Valley. In Galilee the almond trees were flowering. After the rain, the valleys were covered with anemones: red, white, lilac, violet, ravishingly beautiful. "Those are the lilies of the field Jesus talked about", said Bargil in the co-pilot seat. "They are the same flowers that, every spring, every year, he and Mary had before their eyes—a true miracle of Holy Land flowers. They last only a few weeks. They are their true flowers."

"And what did she actually pray?"

"The same things that are still prayed today in the synagogues. The same prayers we pray on Mount Zion and which, for fifteen centuries, we Benedictines have prayed everywhere. Like her Son and the apostles, she prayed above all, the 150 Jewish psalms, by means of which the monks, from the early Middle Ages, taught Christians to read and write." He laughed quietly: "Unlike Jews, Christians had to be bullied little by little into learning to read. This is why in the high Middle Ages, the Dominicans spread the rosary as a simplified breviary for the Christian rank and file. Paralleling the 150 psalms, 150 Hail Marys could be said, to which was joined contemplation of fifteen images taken from the life of Jesus and Mary. Almost all of them referred to Jerusalem, the Temple, the crucifixion, the Resurrection or the Assumption of Mary into heaven. The rosary

was the psalter for everyone, especially the illiterate. Anyone could learn a Hail Mary, and everyone could contemplate images. The rosary could be written ideographically,
while the psalms could not. The rosary was completely paint-
able. Probably for this reason—and for a long time—
Benedictines looked down upon it. Even today, we scarcely
ever pray the rosary. We continue praying the psalter as did
Jesus and Mary."

Above the steering wheel, I noted the twists and turns
of the Allon road, which was taking us across Judea and
Samaria. Not one single vehicle approached from the opposite direction. My gaze wandered over the roads and hills,
as if for the last time, lowered to the Jordan Valley, rising
into Galilee and higher still toward Mount Tabor, behind
which was Nazareth and, farther along, the little village of
Cana. Mary must have been doing something similar when
she commanded Juan Diego to cut "Castilian roses"; she
certainly grew up among flowers. There is no doubt about
this.

Finally, the Lake of Gennesaret emerged among the euca-
lyptus trees. Driving the length of the western shore, we
arrived at the small northern city of Tiberias. In the last
three years of her Son's life, Mary spent more time here
with his followers than anywhere else, in these fields, now
covered with ruins, between Bethsaida, Capernaum and Tabgha, where no season is more beautiful than February and
March. We spent our last night in Tabgha. On our last morning, a kingfisher flew in circles above the bush in front of
our window. It was emerald blue. A feathered and flying
jewel. In the early morning sun, the lake was a sparkling,
silvery field of stars. Clouds piled up high in the sky over
Galilee, like ships in full sail. One last time, Bargil strode
along with us through the damp grass on the Hill of the
Beatitudes above the lake shore.

From here, Haifa is only an hour away by car. With our baggage and a pinch of earth from Jerusalem for our future grave, we left the Holy Land on a freighter (since passenger ships no longer traveled this route). The last glimpse of land we got in the twilight was a faint twinkling of lights above and upon both Mount Carmel and Haifa in the distance. I had learned that there, on the mountaintop, the Carmelite Order had been born, the only Western cloistered order originating in Mary's native land. After the conquest of the Holy Land by the crusaders, some of them had retreated to Mount Carmel to dedicate themselves, above all, to the veneration of Mary. It is the order of the Spanish Teresa of Avila, the Palestinian Mariam Baouardy of Ibillin and the highly educated Edith Stein, whose ashes rained down on Birkenau, in Poland. It is also the order of the sisters who today, on Tepeyac Hill in Mexico, maintain a convent of perpetual adoration.

In some medieval chronicles it is said that the Carmelite community owes its beginning to an apparition of Mary on Mount Carmel, on the site where, about two thousand years earlier, the prophet Elijah had challenged the prophets of Baal to a duel of prayers for rain. On the very spot, the crusaders saw Mary above a cloud. The Book of Kings says that Elijah climbed to the top of Mount Carmel and squatted on the ground with his head between his knees. Then he told his servant, "Go out and look seaward!" The servant did so and announced: "I cannot see anything." He told him: "Go again and look!" This happened seven times. At the seventh try, the servant reported: "There is a cloud as small as a human hand rising from the sea." It was the cloud that very shortly darkened the sky to pour itself out as a torrent over the parched earth. The last crusaders believed that it was the same cloud on which, in 1251, the Virgin Mary appeared above the sea to the sixth general of the

Carmelites, Simon Stock. The last glimmer of Israel was a small light above Mount Carmel, an ocean star that had dropped to earth.

The sea was choppy. When the sky became jet black, I went below and, in the opaque light of the cabin and amid the awful din of the ship's engines, picked up Hugh Thomas' *The Conquest of Mexico*, my reading of which had been interrupted in 1999. This was my first free time in a very long time. The book is a treasure trove. Organizing an enormous amount of historical material with colossal erudition, he paints the drama of the Spaniards' encounter with the Aztecs. Nevertheless, in the epilogue, he praises with great admiration "one of the most astonishing successes of the Roman Church" in the almost inexplicably rapid christianization of Mexico, after a recently baptized Amerindian, Juan Diego, "supposedly" received a vision of a dark-skinned Virgin Mary. I could concentrate only with great difficulty and let the book fall, but it was even harder to get to sleep. On the lower wall of the bar in which, at the beginning of the evening, an Egyptian cook had offered us a plate of pasta, there hung an enormous aerial photograph of Jerusalem, showing our house and all the main streets I had traveled during the last two years—and the Garden of Olives, Mount Zion and Mary's tomb.

It was absurd. After two years as a war correspondent, my work had finally led to a kind of log book and journal as an immense report about Mary's Immaculate Conception and ended as an introduction to the birth, life and death of the Mother of God in Jerusalem, the *Morenita* of Mexico, the most famous woman in the world, who is represented in millions of images, but who has become the great unknown.

The ship pitched through the night. The cell phone at my bed indicated that I had received a call to my mailbox while I was above, standing at the ship's rail. Bargil had called me again from *terra firma*: "Paul, Paul", he called into the telephone. He called out as if he were standing at the open door of an empty house, as if expecting an answer from some other room. But I could not call him back, for the ship was already outside of the calling area.

We were the only passengers on the freighter heading for Greece. Ahead of the prow, dolphins leaped with abandon in the waves of the Aegean. We slid by the islands and, at dawn, past Samos and Ephesus, the coastline of Asia Minor far away on the horizon. Farther on, a solitary house stood on a hill; its foundations went back to the first century. At this hour of the day it was wrapped in blue light and the song of nightingales from the woods nearby. Before they were expelled, the Greeks called the walled enclosure *Panaghia Capouli*, the House of the Most Holy. Within its walls flows a fountain the Turks call *Hazreti Meryam Ana Suyu*, that is, "the Fountain of the Holy Virgin Mary".

It is a particularly beautiful place, whose red earth, even by day, is veiled in fog. Popes have visited it. In one of her visions, the seer Anne Catherine Emmerich saw Mary and the apostle John near the ancient shrine of the goddess Artemis, where Paul had provoked a riot as he announced the new gospel in Ephesus. Four hundred years later the city witnessed jubilant torchlight processions when the Council of Ephesus proclaimed that Mary had a right to be called God-Bearer, Mother of God. Indisputably, Christian veneration of Mary began in Ephesus. But I had also asked Bargil Pixner whether Mary had really lived or even died here.

His answer: "After the death of her Son, she may have lived there for some time, probably with John, but surely, not with him alone. Catherine Emmerich's visions are not disputed. Because, however, the visionary did not record them herself, but rather the poet Clemens Brentano gave literary shape to them, they are not in detail very reliable with respect to what she really saw. In any event, Ephesus has a special place in the history of the veneration of Mary. Mary may also have been in other places around the Mediterranean, if she was even seen as far away as Spanish Saragossa. Now, who could prove or disprove it today? So why could Mary not have been in Ephesus, as an ancient tradition claims? John, whose tomb is still venerated, certainly lived here for a time. But Mary certainly did not die in Ephesus. She died in Jerusalem, as the beautiful "house of Mary" in Ephesus makes obvious. For there is no grave. If her tomb had once been there—like that of John—today it would be more venerated than the house. But there is only one tomb—in Jerusalem." For Bargil, nothing else was worth discussing.

At a layover in Patras, so as not to lose any time, we took a taxi to the church of Saint Andrew. Before our arrival in Rome I wanted to see the sarcophagus of the first apostle, whose birthplace Bargil had discovered and excavated years before at the Lake of Gennesaret.

When the cabdriver left us at the main entrance, we discovered that there is no sarcophagus in Patras as in the tombs of the apostles in Rome. Instead, there is a side chapel of the basilica in which the crown of the apostle Andrew's skull is displayed under a crystal container so that believers may kiss it. The suture of the apostle's skull lay before our eyes like the course of the Jordan River painted on ancient parchment. Under this crown had moved the two eyes that saw Jesus, that saw Mary and saw her die. Andrew helped move her to the tomb. We almost missed our boat.

The wind came up as the ferry left the dock. The Gulf of Corinth spread out, perfectly blue, before the prow. To the west we could make out the hills and mountains, which, from both sides of the mainland—north and south—kept advancing. They were finally swallowed by the sea in the straits, toward which our boat was threading its way in a great curve from Patras to the Adriatic Sea. I clung firmly to the deck watching the brilliant rise and fall of the waves in the Bay of Lepanto. Here, on October 7, 1571, was fought the furious naval battle, compared to which the Japanese attack on Pearl Harbor or the terrorist attack on the Twin Towers in New York seem mere skirmishes in world history. In the last thousand years, perhaps only one battle so decisively changed the history of Europe—the siege of Vienna, 112 years later. The naval battle of Lepanto, in one day, cost 40,000 dead and innumerable wounded. It had a three-hundred-year history behind it.

In the fourteenth century, the Ottomans conquered most of the Balkans. In 1453 Christian Constantinople fell. In the first decades of the sixteenth century, the Near East had submitted. In 1529, Vienna was besieged by the Turks. In 1571 Cyprus, which belonged to Venice, fell. Thereafter, the Ottoman Empire dominated the eastern Mediterranean. Now Crete, the last Venetian stronghold for commerce with the East, was in danger. The Pope saw that Selim II, son of Süleyman the Magnificent, was menacing not only Italy, but the whole of Christendom. Islamization threatened all of Europe. The advance of the Turks seemed unstoppable. In this situation, Pius V succeeded in forming a defensive alliance between Venetians and Spaniards. Many Western rulers also sent mercenaries to the largest army the West had ever mustered against the Turks.

So, at dawn on October 7, as the Christian fleet sailed and rowed from the west into the Ionian Sea through the strait, they encountered the Turkish ships. The Turkish fleet lay in a crescent, and their ships were strung like beads on a rosary from the coast of Greece in the north to the coast of Peloponnese in the south. At their back the Christians saw a second chain. It was a perfect trap. The heroes of the Christian naval expedition were in a position hopelessly inferior to that of Ali Paşa's janissaries. The commander of the Muslim fleet was a strategic genius. The two large squadrons of Venice and Spain were joined by the smaller flotillas of Parma and Savoy, which had joined forces with Genoa under the command of Andrea Doria. The wind blew all these naval forces into the trap the Turkish admiral had laid. The commander-in-chief of the Christian fleet was Don John of Austria, a half brother of Philip II of Spain. He was twenty-four years old, the same age as Andrea Doria.

Miguel de Cervantes Saavedra was on one of the ships. He, too, was twenty-four. On that day he took two harquebus shots to the chest, as a third destroyed his left hand; years later the Spaniard would write *Don Quixote* with his right hand. On this day the Holy League, the cream of Europe, fought the Crescent from the east. This was the first time a disunited Christendom had ever joined forces. The Savoyard flagship flew an immense standard, with a silhouette of the Crucified on the Holy Shroud embroidered in heavy brocade over an emblem of the sun. But this standard hung limp from the mast from lack of wind. Almost five hundred ships and about two hundred thousand men faced each other on the sea. But from the beginning of the battle, the Christians were hopelessly inferior to the Turkish naval power.

Storm petrels circled over the waves in anticipation. Then, at almost nine in the morning, the sky grew dark. The greatest hope of the Europeans was in six galleons, heavy sailing ships assisted by oars but difficult to maneuver. They could scarcely use their long-distance cannons here. For this, they needed a fair wind. Notwithstanding, Andrea Doria finally raised the cry: "Long live Mary!" and hurled himself into battle. He was immediately outmaneuvered, his flag-ship forced aside, and his contingent of ships separated from the main fleet. The Turkish admiral Uluch Ali was busy sinking the Genoese ships one by one. It was the begin-ning of the end. Don John of Austria's flagship was boarded by the Turks. They took full advantage of their superiority everywhere: they had better strategy, they were more skill-ful fighters, and they had an insatiable will to win.

For there would be enormous booty. Beyond the Bay of Lepanto and the Christian fleet lay Venice, wide open like an abandoned treasure, and then Bari, Rome, Naples and the rest of the western ports. Desperate, Andrea Doria hurled himself to his cabin below deck and fell to his knees before a new miraculous image of Mary. Now only you, Queen of Heaven, can help me—he begged her—if everything is not to be lost. That is, if Christendom is still dear and beloved to you. In tears, the young commander prayed to this for-eign Virgin with the cross medallion.

It was the first copy of the *Morenita* to reach Europe; it was María of Guadalupe. The year before, Alonso Montú-far, the new archbishop of Mexico, had had it made and had shipped it as a gift to the king of Spain. Philip II had passed it on to John of Austria, who, in turn, entrusted the Madonna to Admiral Andrea Doria, a man of his own age, as a "pallium" to bring good fortune, like a protective cloak in the decisive duel at arms.

When Andrea Doria returned to the deck, the wind had changed. A storm unleashed itself and swept the Turkish ships out of formation, dispersing them. Suddenly the Euro-peans could use the strength and scope of their firepower. The Spaniards boarded Ali Paşa's flagship and beheaded Selim's best admiral right on the deck. The Turks panicked and were unable to maneuver. Those who could swim tried to reach land through a blood-red sea. Those who could not, clung to flotsam. It was a horrific battle, an overwhelming victory for Christendom. Between the morning of October 7, 1571, and early afternoon, here on these waves, in this bay, at least thirty thousand Turks and 7,600 Christians died. (Four hundred years later, in World Wars I and II, the German submarine fleet lost 33,472 men.) On that day, fifteen thousand Christians were freed from the Turkish galleys where they had been chained to their oars. Very dramatically and for the first time, the victory put a stop to the triumphant spread of Ottoman Islam to the West. From that day, Turkish sea power kept declining.

I had read many accounts of all this, including many accounts of the battle, without finding a single mention of the Virgin's intervention. They all mention only the favorable wind. It is difficult to identify historical sources. The principal witness about the number of mortalities is the chronicler Wilhelm Dilich, who was born in the year of the battle.

Only three things are certain. First, against all likelihood, the Christians won the battle decisively. Second, afterward, the Genoese fleet attributed the victory to the Virgin of Guadalupe. Third, it is certain that Andrea Doria carried the first copy of the apocalyptic Madonna of Guadalupe to reach Europe. I saw it with my own eyes after I returned from my first trip to Mexico and before I set out for Jerusalem.

In July 1999, many hours from France, we traveled over a highway flanked by oleander that went through the mountains, tunnels and bridges of Liguria, above the sea, past the colossal city of Genoa, tucked into two valleys. Then we climbed the Apennines, along a road full of dangerous curves, until, finally, we reached our destination, a tiny church in a high valley, where we parked our car under a broad chestnut tree. We were at Santa Stefano d'Aveto.

With stiff legs we crossed over the main gate, pushed open a side door, searched in the half-light for the image of the Madonna, and then stopped to the right of a painting of Christ's face covered in blood, with bloodied red hair, and, the crown of thorns removed, full of puncture wounds on brow and temples. But not a trace of the Madonna we had traveled so far to see. We rang the rectory bell. From a window, the sacristan yelled that we had to go to the next village.

In the next village, a few twists and turns higher, the door was wide open to a church full of light. It was late afternoon. About twenty women and a few men were praying the rosary: *Ave Maria, piena di grazia, il Signore è con te* ... Like links in an endless chain the parts of the prayer were intertwined: Amen, Ave, Amen, Ave, Amen, Ave ... But all my attention was focused on the *Morenita* in a richly decorated frame, very high up above the main altar. Yes, surely, this had to be the one. The first authenticated copy of the Virgin of Mexico, painted in exact detail and with great skill. Surrounded by the rays of the sun, in an oval of clouds, with the stars on her cloak, with a black moon at her feet, with her four praying fingers, with the small feathered man at the hem of her clothing, with the translucent veil of flowers, with lowered eyes and bronzed skin, with the folds of her robe and her cloak. Nothing was missing. The copyist had added only a nine-pointed crown. Finally, this copy also bears witness that, at least since 1570, the original has not changed color because of environmental pollution or climatic conditions.

After the battle of Lepanto, the image had been in the possession of the Doria family, in the Malaspina Castle, outside Genoa, until Cardinal Giuseppe Doria willed it, in 1811, to the tiny highland parish of Santa Stefano d'Aveto, whose church became a shrine for pilgrims.

A year after the naval victory, Pope Pius V made October 7 a new feast and added it to the Catholic liturgical
calendar. It was called Our Lady of Victory, but was soon
changed to Our Lady of the Rosary. The Venetian senate
then moved that, below the painting of the battle of Lepanto,
there should appear the words: "The victory was ours, not
because of power or arms or admirals, but because of Mary
of the Rosary." Many cities added to their shields the image
of Mary standing on a crescent moon.

This overwhelming event gave rise to the ceiling decoration of Santa Maria in Aracoeli on Rome's Capitoline Hill
and to the innumerable images in many baroque churches
in the Western Hemisphere, including the church of the
Visitation in Ain Karim, near Jerusalem, where Mary and
Elizabeth are supposed to have met. To secure a good outcome of the battle, Pius V had called Western Christendom to a prayerful offensive by means of the rosary. While
the battle was still raging at sea, in Rome the rosary
confraternities processed through the streets praying the rosary.
Through the documents in the Vatican of the later canonization of Pius V, we know that the Pope confided to his
most trustworthy associates that he had had a vision of the
triumph of the Christians. Afterward he added to the Hail
Mary a second part, commonly used today, beginning: "Holy
Mary, Mother of God!" (Before that, it had consisted only
of the greeting of the angel Gabriel to Mary in Nazareth
and the greeting of her cousin Elizabeth in the hill country
of Judea: "Hail, Mary! The Lord is with you, blessed are
you among women and blessed is the fruit of your womb,
Jesus.")

Shortly afterward, in Mexico, the rumor spread that the
Pope had taken the additional part straight from the greeting with which the Virgin introduced herself to Juan Diego
in the half-light of dawn on Tepeyac Hill, December 9,

1531: "Know and understand, smallest of my sons! I am the most holy, ever-virgin Mary, Mother of the true God."

The next morning our ship dropped anchor in the harbor of Ancona. It was a Sunday. Fifteen minutes by car, south from the port, on the road to Rome, we celebrated the first Mass in our new homeland on a laurel-covered hill near the highway. The great Basilica della Santa Casa in the little city of Loreto, on a hill near the Adriatic coast, is the most important Marian shrine among the 1500 Italian churches dedicated to Mary, because here, so they say, and not in Nazareth, the House of the Incarnation has been venerated since the fifteenth century. In a house on a hill in the March of Ancona, Mary was thought to have conceived her Son. For centuries millions of European pilgrims, who have harbored no doubts about all this, have been drawn to this place. In this *Santa Casa* they venerated the house in which the archangel Gabriel announced to the Virgin the birth of a Son without the intervention of a man. It is said that, later, *angeli* transported the house through the air on their shoulders to this spot. Very recently, the Vatican discovered documents from which scholars deduce that, in 1294, a certain Niceforos Angeli, of Palestine, made a gift to the son of the king of Naples of "holy stones carried from the house of our Lady, Virgin and Mother of God". *Angeli*, that is, angels, did in fact transport the Holy House from Palestine to Italy. All the stones in this little house are foreign to the region, but not foreign to the region above Gennesaret, which we had left less than a week before.

Even from the highway along the seacoast to Pescara, one can see the dome that arches over the forty-square-yard room. Inside the basilica, a sumptuous marble shrine adorns the empty space. The room of Loreto is made of stones cut in the style of Palestinian Nabateans. They are red, white, black, gray and yellow and have been kissed and worn smooth up to eye-level. In this house of Joseph the carpenter, Mary had lived many years; as a child, Jesus had played here, and within its walls he had grown up. And where else but between these walls would Joseph have died? An ancient door lintel can be discerned on the walls that at some time must have extended over the room's only door.

As I leaned on the doorpost, I was struck anew by the memory of the dialogue between Mary and Juan Diego, the widower in Mexico. An altar closes off the front part of the room. Over this altar is a black Madonna in a golden niche, decorated as extravagantly as the miraculous image of the Virgin in the original Guadalupe in southern Spain. Though this room is never empty, it is always very silent.

At the main entrance we picked up a souvenir copy of the Litany of Loreto, which originated here. As I drove across the Italian Marches, my wife read aloud, in Latin and German, one of the most beautiful texts in the literature of prayer: Kyrie eleison, Christe eleison, Kyrie eleison, Mater divinae gratiae, Mater purissima, Mater castissima, ora pro nobis. Pray for us! Holy Mary, Holy Mother of God, Holy Virgin of virgins, Mother of divine grace, Mother most amiable, Mother most admirable, Mother of good counsel, Mother of Golgotha, surrounded by the sun, crowned with stars, Virgin most powerful, Virgin most merciful. Mirror of justice, Seat of wisdom, Vessel of honor, Mystical Rose, Tower of David, Tower of ivory, House of gold, Ark of the covenant, Gate of heaven, Morning Star, Health of the sick, Refuge of sinners, Comforter of the afflicted, Help of Christians, Queen of angels, Queen of patriarchs, Queen of prophets, Queen of apostles, Queen of martyrs, Queen of all the saints, Queen assumed into heaven, You, Queen of the most holy rosary, Queen of families, Queen of peace, Queen of the heavenly Jerusalem ... pray for us, pray for us, pray for us ...

Late that same afternoon we arrived in Rome, two years to the date of our arrival in Jerusalem. From Israel, we had rented a house in the Via delle Grazie on the Tiber, the street of graces, and we discovered that it belonged to the parish of Santa Maria in Traspontina church, where Our Lady of Mount Carmel is venerated.

A few days after our arrival, I noticed that on a street corner farther up, a woman was blessing herself before a mosaic of a Madonna in which Mary, framed by a laurel wreath and black marble, with a distracted look nursing the ecstatic Child on her arm and covered in a cloak of stars, with a grill of roses before her. I went up, moved the flower pots to one side and read the inscription below the image: "Hail in this image the most holy Virgin Mary, full of grace, whom brother Albenzio de Rossi brought to Rome from Jerusalem in 1587."

While we were still waiting for the moving van, I wanted to look for the tomb of the man who had prevented Europe from becoming Muslim. Pius V, dressed in white and violet, lies in a glass coffin in the Sistine Chapel of Saint Mary Major. Above the coffin, to the left, a scene of the battle of Lepanto is reproduced in marble. A tour guide was telling a group of pilgrims from Washington, D.C., that Pius V was the pope who introduced the use of the white cassock for the bishops of Rome on Peter's chair; before him, they had dressed in red like all other cardinals. Then he took the group to the crypt under the main altar, where pieces of the manger in Bethlehem were displayed under glass. Lastly, he took them to the Pauline chapel, where lovers of Rome are drawn to an ancient image of Mary over the altar, the *Salus Populi Romani*, Protrectress (or Health) of the Roman People. The docent smilingly told the pilgrims traveling from the capital of the most recent empire that Romans thought that Luke personally painted the image. Scientists, on the other hand, are still arguing if it comes from the eighth or the thirteenth century. But Romans are certain that Helen, the mother of the emperor Constantine, brought the image to this Marian basilica, the most ancient in Rome, in the fourth century.

The previous occupant of our new residence had been a priest who died the previous summer, at ninety years of age. In the 1950s, he had been working in Jerusalem at the request of Pope Pius XII. I would have liked to meet him. As we were setting up the rooms, our neighbors from below came up to tell us that, previously, a life-size image of a Mexican Madonna had hung on our dining-room wall. The sister of the deceased had given it away.

The *Morenita* had been awaiting us here. But not only us. In a thousand images Mary awaits the visitor on every corner, in every nook and cranny, down even the most hidden alleys. In the very ancient church of San Nicola in Carcere, fronting Tiber Island, a Mass of thanksgiving is celebrated in a side chapel on the twelfth of every month, under an ancient painting brought from Mexico. It seems as if all the beauty of Christian Rome is dedicated to her. I have never seen a city more Marian. Meanwhile, on television, images of Bethlehem shine out, which in close-ups show a statue of the Queen of Peace that has just been riddled with bullets: the nose shot off, the mouth bashed in, outstretched hands torn off, clothing in tatters, and at her right breast, a hole the size of a fist.

Also, in the kiosk next to Saint Peter's square, the same picture appears in every newspaper. We had not yet finished hanging our pictures on the walls when we got a call from Jerusalem: Bargil Pixner had died suddenly. His Benedictine brothers had buried him in their garden on Mount Zion, and they had laid his cane alongside the wall nearby, less than a hundred yards behind Mary's *mikva*, which he had excavated higher up.

CHAPTER TWENTY-TWO

A STAR-STUDDED FIELD OF LOVE

Nights without sleep; flowers dancing and a magic triangle of views about the inclusion of an old Indian in the list of saints. Mary's star-studded cloak around the hips of Christ crucified, and a star-studded field of love for Peter's successor.

So my trip to Jerusalem ended—and was extended—in Rome, the trip that had started three years earlier with a "letter from heaven". I was now unexpectedly sitting on the same plane with Aura. Of course I had not forgotten what she had said to me on March 25, 2000, in the Garden of Gethsemane. I kept looking out the window of the plane, even though the sky had become overcast. Twilight was falling over Mexico City as the plane prepared to put down. No flashing mirrors greeted us from the ground, only the lights of the megacity in mist and drizzle. I saw the enormous city below the plane and looked at Aura. She laughed: "What do you expect in this weather and this light?" I looked down again. The Pope was sitting in the forward part of the plane, in a cabin constructed especially for him, and he, too, was looking at the city.

If someone had asked me how I had embarked on this trip with the Pope, I could not have explained it. I could never have planned or organized all this. Neither love nor money would have been enough to get me a ticket from the Vatican. Or, above all, to have me sent these years as correspondent from Jerusalem to Rome. I had been granted wishes I did not even know I had; I could never have imagined it enough to fantasize about it. My life had become as mysterious as the city below, which came to meet us in the failing light, as mysterious as the Pope whom I again had the privilege of accompanying on this trip.

The old pontiff was scarcely able to walk or speak; nevertheless, he still sang and could string together historic moments. While I was still in Jerusalem, seven months earlier, on December 12, the anniversary of Mary's apparition on Tepeyac Hill, he had opened, with a click of a mouse on a laptop in the Vatican, a website on the Virgin of Guadalupe. The program, which intended to make the most-visited Marian shrine available also to virtual pilgrims, was called "Fuerza de la fe", which was now the program of his visit, "The Strength of Faith".

A cannon salute greeted us at the airport, followed by a reception, in a festively decorated hangar by the runway, attended by the nation's highest dignitaries. Even President Fox was there. For the first time in the recent history of the nation of believers, who had endured a century of radical hostility and rigorous fanaticism regarding the separation of Church and state power, a president was there to kiss the Pope's trembling hand. The man who the next day would canonize the visionary Juan Diego in the Guadalupe basilica had an enormous significance for the nation, the president said in his speech of welcome, as the basilica was "Mexico's shrine of the presence of the Patroness of Mexico, the Mother of God of Guadalupe. It is the most precious and most beautiful possession of the Mexican people."

At the hotel I got a new press card for the next three days, where, on a kind of credit card, my photo beneath a glimmering silvery photo of the Pope, Juan Diego and the Virgin of Guadalupe was fused on top of a cross. By its side: 5th Visit of John Paul II—July 30, 31 and August 1, 2002.

His fifth trip to Mexico took John Paul II once more to where he had begun his trips in January 1979. María of Guadalupe is the secret of his mysteriously powerful pontificate. He dedicated his service or ministry to her as, perhaps, only some medieval knights before him had done before leaving for Jerusalem. "Since January 29, 1979, she has been directing my steps", he said fearlessly. That was the first time he saw her image. He had come to the image of María of Guadalupe even before shaking up Poland and the Soviet bloc with his first visit. Now he kept it on his desk.

After we left for the basilica on Tepeyac, a hummingbird darted through the roses in front of the hotel. Everywhere during the last three years, birds and flowers had reminded me of the widower Juan Diego, soon to be inscribed among the saints. The brighter they were, the more they reminded me, and the most beautiful species most of all.

Through the metropolitan chaos, under police escort with flashing lights, a bus carried the journalists from the Pope's plane to the shrine where the Pope wanted to canonize Juan Diego immediately. Behind me were nights with almost no sleep, filled with work, work, work. Three hours of sleep, night before last, four hours, the night before that, last night, up until one, writing my penultimate article, up at seven to write the last one, looking forward to writing the next one in the afternoon. The Pope left us breathless with his speed through time and climate zones past fixed deadlines in far-off Berlin. I no longer even knew what I had written during the week or what had or had not been published. Before I left Rome, pickpockets had stolen my cell phone. It had been a long time since I had spent a week without a telephone in my pocket.

Now I had on my best suit and bow tie. On the bus I noticed that the fabric of my expensive pants was already frayed, even though I had not worn them more than a couple of times in the past ten years. Through the window I looked at the mountains surrounding the sea of buildings. It looked like rain. At dinner in Guatemala the previous afternoon I had heard colleagues say that today the Pope was going to canonize a phantom. Before the canonization, the historian Eduardo Chávez Sánchez published a heavily researched tome proving, with laborious precision, the historical authenticity of the Amerindian visionary. This only confirmed two of my neighbors at table in their suspicions.

The northern part of the city was completely deserted; soldiers blocked all points of access. During the previous visit of the Pope, two million people had made it absolutely impossible to get anywhere. The year before, when the canonization of the Amerindian was announced, there was talk of the largest celebration of the Eucharist in the history of the Catholic Church ("with twenty million people attending"); now the police were rigorously limiting the number of visitors allowed. Were they afraid that uncontrollable masses of people would take the shrine by storm and rip it to pieces out of sheer love? A Mexico City without people is an unforgettable image.

The tent-shaped roof of the new Basilica of Guadalupe finally rose above the rooftops into the sky before us, like the cone of a volcano, like one of those smoking volcanoes that just days before surrounded the racetrack in Guatemala while the Pope canonized Brother Pedro for the Mayan people. The streets of Guatemala covered in flowers, became, in Mexico, boulevards strewn with orchids all the way to the image of Mary in the basilica.

On top of all this, the jubilation when, appearing in the doorway, the stooped Pope was the first to lift his eyes toward her, before whom, twenty-three years before, he had begun his pilgrim life in the shoes of the fisherman. In our day, she has no greater lover than he. When he lifted a hand in blessing, a storm of joy swept over the crowd. When, near the altar, he sank into a seat, he lifted both arms. His first words were: "I praise you, Father, Lord of heaven and earth, because you have hidden all this from the wise and learned and have revealed it to the simple and to children" (Mt 11:25). "There are ten thousand people in a basilica that can hold only six thousand", asserted Andrew, a clown without his makeup, who was a volunteer providing crowd control in the back rows. "There are 17,000 in the forecourt of the basilica and five million on the other side of the traffic barricades."

In the last ten days, the Pope, with the strength of a weightlifter, had kept the journalists at a trot. But now his head had almost sunk into his shoulders. His miter, if not falling off, was sliding down his head. The pointed bishop's hat was at a quarter to twelve. The exertions of the last week were etched in his face. But, when in a loud voice he began to inscribe Juan Diego "in the catalogue of saints", Mexico was beside itself. Maracas in thousands of hands filled the space with their sound; shell horns and drums resounded; a procession of Aztecs in great peacock headdresses came forward dancing slowly through the main door in a hypnotic rhythm, danced with a measured tread before the Pope, circled the altar like a living floral arrangement, performed a feather dance under the image of the Virgin, until the dancers fell before a nearby cross, from which hung Mary's Son, whose hips were draped with the starry cloak of the Mother. At the end of the procession, an old image of Juan Diego was carried in and placed to the right of Mary. Now, he was looking at her as he had 471 years before. Women in multicolored fiesta costumes placed braziers of burning copal, the ancient Aztec incense, below the "Speaking Eagle". Surely, that day, the eagle himself was smiling and probably, now as then, was saying about himself: "Am I worthy or deserving of what I am seeing? Or am I still dreaming? Where am I? Am I perhaps already in heaven?" It was a dream, a celebration like no other.

The rattles seemed to go on forever. "After long reflection and testing, after repeated prayers for divine help and after much consultation with my brother bishops, by the authority of our Lord Jesus Christ, of the apostles Peter and Paul and my own, I declare blessed Juan Diego Cuauhtlatoatzin a saint and inscribe him officially in the catalogue of the saints; from this day forward, he should be venerated as such throughout the Church." Unceasing jubilation and rattles.

The Eucharistic celebration began. The first reading was from Paul's First Letter to the Corinthians: "But God chose what is foolish in the world to shame the wise, God chose what is weak in the world to shame the strong, God chose what is low and despised in the world, even things that are not, to reduce to nothing things that are" (1 Cor 1:27–28). Then the Gospel was proclaimed in Nahuatl and Spanish: *Immanon, Jesutzin omotlahtolti, ohmitlahui: "Nehuatl nimitzmoteochihuilia, tatahtzin, ilhuicatl ihuan tlalticpac tlacatecuhtzintli, ipampa inin tlamantili otiquimmotlatilihi in talmatinimeh in mozcalianime ihuan otquimmonextilili in tziquitzitzin. . . .* At that time Jesus declared, 'I thank you, Father, Lord of heaven and earth, that you have hidden these things from the wise and understanding and revealed them to infants'" (Mt 11:25). Don Guido from Radio Telepace placed a microphone before me, asking me to say a few words for the Vatican Radio listeners worldwide.

I felt as if I were dozing. Where was I? Three years after first hearing the story of the Virgin María of Guadalupe, I suddenly found myself with the Pope, who had returned to say good-bye to his most beloved image—although not nearly as close to her image as I had been the first time. From the last row in the basilica, with binoculars, I could see how the smoke of the incense rose in a heavy fog to the image; and she emerged once more from this fog as from the clouds, as she had in her first apparition.

It was yet another triumph. Nevertheless, in recent years North American sects had bought whole María of Guadalupe villages with their dollars or also, sometimes, with forty sewing machines. On this day, a new massacre in Jerusalem swept the Pope out of the headlines and stories once again. "Today he'll only get twenty seconds", a colleague complained about an American transmission. Somewhere in the megacity two shots had been fired. Could this possibly have been an attempt against the Pope? Like a small cloud, the smoke of the censers permeated the basilica and hung over the Pope. From his new image, Juan Diego looked up toward his old tilma, which now hung on the lower wall, like a delicate painting set in a heavy frame of gold and silver roses. But on this day, Mary had lowered her gaze totally toward the old man with white hair who was at the altar dressed in ancient Roman feast-day vestments. It was a magic triangle of glances. Juan Diego raised his eyes to Mary; Mary lowered her glance to John Paul; the Pope gazed inward, his head bowed. When he raised his hand with the host, his face still and intent, he leaned his hands on the altar, his legs having become weak. But on Mary's face again that inward-turning half smile of an unborn: "Juan, dear; dearest Juan Diego!"

My room in the large modern hotel could not be compared with the hotel of my first trip. Here everything was in working order. It was large, well lit, with a hermetically sealed window, on the sixteenth floor, with a view over the rooftops of Mexico City—and sinfully expensive. That night, when I sent my story to Berlin, I was so exhausted I could scarcely eat. Not even a tequila could awaken my appetite.

I had hired a taxi to drive me through the rain and the city at night to the main plaza, the Zócalo, and the old cathedral of Mexico City. Would the Amerindians perhaps dance again in the enormous plaza—and the girl who could fly like an eagle—all of which had never left my mind ever since? The windshield wipers battled with torrents of water. The windows steamed up. The cabdriver was a newly converted evangelical who had not only learned a crude American English, but wanted straight off to convert me with it. More, he wanted to warn me against the use of images. And, naturally, against the Pope. It was raining so hard in the Zócalo that there was no question of getting out of the taxi. The driver said that he "had been a bad Catholic", but now, at last, had become "a good Christian" who could not wait to rise to Jesus at the moment of his death. When he left me at the hotel, he snatched a Bible from the back seat to show me the place in the book of Genesis where the use of images was forbidden.

Next morning we traveled by car to the Basilica of Guadalupe, once more to the *Morenita*, under whose gaze the Pope beatified two Amerindians martyred in 1700. Again there were feather dances, but this time with other rhythms, other flowers, other perfumes; then the Pope gave the blessing, and an Amerindian woman dressed in multicolored swaths of wool offered me a branch from a bunch of aromatic *Yodo* with which she had stroked the Pope. Then, by bus with the flashing lights of the escort, we went directly from the basilica to the airport.

The long route was a narrow passage through human beings, all waiting, all gesturing. As the Pope again struggled step by step up to the handrail of the gangway to the front door of the plane, I again stuck my head out the back door. In the hatchway, the Pope turned and made the biggest sign of the cross I ever saw him make over Mexico. At three fifteen the plane began to taxi to the runway. At that moment I saw something like a lightning flash begin along the airstrip. Then it did not cease until it had spread over the whole horizon. I pressed my nose to the window. It was not an electrical storm. Along the whole long strip, clusters of human beings behind the barricades were sending messages of light with mirrors large and small, pieces of glass, from trees and rooftops, behind every shrub. Banners streamed from their midst, waving without end.

When the plane finally took off, millions must have been gathered on the hills and in the streets of the city. Brilliant flashes and sparkles of light crossed the space toward us from everywhere, from every corner, street and alley. Cutting through scattered patches of fog and clouds, the flashes flamed out toward us, flashes great and small, by which the Mexicans wanted to shift the sun's light like an explosion from the sea of houses to the Pope who was saying good-bye to them. It was as if heaven and earth had joined in a sea of sparks, an image as impossible to reproduce as that of the Madonna who was among them.

On his journeys, the Pope really strung together a series of great moments, but these moments were incredible: a gigantic city glimmering with affection in the bright afternoon; the sparkling veneration of a whole nation for him and for his great love. This was the quintessence of the whole trip. The flickering jumped from house to house, from roof to roof, as if lighting up automatically, like sparks in a field of stubble. It was no spectacle of nature, but rather one of a unique culture. I thought about the poor people who had been waiting down there for hours, mirror in hand, who might have been overshadowed by a cloud at the decisive moment when we passed over.

Not one of the people down there could see what we in the plane were seeing or know how many of us there were. There were seventy journalists altogether; forward, there were the Pope and some thirty of his Vatican entourage. With the final lessening of pressure, some colleagues seated in the middle of the plane had fallen asleep, others had adjusted their sleep shades in preparation for sleep, and others, exhausted, were paging through newspapers. Aura, whom I had first seen smiling two years before in Jerusalem, was laughing. How many people have ever seen anything like this? What was it? Heaven had touched earth; a field of stars had covered the city in broad daylight; flashes leapt from house to house. The remodeled Aeromexico plane turned one last time, flying low in a farewell swing over the sea of houses of the metropolis, which is home to three times the population of Switzerland and twice as large as London.

Now once again we flew over the basilica where the *Morenita* is venerated. For the old, bent Pope, who was looking at all this from the window of his forward cabin, the starry field of love covered the enormous Mexico City, not for a brief moment and not only for the time it took to sing a song. It lasted seventeen whole minutes, until a cloud finally swallowed us up, and we broke through into the clear blue of the sky.

CHAPTER TWENTY-THREE

MIRIAM, MARYAM, MARÍA

Returning with the Pope from Mexico to Rome; dawn in the cosmos; blessing-fatigue; a mother holding a newborn; a burning heart; a window to heaven; face to face with the Virgin María of Guadalupe.

It got dark. In his separate cabin in the front of the plane to the right, a bed had been installed for the Pope; he was asleep under an image of the *Morenita*. It was not a quiet night. Because of stormy winds, the plane was flying at very high altitude, at more than 36,000 feet. My neighbor from the CNN network was asleep; almost all my colleagues were asleep. But when I raised the curtain on the window a little, it was already becoming light again below us, at first very slowly, because we were flying against the clock. A thick, undulating blanket of clouds spread from horizon to horizon, immensely fragile and soft. We were already over Spain. In the distance, at first light, the outer fringes of cloud were already turning a soft pink.

Suddenly below us the horizon turned that unmistakable shade which I had last seen three years before on the tilma, right behind the *Morenita*. It is the background color from which the Virgin of Guadalupe emerges; that unearthly dawn-pink, above the clouds, and not the usual earthly dawn-red, not even that seen over the desert or the ocean. Perhaps astronauts can see it better. The open sky that no painter can capture. That was the precise color. I will not be able to forget it to my dying day.

It happened before I was sent to Jerusalem, before I met Mathias Döpfner, before eternity itself; it happened three years ago on the last morning before I left Mexico. The night before, the view from Tepeyac Hill had been extraordinarily clear. The rain had washed away the smog. Suddenly, before me lay the enormous city, truly like the largest city on earth, it seemed like the center of the cosmos, very like the place where God descended to earth.

The outline of the mountains circled the city like points in a crown. From the top of the Tepeyac I scanned the city with my binoculars again, in all directions; the city that a week before I had explored on foot, by cab and by metro. Now I noticed that the hill of the apparitions lay due north of the Mexico City cathedral. Thus the extension of the street that in my line of sight leads from the foot of the hill to it must have been the very path that Juan Diego took to the ancient Aztec capital. A glance could take in the great pyramid, whose foundations are still next to the cathedral, the last remnant of the temple complex that dominated what was once the heart of the ancient empire of the Mexicans. By Cortés' command, after the destruction of Tenochtitlán, the capital was to be rebuilt even more magnificently. More men worked on the project "than had in the construction of Solomon's temple in Jerusalem", wrote the Franciscan Brother Motolinía. In sixteenth-century Europe, which built feverishly, "no construction project even remotely equaled the magnitude, the ambition and the opulence of this undertaking", I had read in Hugh Thomas' book. Now in the megametropolis, something of all this can be detected only if one consciously searches for it.

In the days previous, each and every day, for many hours, I had looked carefully at the image of Mary than at any other wonder of the world: close up, far away, with the naked eye, with binoculars. Every day I went to meet her in a different way. As in no other church, I saw tears all around me. Perhaps the colors shift according to the quantity

of tears, from every corner, on every day, and also according to the heaviness and pain that are raised up to her every
day. Depending on the distance, the colors seem different.
From one specific perspective, the gold turns to silver; from
another, it turns black. From afar, one has the impression
that her eyes are closed, as they are downcast. Close up,
seen from below, it was as if one were gazing, in the folds
of her gown, into some Gothic space, yet living, breathing,
of perfect stature and perfectly proportioned. The image
sheds light. A supernatural shimmer surrounds the Virgin,
like that of velvet or silk. The golden roses are not woven
into her gown but float around her body between gown
and mantle, with no relation to the folds of her robe, as if
on some kind of gauzy and completely invisible veil.

The *Immaculata*, the *Purísima*. The apparitions of Mary
announce the return of Christ, I had read somewhere. She
was already present before his birth in Bethlehem and before
the birth of Christendom on Mount Zion. Wherever she
now appears, she would remain the foremost messenger of
his return for the Last Judgment. From the other side of
the cosmos, she would be looking at whoever is contemplating her, Don Mario had said. Standing beneath her, with
binoculars, was like surfing stellar space. I would never get
enough of it. As at my last visit to Turin, as I entered, on
this morning of my good-bye visit, the Benedictus was being
sung, this time in Spanish: "Bendito sea el Señor, Dios de
Israel—Blessed be the Lord, the God of Israel!"

"Monsignor!" I said to Monsignor Warnholtz in the crypt
of the church, on the last morning before my afternoon
flight back to Europe, "You have to help me out today." I
had visited Carlos Warnholtz for the first time a few days
earlier. He is a tall man, a canon lawyer, liturgist and moral
theologian of seventy-four, who was a professor for forty-
five years and now volunteered in the basilica, where he

had a modern, well-furnished office on the first floor. I was in admiration of his elegant tailored suit, after having come to know Don Mario in his white vestments and Don Guerrero a bit neglected in black.

Don Carlos had shown me the Aztec text of the *Nican Mopohua*. At his side, full of wonder but understanding nothing, I had looked at the strange writing as though it were a missing manuscript of Rabbi Löw from ancient Prague. This priest with a German name was a winking skeptic and a charming conversationalist who called the Virgin *Morenita* or also *Virgencita*. But unfortunately he amounted to nothing, he complained: "All I do is bless, bless, bless. All day long without stopping, bless!" Bless people, bless crosses, rosaries, images of the Virgin, statues of Juan Diego and Saint Jude Thaddeus. There are 1600 confraternities of pilgrims. The main altar, below the miraculous image, is always in use: the church is always crammed, Mass after Mass—as if this, and not Rome or Jerusalem, were the heart of Christendom. An especially beautiful day is the feast of the bird sellers, when the central corridor's balustrades to the right and left of the miraculous image are totally filled with the most beautiful birdcages for all imaginable types of songbirds with the most beautiful voices and most exquisite plumage; but then the church is crammed to the bursting point, which makes even more work for him. But even on ordinary days there is Mass every hour, from six in the morning to eight at night, always for a new group. Every year, millions of pilgrims, rivers of people, pass beneath the Virgin, and what they want most is to be blessed, one by one. So I, too, asked him for his blessing, which he gave me on the threshold with a sigh.

"You know that I came here especially from Germany", I said before the good-byes. "I want, need to write a book about the Virgin of Guadalupe. Would you be able to help me get closer to her? As close as possible?" He looked at me closely, pausing to think, and nodded: "OK, come along."

In front of the basilica I had bought the most beautiful bouquet of flowers from a flower stall—roses and carnations in a porcelain vase—and, like a true Mexican, had placed it as close as possible along the Virgin's line of vision. Then we went into the basement, past two guards in the information section, through a door set into the cement wall, and took an elevator up to an enormous sacristy where various clergymen were milling around. I was in a dream state as I followed him through a side door on the left, leading to the area around the main altar. The church was at the bursting point; the seats around the altar were filled with priests. Norberto Rivera Carrera, the cardinal archbishop and primate of Mexico, was preaching from his episcopal chair. Don Carlos led me to a place exactly behind his chair, shoulder to shoulder with the archbishop, where the image of the Virgin is hanging on the wall only about two or three yards behind him, and he stood only a couple of steps away. It would have been impossible to get any closer to the Virgin. I had my binoculars in hand.

How long was I standing there before her—five minutes? Ten? Time stood still, my biological clock stopped. At two yards, with binoculars, I set about carefully reexamining the Virgin as a cosmic apparition, as a constellation in the Milky Way. She is multidimensional: two, three, four, five, six, seven dimensions. And yes, she really is pregnant. Otherwise, the expression on her face would be completely incomprehensible. She is Mary of the Visitation. She is the Mother of the Magnificat. This is how she had to have gone to visit her cousin Elizabeth in the Judean hills, with that same look on her face:

My soul magnifies the Lord,
and my spirit rejoices in God my Savior, ...
for he who is mighty has done great things for me,
and holy is his name. ...
He has shown strength with his arm,
he has scattered the proud in the imagination of their hearts,
he has put down the mighty from their thrones,
and exalted those of low degree. (Lk 1:46–52)

It is a unique moment of her existence. As closely united as she was to her Son in his Passion and death, she was never again as closely united to him as during her pregnancy. This is the period of the greatest closeness of her life to his. The Lord is with her. The small face at her feet looks pensively up past me.

Then suddenly I recognized myself in him, but when I was too young to remember. An old dream suddenly awakened in me. I am in bed, and in the next room I hear a woman sighing and groaning; I get up, go to the other room and see my mother, smiling and exhausted, lying on pillows, with a newborn in her arms. I go up to her and the newborn and see that it is myself, with eyes closed. I wake up.

Suddenly I felt myself as light as if I had wings. My heart was beating in my throat. My breathing had become an *Ave*. The image was breathing. All that I had seen of her before was erased—as was every line of this book and every experience of my life. Whoever would want to could settle the disputes about the formation of the image, if it was painted or what was painted or not painted. Here there was no dissension. Here there was a person in front of me, not an image, even though her face seemed like an ancient photo, a slide of an existence that was in a window of an alternate world on a new horizon of a four-hundred-year-old dawning, a delicious face, like the most mature wine, "a little darker than a pearl", a face like a radiant monstrance.

Here was the real City of the Dawn, next to her, around her. The clouds opened almond-shaped, and so, too, her mantle fell apart at the golden trim, as the intersection, so to speak, between heaven and earth, between being and that which exists. Her dress shone like the sun. The sea-green-blue of her cloak was unfaded from the day Miguel Cabrera described it in 1756. Peace shed light behind her. A paradisial brilliance like velvet and silk surrounded the Virgin. "You are beautiful, full of beauty, daughter of Jerusalem, rising in the morning like the red of dawn." She is the Queen of the Song of Solomon. O my child! Forgive me for coming so late. But you know that I had a great deal to do. O, *Morenita!* My *Morenita!* O my little Miriam, Maryam, María!

"Am not I, your Mother, here?" Her fathomless eyes answer yet again—in German, Spanish, English, French, Italian, Aramaic, Arabic, Nahuatl, in all the languages on earth. It is a miracle, her eyes say, a totally new way, against all expectations, a totally unexpected turning is always possible. An indescribable, preoccupied grief plays about her lips. "Now, so that there be realized what my merciful glance desires: *Auh inic huelnelteiz in nicnemilia in noteic-noittalliz ma xiauh in ompa in itecpanchan.*"

She opened to me like a flower, from inside out. I clung to the binoculars for dear life. Her beating heart shone through her clothing: "the delectable fruit of the cactus for the eagle", her heart shone within her left hand. A flame flared above the place of the bubbling aorta. I could not do what the Aztecs did; I could not read what the flowers on her mantle were saying or read its stars or its unique, enigmatic details. I knew of visions only through books. In this moment I was aware of only one thing: how her left leg under her robe was flexed to take a step forward. She was approaching me; she approaches us from another world.

Voltaire was wrong. Whoever says that no one has ever returned from the other world not only does not believe in Christ's Resurrection but also makes no attempt to peer into this world. Here, anyone with open eyes can see that there is another world, that death is not the final blow, that what we do matters. That there is a place behind all our places. From there the Virgin Mary has come, through the burning red of all the apocalypses. She is here at the door. At heaven's gate.

Empires and ideologies have come and gone since Mary came here to meet men. Here dawn has been captured. The world will never again be what we have known it to be. But she is coming. She still keeps coming. She meets us in wars and floods, in blood and tears, in blasts and volleys of bullets, in falling buildings just built, collapsing towers, drums, shouts, horns, thunder of cannons and gunfire, ghosts and phantoms, terror and death, storm and wind and climate change, crashing databases, falling gods and idols, layoffs and joblessness, anguish and fear, trembling and uncertainty, dreams and nightmares. Through broken friendships, marriages and families, through broken arms, hearts, oaths and promises. Through broken trust and a broken world. Through all false doctrines, through every false appearance. Not to mention all lies. She comes for sinners and saints, for Jews and Muslims, for Israelis and Palestinians, for west and east, for north and south, for black and white, for red and yellow, for Christians, Hindus, Buddhists, agnostics, atheists and nihilists. Naturally, she also comes for the first cloned human being, if human beings refuse to stop even before this ultimate crime. She comes for everyone.

In the Basilica of Our Lady of Guadalupe, in northern Mexico City, anyone can look at her image. The Virgin

Mary was there and is there. She comes from the place where all tears are wiped away, with one foot in front of the other. She comes to us, pregnant. If only she could come sooner—and if possible, first to Jerusalem!

APPENDIX

FACSIMILE OF THE NAHUATL
EDITION OF THE *NICAN MOPOHUA*
PUBLISHED IN 1649

IMAGEN

DE

LA VIRGEN MARIA

MADRE DE DIOS DE GVADALVPE,

MILAGROSAMENTE APARECIDA EN LA CIVDAD DE MEXICO.

CELEBRADA

En su Historia, con la Profecia del capitulo doze del Apocalipsis. A devocion del Bachiller Miguel Sanchez Presbitero.

DEDICADA.

AL SEÑOR DOCTOR DON PEDRO DE BARRIENTOS Lonelin, del Consejo de su Magestad, Tesorero de la Santa Yglesia Metropolitana de Mexico, Governador, Prouisor, y Vicario de todos los Conventos de Religiosas de esta Ciudad, Consultor del Santo Officio de la Inquisicion. Comisserio Apostolico de la Santa Cruzada en todos los Reynos, y Prouincias de este Nueua España, &c.

Año de 1648.

CON LICENCIA. Y PRIVILEGIO,
En Mexico, En la Imprenta de la Viuda de Bernardo Calderon.
Vendese en su tienda en la calle de San Agustin.

HVEI

TLAMAHVIÇOLTICA,

OMONEXITI IN ILHVICAC TLATÓCA ÇIHVAPILLI

SANTA MARIA,

TOTLAÇONANTZIN

GVADALVPE IN NICAN HVEI ALTEPE-
NAHVAC MEXICO ITOCAYÒCAN TEPEYACAC.

Impreſſo con licencia en MEXICO : en la Imprenta de Iuan Ruyz.
Año de 1 6 4 9.

✠

NICAN

MOPOHVA,

MOTECPANA INQVENIN

.YANCVICAN HVEITLAMAHVIÇOLTICA
MONEXITI INÇENQVIZCA ICHPOCHTLI
SANCTA MARIA DIOS YNANTZIN TOÇI-
HVAPILLATOCATZIN, IN ONCAN
TEPEYACAC MOTENEHVA
GVADALVPE.

Acattopa quimottititzino

maçehualtzintli itoca Iuan Diego; Auh çatepan
nexiti initlaçò Ixiptlatzin ynixpan yancuican Ob:
D. Fray Iuan de Sumarraga. Ihuan inixquich tla
huiçolli ye quimochihuilia. ⌐

E iuh matlac xihuitl in opeuuak
atl in tepetl Mèxico, ynyecomoma
in mitl, in chimalli, in ye nohuia
ontlamatcamani in ahuàcan, intepe-
huàcan; in macaçan yeopeuh, yex
tla; ye cueponi intlaneltoquiliztli
iniximachocatzin inipalnemohuani
nelli Teotl DIOS. In huel iquac inipan Xihuitl mihto
y quinientos, y treinta y vno, quiniuh iquezquilhuial
in metztli Diziembre mochiuh oncatca çe mai tzint i,

A

tzintli, icnotlápiltzintli itoca catca Iuan Diego, iuh mi-
tôa ompa chane catca in Quauhtitlan, auh inica Teoyotl
oc mochompa pohuia in Tlatilolco, auh Sabado catca
huel oc yohipatzinco, qui hual tepoztocaya in Teoyotl,
yhuan ininetititlaniz; auh in àcico ininahuac tepetzintli initocaydcan Tepeyacac yctlatlalchipahua, concac
inicpac tepetzintli cuicoa, yuhquin nepapan tlaçototo-
mecuica, catahuani inintozqui, iuhquin quinánanquilia
Tepetl, huelçenca teyolquimà, tehuellamachti inin cuic,
quiçenpanahuia in coyoltototl, intzinitzcan, ihuan yn-
ocçeçain tlaçototome ic cuica: quimotztimoquetz in
Iuan Diego quimòlhui cuix nolhuil, cuix nomàçehual in-
yeniccaqui? àço çannictemiqui? àço çanniccochitlehua,
canin yenica, canin yoninozca, cuix yeoncan in inquito-
chuaque huehuetque tachtohuan, tocòcolhuan in xochi-
pan intonacatlalpan? cuix yeoncan in inilhuicatlal-
ompa on itztîcaya inicpac tepetzintli intonatiuh
içayanpa in ompa hualquiz tia inilhuicac tlaçòcuicatl.
h inoyuh çeuhtiquiz in cuicatl in omocactimoman in
cquicaqui hualnotzalo inicpac tepetzintli, quilhuia
antzin Iuan Diegotzin; ninari çayeêmòtlapaloa inic
pa yaz incanin notzalo, àquen mochihua yni yollo,
noçe itla ic miçahuia, yeçe huel paqui mohuella-
machtia, qui tlecahuîca intepetzintli, ompa itzta incápa
hualnotzaloc, auh inye àçitiuh inicpac tepetzintli, inye
oquimottili çe çihuapilli oncan moquetzindticac, qui-
hualmonochili inic onyaz ininahuactzinco; auh in oyuh
àcito inixpantzinco, cenca quimomahuiçalhui inqueni-
huellaçenpanahuia inicçenquizca mahuizticatzintli, ini-
pàcuentzin iuhquin tonatiuh icmotonameyotia inicpe-
mina ca, auh intetl, intexcalli inic itechmoquetza, inic qui-
quiztia ini tlanexyotzin yuhqui intlaçò chalchihuitl, nia-
li; inic neci yuhquin ayauh coçamalòcueçueyoca
in

2

intlalli; auh inmizquitl, ynnopalli, ihuan occequi nepa:
panxiuhtotontin oncan mochichihuani yuhquin quetza:
lietztli, yuhqui inteoxihuitl ini atlapallo icneci; auh ini:
quauhyo, ini huitzyo, ini ahuayo yuhqui incoztic teocuil:
tlatl icpepetlaca. Ixpātzinco mopechtecac, quicac iniyo-:
tzin, ini tlatoltzin inhuelçonca tehuellamiachti, inhueltec::
piltic yuhqui inquimoçoçonahuilia, quimotlatlaçotilia,.
quimolhuili, tlaxiccaqui no xocoyouh Iuantzincampa:
incimohuica? auh inyehuatl quimonanquililiNotecuiyoe,
Çihuapille Nochpochtzine ca ompa nonaçiz mochan-:
tzinco Mexico Tlatilolco, nocon tepotztoca inteoyetl,:
intechmomaquilia, intechmomachtilia inixiptlahuan in:
tlacatl inTotecuiyo, intoteopixcahuan. Niman yeic qui-
mononochilia, quimixpatilia initlaçotlanequiliztzin, qui-:
molhuilia, Maxiemati, mahuelyuhye inmoyolio no xo:
coyouh canehuatl inniçēquizca cemicac ichpochtli Sāti:
tā Maria inninantzin inhuelnelli Teotl Dios ic, acacornos:
huani, inteyocoyani, in Tloque Nahuaque, in ilhuicahua,
in Tlalticpaque, huelnicnequi, cenca niquelehuia inic
nican nechquechilizque noteocaltzin inoncan nic nex:
tiz, nicpantlaçaz, niētemacaz in ixquich notetlaçotla-
liz, noteicnoyttaliz, innotepalehuiliz, innotemanahuiliz
cañel nehuatl in na moicnohuācanantzin intehuati ihuan
in ixquichtin inic nican tlalpan ançepantlaca, ihuan in
occequin nepapantlaca notetlaçotlacahuan in notechmo-
tzatzilia, innech temoa innotech motemachilia, cā oncan niquincaquiliz inin choquiz, inin tlaocol inic nicyec:
tiliz, nic patiz inixquich. iepapan in netoliniliz, into:
nehuiz, in chichinaquiliz. Auh inic huelneltiz in nic ne:
tilia in innoteicno yttaliz ma xiauh in ompa ini teepā-
chan in Mexico Obispo, auhtiquilhuiz inquenin nehuatl
ninitztitlāni inic ticyxpantiz inquenin huelçenca nic-
elehuia inic ma nican nechcalti, nechquechiliz nican in

tlālmantli no teocal;huelmoch ticpohuiliz inixquich in
otiquittac, oticmahuiçò, ihuan intlein oticcac; auhma
yuhye inmoyollo cahuel nictlaçòcamatiz,auhcaniquix-
tlahuaz, ca icnimitz cuiltonoz,nimitztlamachtiz,yhuā
miec oncan ticmàçehuaz ic nicquepcayotiz ynmociahui-
liz inmotlatequipanoliz inic ticnemilitiuh intlein ie nimitztitlani: òcaycoticcac noxocoyouh ynniiyo innotlàtol maximohuicatiuh ma ixquich mo tlàpal xicmochi-
huili. Auh niman ic ixpantzinco onmo pechtecac quimolhuili no tecuiyoè,Çihuapillè caye ni yauh innic nel-
tiliz, inmiyòtzin , inmotlàtoltzin , ma ocnimitznotlal-
cahuili innimocno maçehual. Niman ic hualtemoc inic
quineltiliciuh ini netitlaniz connamiquizco incuep òtli
i̱ uallamelahua Mexico.

　In o àcico itic altepetl, niman ic tlamelauh ini Tec-
ṇ chantzinco Obiſpo inhuelyancuican hualmohuicac
ṇ ... ōm tlàtoihuani itocatzin catca,D. Fray Iuan de Su-
1a̍rraga S. Franciſco Teopixqui. Auh in o àcito niman
ic moyèyecva inic quimottiliz, quintlatlauhtia initetla-
yecoiticahuan, initlannencahuan inic conittotihuè, ye-
achi huècauhtica inconnotzaco, in ye omotlanahuatili in
Tlàtohuani Obiſpo inic calaquiz. Auh inoncalac niman
ixpantzinco motlanquaquetz , mopechtecac, niman ye
ic quimixpantilia quimopohuililia yniyotzin ynitlàtol-
tzin ilhuicac Çihuapilli, ini netitlaniz: no ihuan quimolhuilia inixquich oquimahuiçò, in oquittac, in oquicac.
Auh in oquicac inmochi itlatol,inetitlaniz iuhquin àmo
çenca monelchiuhtzino, quimonanquilili, quimolhuili
nopiltzè ma ocçeppa tihuallaz,oc ihuian nimitzcaquiz,
hueloc itzinècan niquittaz , nic nemiliz intlein ic otihualla inmotlanequiliz, inmotlaelehuiliz . Hualquiz-
tlaocoxtihuitz, inic àmo nimam oneltic ininetitlaniz...

　Niman hualmoquep izça ye iquàc ipan çemilhuitl,
　　　　　　　　　　　　　　　　　　　　niman

3

niman oncā huallamelauh inicpac tepetzintli, auh ipan-
tzinco àçito in ilhuicac Çihuapilli izçan ye oncan incanin acattopa quimottili, quimochialitica; auh in oiuh-
quimottili ixpantzinco mopechtecac motlalchitlaz quimolhuili, notecuiyoè, tlacatlè, Çihuápillè, no xocoyóhuè,
Nochpochtzinè caonihuia in ompa otinechmotitlanili,
ca onic neltilito in miiyotzin in motlàtoltzin maçihui
in ohuihuitica in onicalac inompa iyeyan teopixca Tlàtohuani, ca oniquittac, ca oixpan nidlali inmiiyotzin,
in motlàtoltzin inyuh otinech monànahuatili, oneci-
pacca celi, auh òquiyec cac; yece inic onech nanquili, yuhquin àmo iyollo ômàcic, àmo monelchihua, onechilhui
oceppa tihuallaz, oc ihuiyan nimitzcaquiz, hueloc itzinècan niquittaz intlein ic otihualla motlayelchuiliz, mo-
tlanequiliz. Huelitech oniquittac inyuh onech nanquili:
camomati inmoteocaltzin ticmonequiltia mitzmo chi-
huililizq nican àço çan nèhuatl nic yòyocoya, acaçomoi
motencopatzinco; caçenca nimitznotlatlauhtilia notecui
yoè, Çihuápillè Nochpochtzinè manoçoàca çeme intlaçò:
pipiltin iniximacho, inixtilò, in mahuiztilò itechxicmo-la
cahuili inquitquiz, yn quihuicaz in miiyotzin, yn motlàtoltzin, inic neltocoz; canel nicnotlapaltzintli, cani:
mecapalli, cani cacaxtli, cani cuitlapilli, canatlapalli, ca:
nitcòcani nimamaloni, càmo.no nènemian, càmo none:
quetzayan in ompa tinech mihualia Nochpochtzinè, No
xocoyohuè, Tlacatlè, Çihuápillè, ma xinech motlapòpol-
huili nic tequipachoz in mixtzin, in moyollotzin, ipan-
niyaz, ipan nihuetziz inmoçomaltzin, inmoqualantzin:
Tlacatlè Notecuiyoè. Quimonanquilili izçenquizca ma-
huiz ichpochtzintli tlaxiccaqui no xocoyouh mahuelo
iuhye inmoyollo càmo tlaçotin innotetlayecolticahuan ,i-
innotîtitlanhuan, inhuel intech nic cahuaz inquitquizq,
in niiyo, innotlàtol, inquineltilizque in notlanequiliz:

yéte huel iuhmonēqui ihié hueltēhuatl ic tinemiz, ipan
ti tlàtoz, huelmomātica neltiz mochihuaz, innoçializ,
iùnotlanequilíz; auh huelnimitz tlatlauhtia no xóco-
yóuh, yhuan nimitztlaqùauh nahuatia cahuel ocçeppa-
tiaz in moztlā tiquittatziuh in Obilpo auh nopampa xic-
nēmachti, huel yuh xic caquiti innoçializ, innotianequi-
liz, inic quineltiliz inquichihuaz neteócal niquitlanilia,
yhuanhuelocceppa xiquiñnui inquenin huelnēhuatl ni
kēmicac ichpochtli Sanҫ Maria in ninantzin Teoti Dios
in ompa nimitztitlani. Auh in Iuan Diego quimonanqui-
líli, quimolhuili noteuiyoè, Çihuapillè, Nochpochtz inè
macamo nic tequipacho in mixtzin, in moyollotzin ca
Çhuelnoçenyollocacopa nonyaz noconneltilitiuh inmiiyo-
ezin inmotlàtoltzin caniman amo nic nocacahualtia, manoçe nic tececocamati in õtli canon yaz canoçõnchihua-
tiuh in motlanequiliztzin, çan huelye in àçocàmo ni-
veccàtoz; intlanoce yconicacoc àcaçomo nineltocoz,
ca tel moztla ye teotlac inye oncalaqui tonatiuh, nic
icuepaquiuh inmiiyotzin inmotlàtoltzin intlein ic nech-
manquiliz in Teopixcatlatohuani, caye nimitznotlalca-
huilia no xocoyohué, Nochpochtzinè tlacatlè, Çihuapillè,
ma oc ximoçehuitzino, niman ic ya inichan moçehuito.
ix. Auh inimoztlayoc Domingo huel oc yòhuatzinco
tlatlayohuatoc ompahuālquiz inichan huallāmelauh in
Tlatilolco, quimattihuitz in Teoyotl, ihuan inic tèpo-
hualoz: nimanyè inicquittaz Teopixca tlàtohuani; auh
àço ycipan màtlaҫli hora inõneçencahualoc inic õmocac
Miſſa, ihuan otepohualoc ic hual xin inichquich maçe-
hualli; auh in yèhuatl Iuan Diego niman ic yà inïteç-
panchantzinco in Tlàtohuani Obiſpo, auh in õ àcito ix-
quichiclàpal quichiuh inic quimottiliz, auh huel ohui-
tica in occeppa quimottili, iexitlantzinco motlanquaquetz, choca, tlaocoya inicquimononochilia, inicquimix-
pantiⱼ

4

hantililia itiiyetz in inytlàtokz iuiin ilhuicac çihuapilli,
inic aço çanen noſtocoz iniinetitlaniz initlanequilztztzin
çenquizca ichpochtli; inic quimochihuililizque, inic
quimo quechililizque initeôcaltzin incanin omotlatene-
liuili incanin quimonequiltia. Auh in Tlàtohuani Obiſpo huel miac tlamantli inicquitlàtlani, quitlatemoli, inic
huel iyollomàciz, campa inquimottili, quenamècztzin-
tli huel mochquimopohuilili in Tlàtohuani Obiſpo. Auh
maçihui inhuel mochquimo meiahuilili in yuhcatzintli,
ihuan inixquich oquittac, oquimahuiçò incahuelyuh neci
ca yehuatzin izçenquizca Ichpochtzintli ini tlaçoma
huiz nanzin in toTemaquixticatzin toTecuiyoīesuChri
to; yece àmo niman ic omonelchiuh quitto ca àmo çan
ica itlàtol, itlaitlaniliz mochihuaz moneltiliz intlein qui
tlani, cahuel oc itlàinezea monequi inic huel neltocoz
inquenin huel yehuatzin quimotitlanilia inilhuicac Çihuapilli. Auh in ô yuh quicac in Iuan Diego quimolhuil:
in Obiſpo tlacatlè, tlatohuaniè maxic mottili catlèhuatl
yez ininezca tic mitlanililia, caniman niyaz nic nitlani:
lilitiuh in ilhuicac cihuapilli onech hualmotitlanili. Auh
in ô quittac in Obiſpo cahuelmonelchihua caniman àtle
ic meleltia, motzotzona niman ic quihua. Auh iſ
yehuitz niman ic quimonahuatilj quezqui inichan tlaça
inhuel intechmotlacanequi, quihual tepotztocazque,
huelquipipiazque campa in yauh, ihuan aquin con itta,
con notza. Tel iuh mochiuh auh in Iuan Diego nimari
ic huailamelauh, quitocac in cuepòtli, auh inquihual te-
potztocaya oncan atlauhtli quiça inahuac tepeyacac
quauhpàntitlan quipoloco, manelocnohuian tlatemòque
acècàn quittaque, çanyuh hualmòquepquè, àmo çaniyo
inic omoxixiuhtlatito, no ihuan ic oquimelelti, oquin:
qualancacuiti: yuhqui nonotzato in Tlàtohuani Obiſpo,
quitlahuellalilique inic àmo quineltocaz, quilhuiq inic
can

çan connoztlacahuilia, çan quipipiqui in tleinquihual-
molhuilia, ànoçe çan oqui temic, çan oqui cochitleuh
intlein quimolhuilia, intlein quimitlanililia; auh huel
yuh quimolhuique intla occeppa huallaz, mocuepaz; oncan quitzitzquizque, ihuan chicahuac qui tlatzacuiltiz-
que inic aocmo çeppa iztlacatiz, tèquamanaz.

··Inimoztlayoc Lunes iniquac qui huicazquia in Iuan
Diego in itla inezca inic neltocoz, aocmo ohualmocuep:
yeica iniquac àçito inichan çe itla catca itoca Iuan Bernardino oitech motlali in cocoliztli,huel tlanauhtoc, oc
quitici nochilito, oc ipan tlàto, yece aocmo inman ye-
huelotlanauh:auh in yeyohuac quitlatlauhti ini Tla in
oc yohuatzinco, oɛtlàtlayohuatoc hual quiçaz, quimo-
nochiliquiuh in oncan Tlatilolco çemein teopixque inic
mohuicaz, quimoyolcuitilitiuh, ihuan quimoçencahui-
litiuh, yè ica cahuelyuhca ini yollo caye inman; caye
oncan inic miquiz ca aoc mehuaz aocmo pàtiz, ··

Auh in Martes huel oc tlàtlayohuatoc in ompahual-
quiz ichan in Iuan Diego inquimonochiliz teopixqui in
ompa Tlatilolco, auh in ye àçitihuitz inahuacrepetzin-
tli tepeyacac iniexitlan quiztica òtli tonatiuh icalaquian-
pa inoncan yeppa quiçani, quito intlaçan nic melahua
òtli manen nech hual mottilitiizçihuapilli ca yeppa nech
motzicalhuiz inic nic huiquiliz tlanezcayotl inteopixca
tlàtohuani inyuh onech monànahuatili; maoɛtechcahua
in tonetequipachol, maoc nicno nochilitihuetzi in teopixqui motolinia innotlàtzin àmo çaquimochialitoc.Ni-
man ic contlacolhui intepetl itzallan ontlècoc yenepa
centlapal Tonatiuh yquiçayanpa quiçato inic içiuhca
àçitiuh Mexico inic àmo quimotzicalhuiz in ilhuicac
çihuapilli inmomati ca inompa ic otlacolo ca àhuelqui-
mottiliz,inhuelnohuiampa motztilitica ‹ Quittac quenin
hualmotemohui icpac. intepetzintli ompahualmotzti-
                                                        litoc

5

Titoc in ompa yeppa conmottiliani, con monamiquilico.
ininacaztlan tepetl, conmoyacatzacuililico, quimolhuili.
Auh noxocoyouh, campa in tiyauh? campa intitztiuh?
Auh in yehuatl cuix achi ic mellelma? cuix noçe pina-
huac? cuix noçe ic miçahui, momauhti? ixpantzinco
mopechtecac, quimotlapalhui, quimolhuili, nochpochtzinè, noxocoyohuè, Çihuapillè maximopaquiltitic quen
otimixtonalti? cuix ticmohuelmachitia in motlaçònaca-
yotzin noTecuiyoè, nopiltzintzinè; niçtequipachoz in
mixtzin in moyollòtzin, ma xicmomachiltitzino nochpochtzinè, ca huellanauhtec çe momaçehualtzin noTla-
huei cocoliztli initech omotlali ca yeppa ic momiquiliz,
auh oc noniçiuhtiuh in mochantzinco Mexico noconno-
nochiliz çemè initlaçòhuan toTecuiyo intoTeopixcahuã,
conmo yolcuitilitiuh, ihuã conmo çencahuilitiuh, canel
yè inic otitlacatque, intic chiaco intomiquiztequiuh. Auh
intla onoçon neltilito, caniman nican occeppa nihualno-
cuepaz, inic non yaz noconitquiz, in miiyotzin in motlàtoltzin Tlacatiè, Nochpochtzinè, maxicchmotlapo-
polhuili, maoc ixquich ica xinechmopaccaiyohuilti càmo
ic nimitznoquelhuia, noxocoyohuè, nopiltzintzinè, ca
niman moztla niquiztihuetziquiuh. Auh in oyuhqui-
mocaquiti itlàtol in Iuan Diego quimonanquilili in ic-
nohuàcaçenquizca ichpochtzintli: Maxiccaqui ma huel
yuh ye in moyollo noxocoyouh macatletlein mitzmauh-
ti, mitztequipacho, macamo quen mochihua in mix in
moyollo, macamo xiquimacaci in cocoliztli, manoçe oc
itlà cocoliztli, còcoc teòpouhqui, cuix àmo nican nicà
nimoNantzin? cuix àmo noçchuallotitlan, nècauhyoti-
tlan in ticà? cuix àmo nèhuatl in nimopaccayeliz? cuix
àmo nocuixanco, nomamalhuazco intica? cuix oc itlà
in motech monequi? macamo oc itlà mitztequipacho,
mitz àmana, macamo mitztequipacho inicocoliz moTlà-

B   tzin

tzin càmo ic miquiz in axcàn itechca; ma huel yuh ye
in moyollo ca ycopàtic : (Auh ca niman huel iquac pà-
tic iniTlàtzin iniuh çatepan machiztic.) Auh in Iuan
Diego in oyuhquicac iniiyotzin, initlàtoltzin inilhuicac
Çihuapilli, huel cenca ic omoyollali, huel ic pachiuh ini
yollo. Auh quimotlatlauhtili inic maçayè quimotitla-
nili inic quittatiuh in Tlàtohuani Obispo in quitqui-
liz itlà inezca, ini neltica, inic quineltocaz. Auh in ilhuicac Çihuapilli niman ic quimonahuatili, inic ontlè-
coz in icpac tepetzintli, inoncan canin yeppa conmot-
tiliaya; quimolhuili xitlèco noxocoyouh in icpac in tepetzintli, auh in canin ótinech ittac, ihuan onimitznàna-
huati oncan tiquittaz onoc nepapan xochitl, xicrètequi,
xic nechico, xicçentlali, niman xic hualtemohui, nican
nixpan xic hualhuica. Auh in Iuan Diego niman ic qui-
tlècahui in tepetzintli, auh in oàcito icpac, çenca quima-
huiçò inixquich onoc, xotlztoc, cuepontoc in nepapan
Caxtillan tlaçòxochitl,in ayamo imochiuhyan; ca nel huel
iquac inmotlàpaltilia izcetl : huel çenca àhuiaxtoc, iuh-
qui in tlaçò epyollòtli inic yohual àhuachyòtoc; niman ic
peuh in quitètequi,huel moch quinechico, quicuixanten.
Auh in oncan icpac tepetzintli ca niman àtle xochitl ini-
mochiuhyan, catexcalla, netzolla, huihuitztla, nòpalla,
mizquitla; auh intla xiuhtotontin mochichikuani iniquac
inipan metztli Diziembre ca moch qui quà, qui pòpolo-
hua izçetl. Auh ca niman ic hualtemoc, quihualmotqui-
lili inilhuicac Çihuapilli in nepapan xochitl oquitètequi-
to, auh in oyuh quimottili imaticatzinco conmocuili;
niman ye ocçeppa icuexanco quihualmotemili, quimolhuili, noxocoyouh inin nepapan xochitl yèhuatl intlane!-
tiliz,in nezcayotl intic huiquiliz in Obispo, nopampa tiquilhuiz ma ic quitta in notlanequiliz, ihuà ic quineltiliz
in notlanequiliz, in noçializ. Auh in tèhuatl intinotitlan

ca

6

ca huel metech netlacaneconi; auh huel·nimitztlaçeauh
nahuatia çan huel icel ixpan Obispo tic çohuaz in motil-
mà, ihuan·tic nextiliz intlein·tic huica; auh huel moch
ticpohuiliz, tiquilhuiz inquenin onimitznahuati inic ti
tlècoz inicpac tepetzintli intic tètequitiuh Xochitl, ihuã
inixquich otiquittac, otic mahuiçò, inic·huel·ticyollòye-
huaz inTeopixcaTlàtohuani; inic niman ipan tlàtoz inic
mochihuaz, moquetzaz in noTeòcal oniquitlanili. Auh
in ocòmonànahuatili in ilhuicac Çihuapilli quihualtocac
in cuepòtli Mexico huallamelahua,ye paçhihuitz, ye yuh
yetihuitz ini yollo ca yecquiçaquiuh,qui yçc itquiz, huel
quimo cuitlahuitihuitz intlein icuixanco yetihuitz in-
manen itlàquimacauh,quimo tlamachtitihuitz iniàhuia-
ca innepapan tlaçò xochitl.

SELECT BIBLIOGRAPHY

Alday, Salvador Carrillo. *El Mensaje Teológico de Guadalupe.* Mexico City, 1982.

Alvarez, Arturo Alvarez. *Cien Personajes en Guadalupe.* Seville, 1995.

Badde, Paul. *Die himmlische Stadt.* Munich, 1999.

Cabrera, Miguel. *Maravilla Americana y conjunto de Raras maravillas: Observadas con la dirección de las Reglas del Arte de la Pintura en la Prodigiosa Imagen de Nuestra Sra. de Guadalupe de México.* Imprenta del Real y más antiguo Colegio de San Idelfonso. Mexico City, 1756. Facsimile edition: Querétaro, 1945.

Callahan, Philip Serna. *The Tilma under Infra-Red Radiation.* Washington, 1981.

Chávez Sánchez, Eduardo. *Juan Diego: Una vida de santidad que marcó la historia.* Mexico City, 2002.

Del Castillo, Diaz. *Die Eroberung Mexikos.* Frankfurt am Main, 1982.

Escalada, Xavier. *Guadalupe, Arte y Esplendor.* Mexico City, 1998.

Fernández, Victor Manuel. *La Virgen de Guadalupe y su Ayate Prodigioso.* Mexico City, 1982.

Franciscan Friars of the Immaculate, eds. *A Handbook on Guadalupe.* New Bedford, Mass., 1997.

Gaertner, Lothar, ed. *La Conquista de México: Die Entdeckung un Eroberung in zeitgenössischen Berichten.* Munich, 1992.

García, Sebastián, O.F.M. *El Monasterio de Guadalupe: Centro de Fe y de Cultura.* Guadalupe (Spain), 1993.

_____. *Guadalupe de Extremadura en America*. Guadalupe (Spain), 1991.

Grignion de Montfort, Louis Marie. *Das goldene Buch der vollkommenen Hingabe an Jesus durch Maria*. Fribourg, 1975.

Guerrero, José Luis. *El Nican Mopohua: Un intento de Exégesis*. Mexico City, 1996.

_____. *Flor y Canto del Nacimiento de México*. Mexico City, 1990.

With regard to Hagia Maria on Mount Zion, see www. hagia-maria-sion.net.

Hierzenberger, Gottfried, and Otto Nedomansky. *Erscheinungen und Botschaften der Gottesmutter Maria*. Augsburg, 1993.

Höffner, Josef. *Christentum und Menschenwürde: Das Anliegen der spanischen Kolonialethik im goldenen Zeitalter*. Trier, 1947.

Janssens, Laurentius, O.S.B. *Das Heiligtum Mariä Heimgang auf dem Berg Zion*. Prague, 1910.

John Paul II. Encyclical *Redemptoris Mater. On the Blessed Virgin Mary in the Life of the Pilgrim Church*. Rome, 1987.

Johnston, Francis. *The Wonder of Guadalupe: The Origin and Cult of the Miraculous Image of the Blessed Virgin in Mexico*. Rockford, Ill.: Tan Books, 1981.

König, Hans Joachim. *Die Entdeckung und Eroberung Amerikas 1492–1550*. Freiburg im Breisgau, 1992.

Meisner, Joachim Cardinal. *Von nun an preisen mich selig alle Geschlechter*. Kevelaer, 1999.

Nebel, Richard. *Santa María Tonantzin, Virgen de Guadalupe: Religiöse Kontinuität und Transformation in México.* Immensee, 1992.

Paz, Octavio. *El Laberinto de la Soledad.* Frankfurt am Main, 1998.

Pelikan, Jaroslav. *Maria: 2000 Jahre in Religion, Kultur und Geschichte.* Freiburg im Breisgau, 1999.

Pimentel, Guadalupe María. *Mi Niña, Dueña de mi Corazon.* Mexico City, 1990.

Pixner, Bargil, O.S.B. *Wege des Messias und Stätten der Urkirche.* Gießen, 1991.

Posener, Alan. *Maria.* Hamburg, 1999.

Ratzinger, Joseph Cardinal, and Hans Urs von Balthasar. *Mary: The Church at the Source.* Translated by Adrian Walker. San Francisco, 1997.

Reichert, Klaus. *Das Hohelied Salomos.* Bi-lingual ed. Munich, 1998.

Rojas Sánchez, Mario. *Traducción del Nican Mopohua del Náhuatl al Castellano.* Huejutla, Mexico, 1978.

Rovira, German, ed. *Im Gewande des Heils.* Essen, 1980.

Sartory, Gertude and Thomas, eds. *Frühwelkende Blumen: Aztekische Gesänge.* Freiburg, 1983.

Schreiner, Klaus. *Maria: Jungfrau, Mutter, Herrscherin.* Munich and Vienna, 1994.

Thomas, Hugh. *Die Eroberung Mexikos: Cortés und Montezuma.* Frankfurt am Main, 1998.

Tönsmann, José Aste. *El Secreto de sus Ojos: Estudio de los Ojos de la Virgen de Guadalupe*. Mexico City, 1998.

Westheim, Paul. *Der Tod in Mexiko*. Hanau, ca. 1986.

Wiesenthal, Simon. *Segel der Hoffnung: Christoph Columbus auf der Suche nach dem gelobten Land*. Berlin, 1991.

WITH THANKS

Together with all persons mentioned by name in the book and with the many not mentioned, I would like cordially to thank my old friend Hans Josef "Hajo" Höltz, of Seville, for his disinterested help in the fortunate realization of this book. And, of course, thanks be to Mary! She has helped from the beginning. Thanks be to God.

Paul Badde
Rome, June 29, 2003

PHOTOGRAPHS

Photograph 1: with permission of the Archdiocese of Mexico.

Photograph 2: with the cordial permission of the Archdiocese of Turin.

Photograph 14: with the cordial permission of Teresa Vaca, Los Angeles, California.

Photographs 3, 4, 5, 6, 7, 8, 9, 10, 11, 12, 13, 15, 16, 17, 18, 19, 20, 21, 22, 23: taken by the author.